Square Knot

HANDICRAFT GUIDE

Square Knotting or

MACRAME

Square Knot Handicraft Guide

Raoul Graumont & Elmer Wenstrom

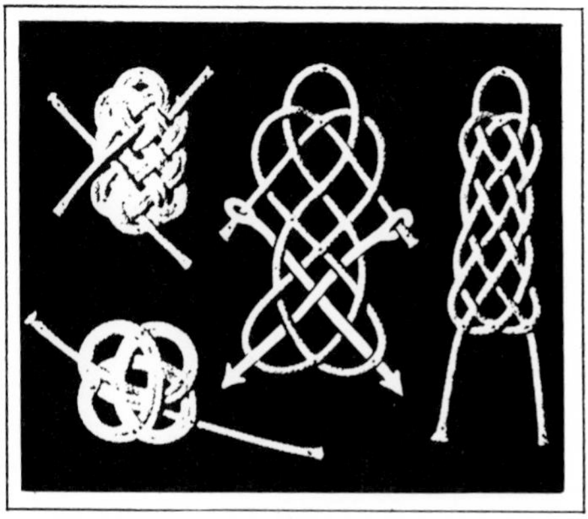

Distributed by Random House
New York

ISBN 0-394-70460-6

Library of Congress Catalog Card Number: 50-5918

Printed in the United States of America

Distributed by RANDOM HOUSE
and in Canada by
RANDOM HOUSE OF CANADA, LTD.

Preface

Square Knot Handicraft Guide embodies the elements of essential skill involved in square knotting and provides graphic, detailed illustrations of the various steps, accompanied by explanatory text.

The earliest form of Square Knot work, which was known as Macramé, is said to have originated in Arabia during the thirteenth century. There is enough available historical data to suggest that it was already an established art in France during the latter part of the fourteenth century. In the years that followed, the fascinating appearance of this unusual work soon made its popularity widespread throughout the world. Its simplicity of execution, requiring very little skill, brought it into instant favor with sailors on their long sea voyages. It is said that as early as the fifteenth century, sailors were using objects they had made from square knot materials to barter with the natives of India and on the China coast and, in later years, even among the North American Indians.

Square Knot work is not only an interesting and practical hobby, but should provide the student with a pleasant pastime to fill many idle hours and give him the personal satisfaction which one realizes from acquiring the ability to create practical designs of beauty and distinction.

In modern times occupational therapists have found it to be an excellent form of diversion for the rehabilitation of convalescent patients in hospitals and institutions, unsurpassed as a diversionary form of activity which develops originality, and initiative, and at the same time provides a light form of recreational exercise.

Since the publication of *Square Knot, Tatting, Fringe and Needle Work* in 1943, which was the first attempt to present modern Square Knot work to the public, there has been a steadily growing demand for a book which would give this popular subject a more thoroughly explained text, along with step-by-step photographic illustrations to simplify the more complicated work in each stage of development. The most difficult-appearing Square Knot designs are in reality quite simple to execute, once the student has mastered a rudimentary knowledge of the work.

Throughout the preparation of this text we have endeavored to present an array of projects sufficiently wide in range of interest and skill to attract the individual craftsman, the instructor and the occupational therapist; while at the same time it has been our purpose to discover precise methods, neither too complex nor burdensome, which would explore and portray each phase of work from simple to more advanced techniques, thus making each characteristic of development more readily understandable, regardless of the age group or level to which the work is carried.

Such an assembly of subject matter presented in this form of sequence is calculated to have an individual appeal that should stimulate creativeness, so that the satisfaction of accomplishment will not only be constructive, but will also bring the reward of personal achievement with knowledge gained by experience which is acquired only in "doing."

All the most practical and popular designs familiar to students the world over will be found in this volume. The methods of construction are in every case the most modern. Among the items listed are such articles as belts, handbags, mats, dog collars, leashes, shade pulls, whistle lanyards, knife lanyards, hat bands, head bands, pillow-tops, doilies, key cases, men's ties, slippers, wrist watch straps, watch fobs, book marks, cigarette cases, camera cases, and center pieces. Comb hangers, sennit braids and a variety of two- and three-strand knot work that is related to Square Knotting is also included.

Hard lay cotton line of 15–18 thread, French DMC #1 or linen cord is sufficient for most types of Square Knot work. Gold and silver metallic cord can also be used to great advantage in the many attractive patterns for women's belts.

Our "key" method of explaining the text, which eliminates confusing repetition, will be of inestimable value, since it comes directly to the point without wasting words and gives a clear description of all designs in simple, understandable language. We hope that this first comprehensive treatise on the Square Knot will add additional interest to this excellent art of bygone years.

Acknowledgments

We are deeply indebted to Arthur S. Whitefield for his kind assistance and constructive criticism throughout the preparation of this volume, and we wish to acknowledge his generous cooperation with gratitude and thanks.

We also wish to thank Eleanor Ewing for the exceptional art work and fine lettering.

Jack Muntzner, likewise, deserves outstanding credit for producing the excellent photographs.

Raoul Graumont
Elmer Wenstrom

Contents

Plate 1—ILLUSTRATED CONSTRUCTION OF THE BASIC SQUARE KNOT

These illustrations portray the construction of the basic knot—Square Knot. They also indicate how to double and loop the strands over a cord to form what is known as a Lark's Head or Cow Hitch. The common method of tying a Square Knot requires two steps or operations and 4 strands. Over and under and through, under, over and through. For convenience the strands have imaginary numbers from left to right: 1, 2, 3 and 4.

Figs. 1A to H embody the step-by-step procedure in each stage of development, as explained in detail with the following text accompanying the illustrations in Plate 2.

Plate 2—TYPICAL SQUARE KNOTS

In this text, it is necessary to use 2 strands as a filler, looped over and held taut by a body hook. To make this body hook, drive a four-inch nail through a small block of wood ⅜″ x 1″ x 3″ and bend the point of the nail back, forming a hook. Place screw eyes in the ends of the block and attach a strong cord to each. This hook is fastened around *your* body and holds the filler cords, leaving the hands free to tie the square knot. (See Plate 49.)

Fig. 2A: The filler (strands 2 and 3) is looped over the body hook and held taut until the knot is completed. When knots are tied around another cord or two, these cords are known as a filler. Take strand 1 and hook it with the second finger of the left hand, holding it to the left of the filler. Then pass it over the filler and hook it with the second finger of the right hand, but at the same time hold on with the left hand so that the filler is between the hands. Then take strand 4 with the thumb and index finger of the right hand and pass it underneath at this point as shown by drawn line. (See Plate 1, Fig. A.)

B: Strand 4 is passed over a section of 1 that was brought to the right, is passed under the filler, and up through the loop and over a

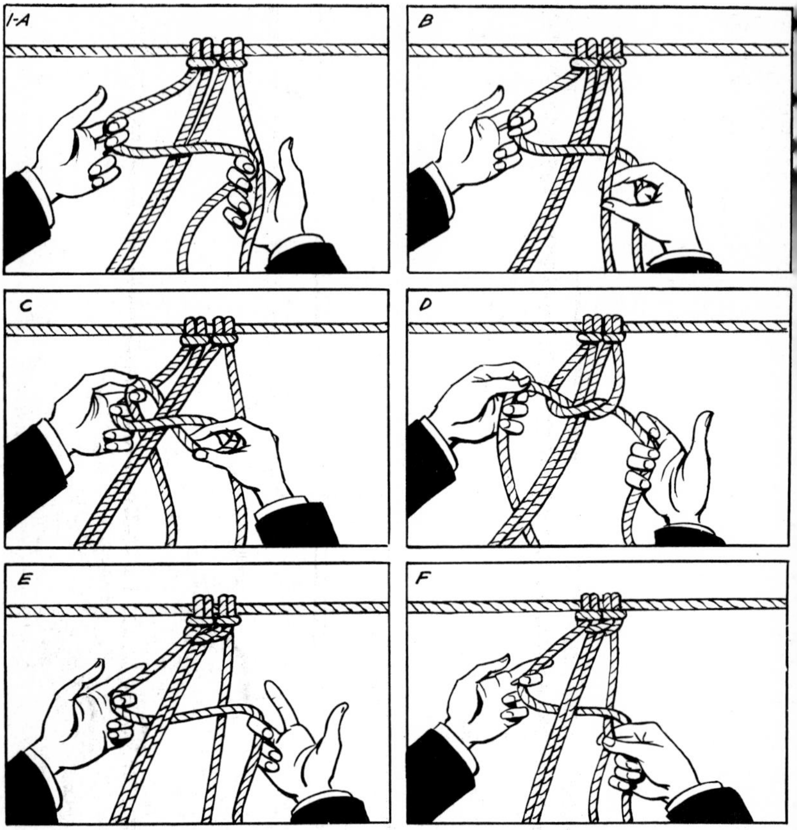

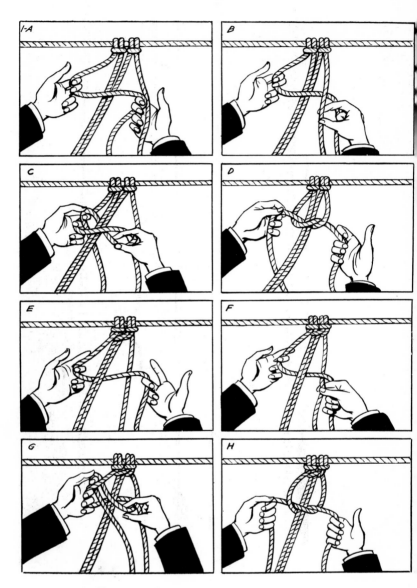

PLATE 1 Illustrated Construction of the Basic Square Knot

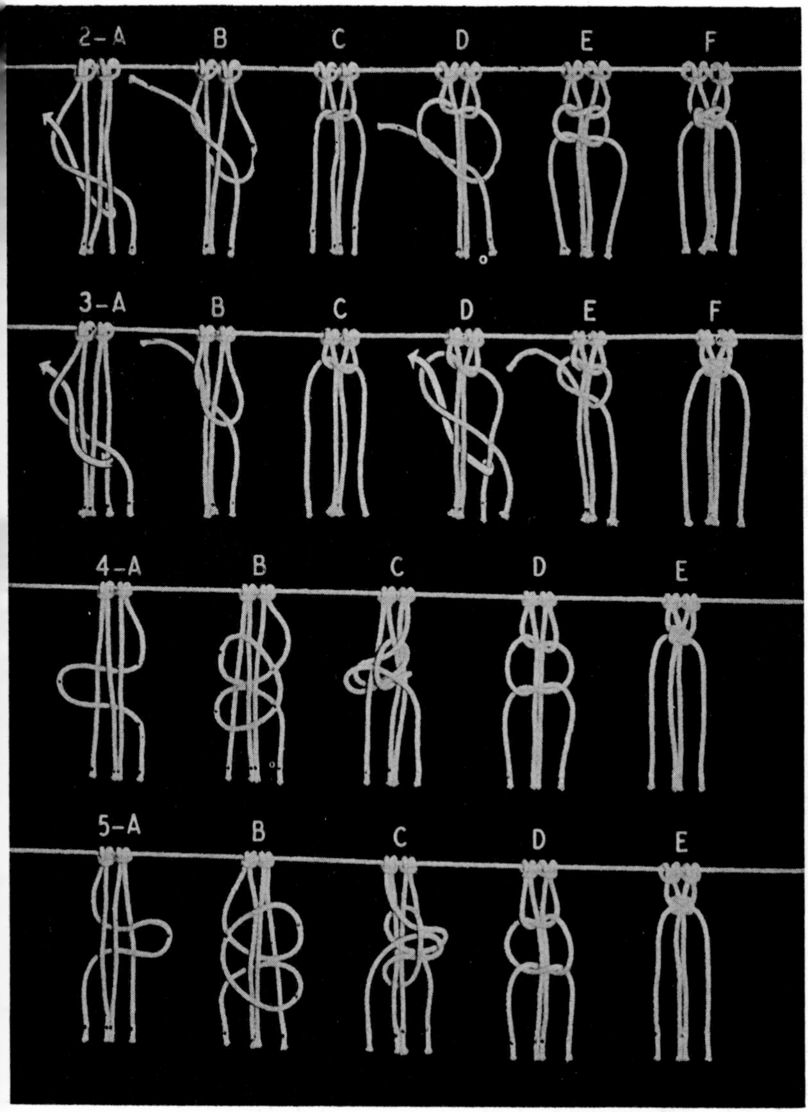

PLATE 2 Typical Square Knots

section of 1 on the left, and is grasped by the thumb and index finger of the left hand. (See Plate 1, Fig. C.) Pull this strand 4 through to the end. (See Plate 1, Fig. D.)

C: Pull strands 1 and 2 taut. This completes the first half of the knot, and forms what is known as a Half Knot.

D: Now renumber the strands from left to right: 1, 2, 3 and 4. Take strand 1 and, hooking it with the second finger of the left hand and keeping it to the left of the filler, pass the end of it under the filler and hold it between the second finger and palm of the right hand. (See Plate 1, Fig. E.) Then take strand 4 with the thumb and index finger of the right hand; bring it under that part of strand 1 which is on the right of the filler, pass it over the filler, and down through the loop made by strand 1 on the left. Seize this cord with the thumb and index finger of the left hand. (See Plate 1, Fig. G.) Pull it through to the end. (See Plate 1, Fig. H.)

F: Pull strands 1 and 4 taut and the square knot is completed. Notice that it points to the lect.

Fig. 3: Illustrations A, B, C, D, E and F show how the knot is formed pointing to the right. The second half of the knot is tied first and thus the order of tying the two halves is reversed. Under, over and through, over and under and through. (See drawn in lines at Figs. A and D.)

Fig. 4A: This illustrates a quick way to tie a square knot pointing to the left. The left hand reaches under the filler and seizes strand 4 with the thumb and index finger. The right hand holds on to the upper and lower part of strand 4 with the thumb and index finger, allowing the left hand to pull a bight to the left.

B: The bight held in the left hand is allowed to slip over the thumb and index finger, and is placed over the filler toward the right.

C: With the thumb and index finger of the left hand seize the part of strand 4 held by the right hand and pull it back through the bight toward the left, forming a double bight. Strand 1 is passed through this double bight on the left.

D: Take the single bight that is on top of the double bight and pull it to the left. This brings the square knot into its proper form.

E: Pull strands 1 and 4 taut and the square knot is complete. The two operations of tying the knot have been performed in one.

Fig. 5: Illustrations A, B, C, D and E show how the knot is formed pointing to the right.

Plate 3—SHADE OR LIGHT PULL

This Shade or Light Pull is made by tying a succession of Square Knots and Half Knots and adding cords at the bottom for the tassel. The amount of cord required is 12⅔ yards. (Always take the cord from the middle of a ball.) This will make a very attractive pull, which will last indefinitely and may be laundered frequently.

Cut 2 strands—one strand 2 feet long and the other 7 feet long. Fasten a clamp vise on the top of the table, double the 2 foot strand over the top of the screw handle of the vise clamp, and fasten the 2 strands to the body hook that all Square Knotters use. (See Plate 49.)

Fig. 6A: Double the 7 foot strand and make a Half Knot or Constrictor Knot about 2 inches down on the two-stranded filler, and continue to make 8 Square Knots in all, one on top of the other. This is known as a Flat. (The Constrictor Knot is firm and symmetrical when used in adding a strand doubled to a filler.) Next make a Spiral by tying the first half of a Square Knot 16 times. Make 8 more Square Knots, 16 more Half Knots, and 8 more Square Knots.

B: Cut 24 strands 8 inches long for the tassel. Place these strands at the bottom of the pull just completed, and fasten them to the pull by tying a Square Knot around their middle with the 2 outside strands from the pull. Let the strands fall down over the knot.

C: Cut 8 strands 18 inches long; these are for forming the crown of the tassel as shown at the beginning in this stage of the operation. Place a ruler on top of the middle of the 8 strands and clamp them down. Number the strands from left to right, 1 to 8. Using strands 4 and 5 as a filler, tie a Square Knot with strands 3 and 6. Using strands 2 and 3 as a filler, tie a Square Knot with strands 1 and 4. Using strands 6 and 7 as a filler, tie a Square Knot with strands 5 and 8.

D: Place the loop of the pull over a nail or over the top of the screw handle of the vise clamp. Then unclamp the 8 strands and take strand 4 in the left hand and strand 5 in the right hand, bringing them around the top of the tassel at the end of the Flat on the pull. Using these two strands as a filler, tie a Square Knot with the nearest strand on the right and the nearest on the left; that is 3 and 6. Let the strands fall down over the tassel. This makes all strands fast to the pull, and there are now 16 working strands. This pictures the foregoing operation as it would appear if it were placed over the top of the shade pull.

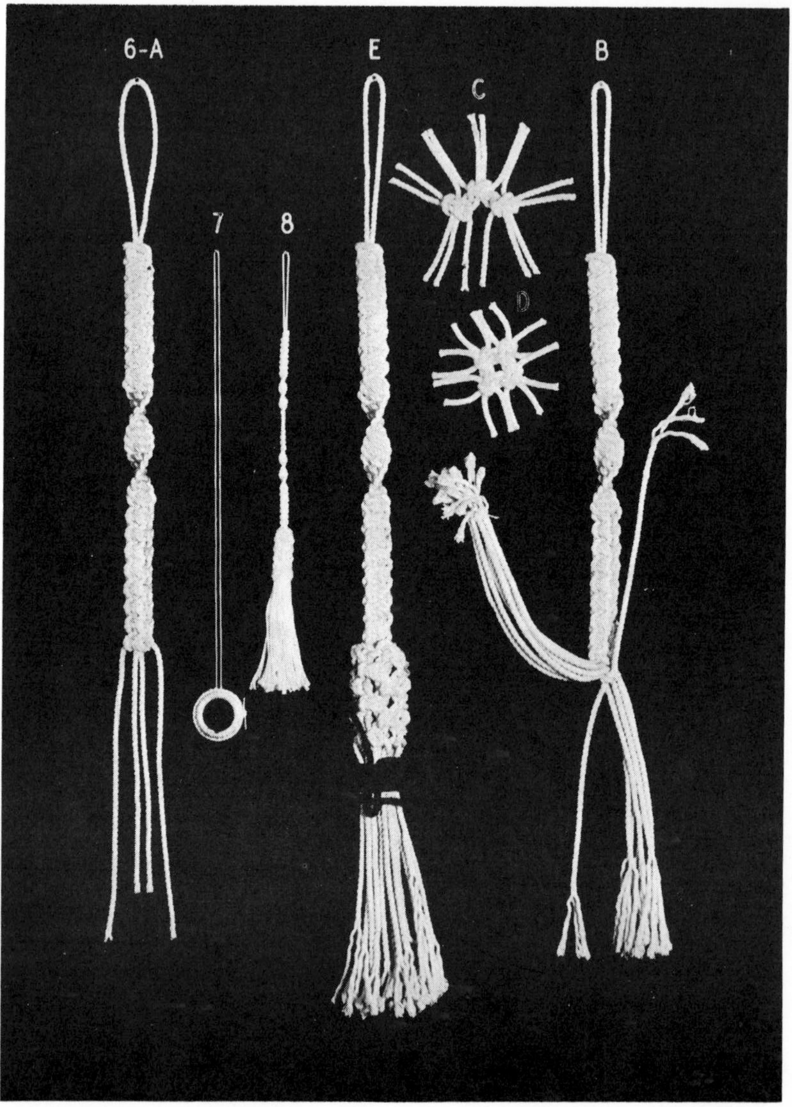

PLATE 3 Shade or Light Pull

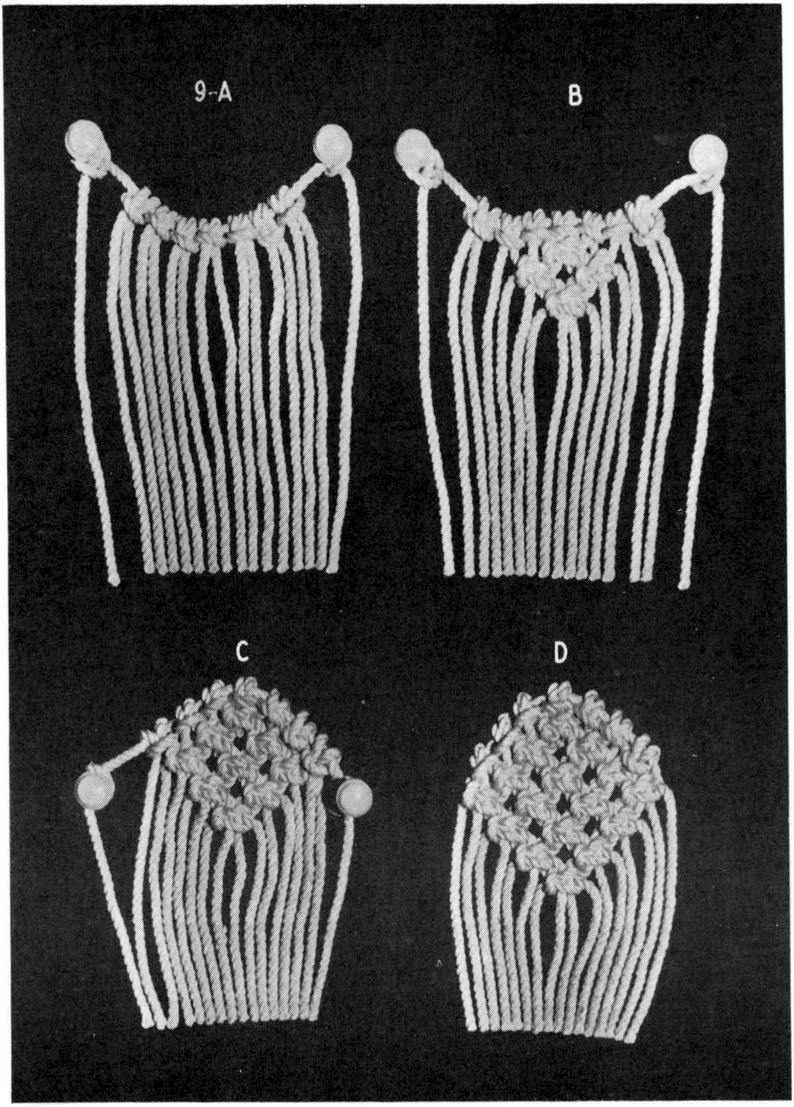

PLATE 4 How to Start a Sixteen-Strand Belt

E: Number the knots in order, 1 to 4. Using the last strand of knot 1 and the first strand of knot 2 as a filler, tie a Square Knot with the nearest strand on the left and the nearest on the right. Take the similar 2 strands between knot 2 and knot 3 and, using these as a filler, tie a Square Knot with the strand on the left and the strand on the right. Take the similar 2 strands between knot 3 and knot 4 and, using these two strands as a filler, tie a Square Knot with the strand on the left and the strand on the right. Take the 2 strands between knot 4 and knot 1 and, using these as a filler, tie a Square Knot with the strand on the left and the strand on the right. This completes a ring of Square Knots. Continue in this manner, tying the knots around the tassel until the crown is the desired length. Practice making this crown with heavy cord. By using 16 strands and tying all Square Knots in one direction, a round crown is formed; by reversing every other row of Square Knots a square crown is formed. This crown is widely used in making women's handbags, dog leashes and lanyards. To put the binding on below the crown, loop about 1 inch of a 12 inch cord on the tassel with the loop downward. Start binding from the top close to the knots. Wind the cord closely over the loop around the tassel until a sufficient number of turns have been taken. Tuck the end through the loop, and with the other end pull the loop half way through the binding. Cut off the ends closely at the top and bottom. A Turk's Head Knot may also be used. (See Plates 49 and 50 for Turk's Heads.)

A beginner should make at least a dozen pulls before proceeding to other articles, in order to become skilled in tying Square Knots. Always keep the anchor or filler cord taut in the body hook, and pull the knots taut.

Fig. 7: Shows a Shade Pull with a Coxcombing (Half Hitches) made around a bone ring, and tied on the outside with a Square Knot where the two ends meet.

Fig. 8: A Finished Shade Pull.

Plate 4—HOW TO START A SIXTEEN-STRAND BELT

It is usually rather difficult for a novice to start a belt in Square Knot work. Therefore, do not become discouraged with an initial failure. The following is presented as the most practical method to accomplish this task.

Special instructions:
Remember that the number of any strand changes whenever its position is shifted. This occurs when Half Hitches are tied.
In tying Square Knots with strands of different colors, observe the following rule: Reverse the Square Knots to the right of the middle of the belt; that is, point them to the right. This will balance the design.

Note these Abbreviations: Square Knot—SK Filler cord—F Half Hitches—HH Remember that two HH are to be tied unless directed otherwise.

Fig. 9A: There are five ways to start a belt. In the first method, cut 8 strands seven times the desired length for a belt without a design. These strands will be doubled, thus making 16. Clamp a board to the top of a table and drive part way into it two nails, 3 inches apart. Push pins may also be used. Double one strand over the two nails and secure it with 2 Clove Hitches, 1 to each nail. Allow some slack between the two nails. Double the other 7 strands in the middle and tie each to the first strand between the two nails by means of a Lark's Head Knot. Number these strands 1 to 16 from left to right. Notice that strands 1 and 16 are tied to the nails.

B: Find the 2 middle strands. They are 8 and 9. Using these 2 middle strands as F, tie SK with strands 7 and 10. Then using strands 6 and 7 as F, tie SK with strands 5 and 8. Next using strands 10 and 11 as F, tie SK with strands 9 and 12. Then using strands 8 and 9 as F, tie SK with strands 7 and 10. This completes 4 Square Knots.

C: Fasten the work to the board with brads or push pins. Using strands 4 and 5 as F, tie SK with strands 3 and 6. Using strands 6 and 7 as F, tie SK with strands 5 and 8. Using strands 12 and 13 as F, tie SK with strands 11 and 14. Using strands 10 and 11 as F, tie SK with strands 9 and 12. Using the 2 middle strands 8 and 9 as F, tie SK with strands 7 and 10. This completes 9 Square Knots in the shape of a diamond.

D: Remove the two nails, freeing the 2 outside strands 1 and 16. In the following sequence of four strands, tie seven SK: 1 to 4, 3 to 6, 5 to 8, 13 to 16, 11 to 14, 9 to 12 and 7 to 10.

In the second method, start from the point with brads or push pins. Place two brads in the board on the table about ¼ inch apart,

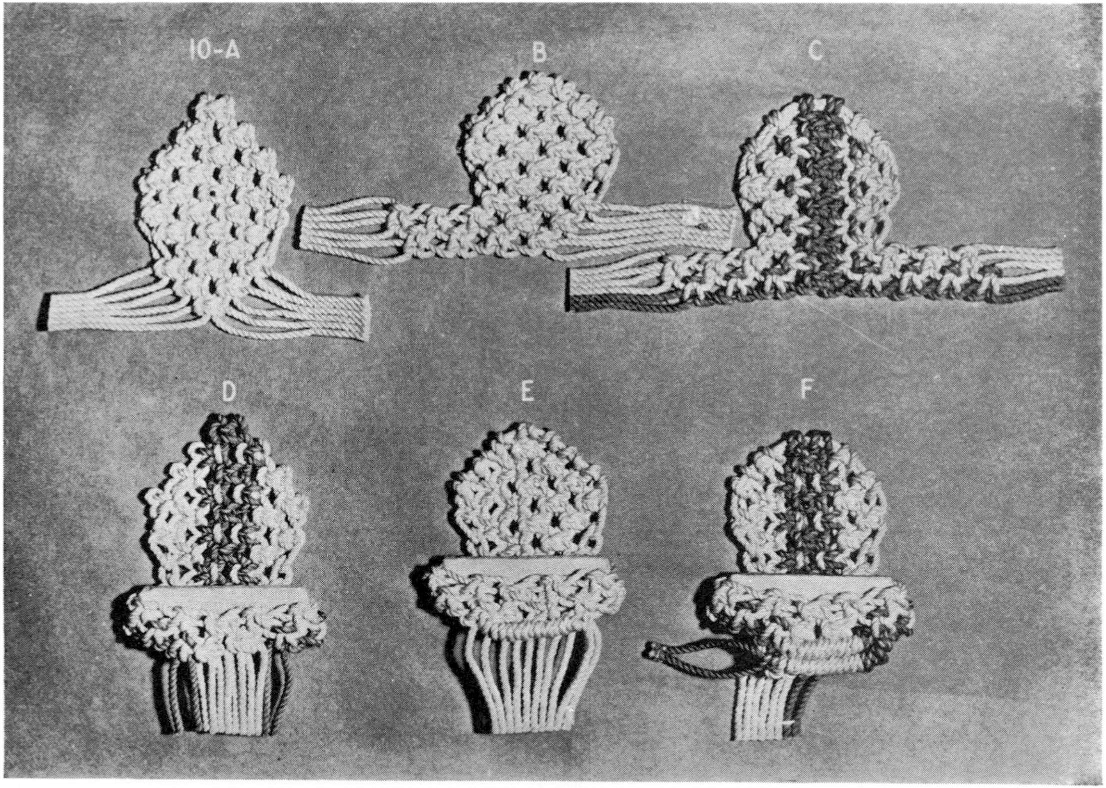
10-A
B
C
D
E
F

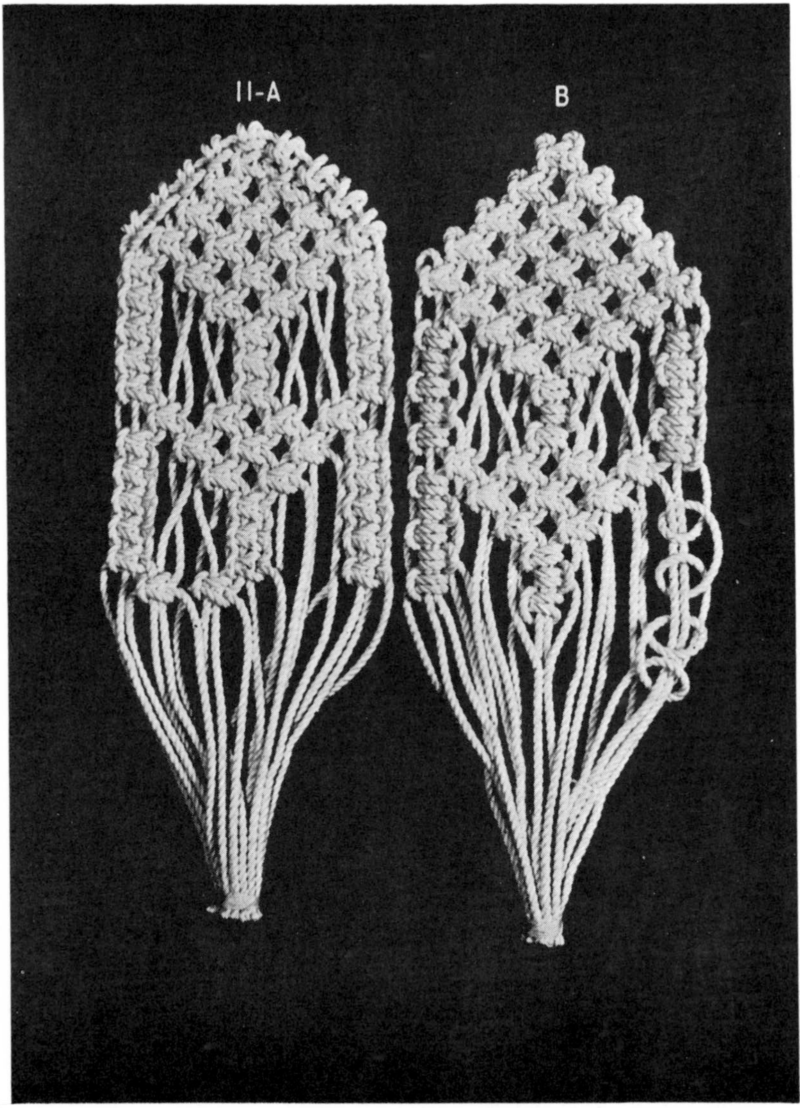

PLATE 6 Open Work Flat Design

and double 2 strands over each brad, tie SK. Then place another brad to the left of this SK, double a strand over brad, and tie SK with the 4 strands on the left. Alternate from left to right in this manner, removing work from brad after adding a strand and pulling the filler strand taut. (See Plate 7.)

In the third method, start from a buckle. Double a strand over the bar, tie a Lark's Head Knot. For a sixteen-strand belt, tie 8 Lark's Head Knots and then tie 4 SK.

In the fourth method, start from the middle of the strands; this necessitates cutting off unused strands at both ends of the belt.

In the fifth method, start with 2 strands as F. Double 2 strands over two nails and secure them with two Clove Hitches, 1 to each nail. Allow some slack between the two nails. Double the required number of strands in the middle and tie each to the 2 strands between the two nails by means of a Lark's Head Knot. This method serves the best purpose when it is necessary to get the 4 colored strands in the middle.

Plate 5—HOW TO MAKE A BELT LOOP

For special instructions and abbreviations see Plate 4.

Fig. 10A: To Form a Belt Loop, work the Square Knots to a point. Cut strands 2, 4, 13 and 15. Then use strand 2 as F, tie *one* HH on it with strand 1. Using strands 2 and 3 as F, tie SK with strands 1 and 4. Using strands 4 and 5 as F, tie SK with strands 3 and 6. Using strand 11 as F, tie *one* HH on it with strand 12. Then using strands 10 and 11 as F, tie SK with strands 9 and 12. Using strands 8 and 9 as F, tie SK with strands 7 and 10. Using strands 6 and 7 as F, tie SK with strands 5 and 8. Then work the belt to a point in the usual manner. This method of eliminating strands is thoroughly illustrated in Plate 81.

Place the belt horizontally in front of you and clamp a ruler or piece of wood on top of the belt near the working end. There are now 6 strands on the near side, and six strands on the far side. These strands are numbered 1 to 6 from the left to the right. Using strands 4 and 6 as F, tie SK with strands 3 and 5. Using strands 2 and 3 as F, tie SK with strands 1 and 4. Tie 4 more SK in this fashion, using first the 4 right strands and then the 4 left strands.

B: Turn the work around and repeat the foregoing instructions on the opposite side.

C: It is very important to turn the work over and bring the two straps together on the reverse or wrong side to form a belt loop. At this point there are 12 working strands. These strands are numbered 1 to 12 from the left to the right. Using strands 6 and 7 as F, tie SK with strands 5 and 8. Using strands 4 and 5 as F, tie SK with strands 3 and 6. Using strands 8 and 9 as F, tie SK with strands 7 and 10. Cut strands 4 and 8 close to the knots. There are now 10 working strands. Renumber the strands from left to right, 1 to 10.

D: Hold strand 2 in the right hand horizontally toward the right. Using this strand as F, tie HH with the left hand, using strands 3 to 9.

E and F: Hold strand 10 in the left hand horizontally toward the left. Using this strand as F, tie HH with the right hand, using strands 9 to 1. While tying the second part of HH with strand 8, tuck strand 9 through loop before making knot taut; then tuck strand 8 through the loop of 7, etc. Turn the belt loop over and pull taut all strands used in tying the last row of HH. On the reverse side bury the F and last strand with which the HH were tied. There are several other ways to form a belt loop, all clearly illustrated in the book.

Do not cut the strands close until the belt is soaked in water and stretched during the course of drying. Do not dry cotton or linen in the sun, as direct sunlight ruins the fibres. After a belt or handbag has been washed in soap and water, rinse first in clear water and then again in water to which a little vinegar has been added.

Plate 6—OPEN WORK FLAT DESIGN

For special instructions and abbreviations see Plate 4.

Fig. 11A: This Design with a combination open work Flat is very easily and quickly made.

Cut 10 strands 10 times the desired length. These strands are doubled, making 20 in all. Number the strands from left to right 1 to 20.

Work the belt to a point in the usual manner. Then tie 4 SK from each edge toward the middle.

*Next tie a Flat of 3 SK with 9 to 12, and two more Flats of 5 SK with 1 to 4 and 17 to 20.

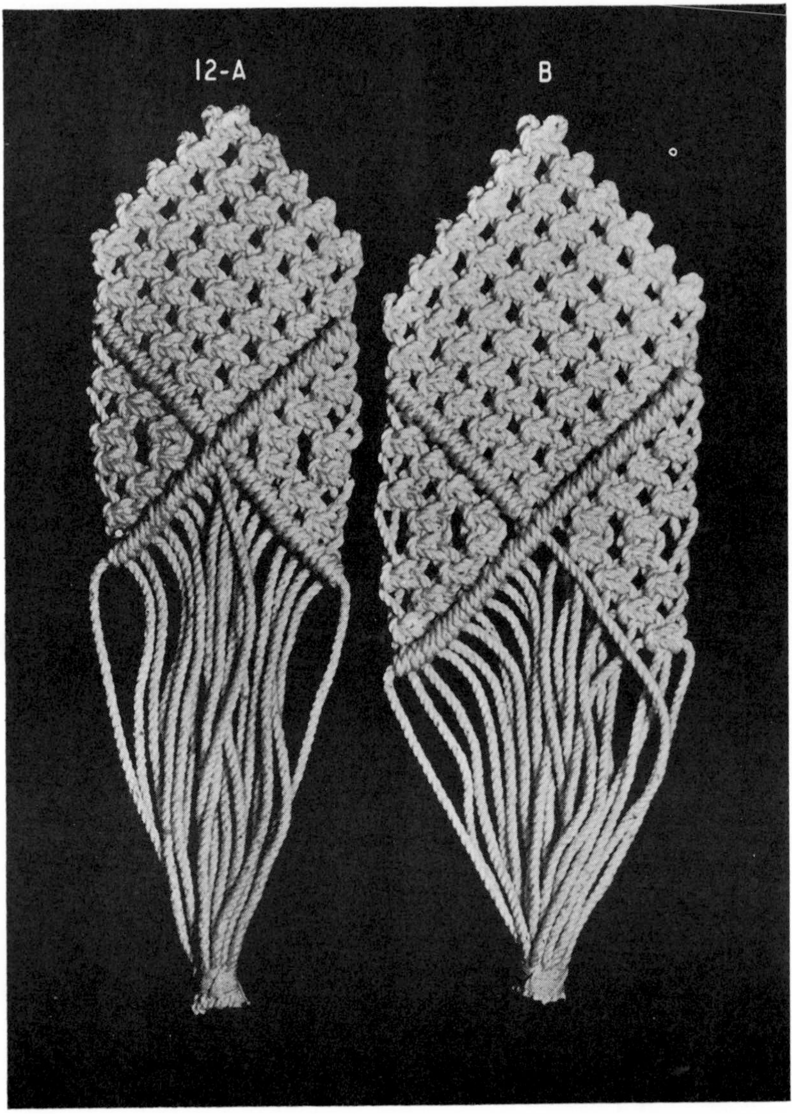

PLATE 7 Single Bar Diamond Design

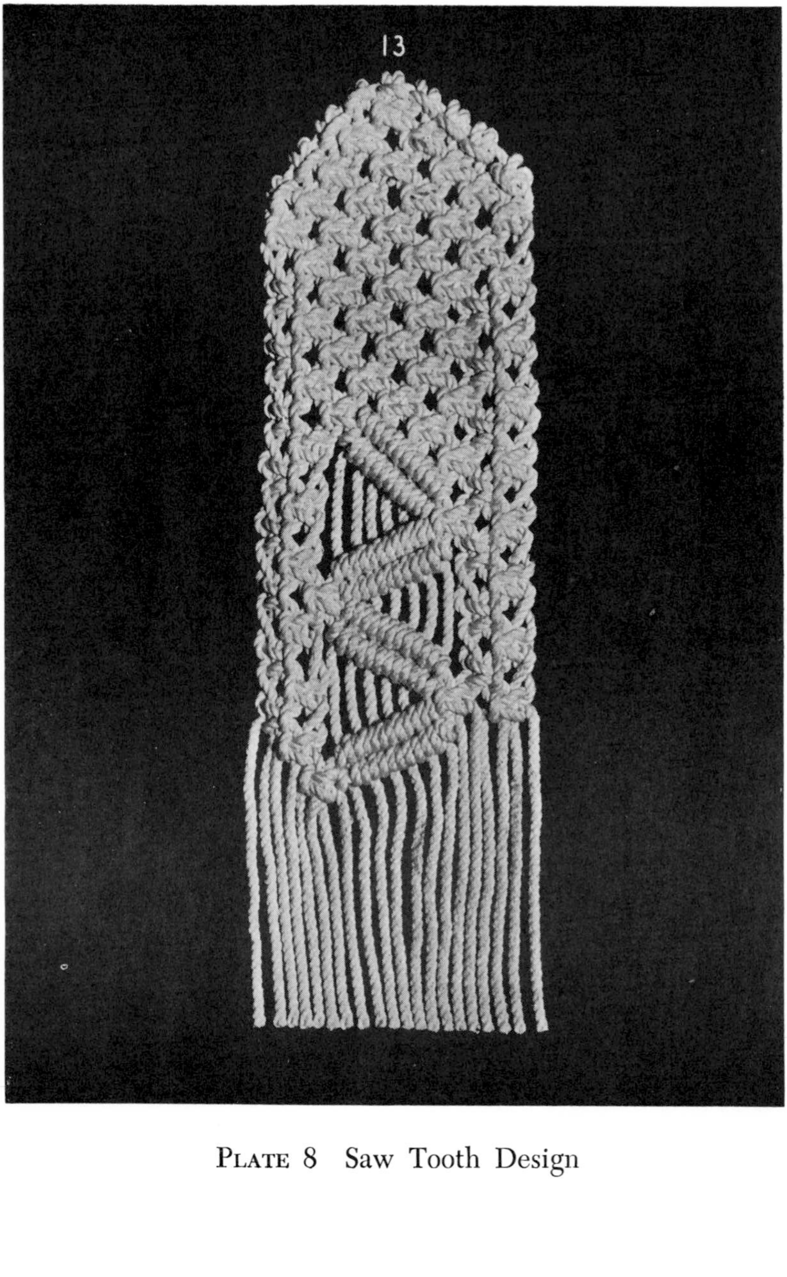

PLATE 8 Saw Tooth Design

Tie SK with 3 to 6, 7 to 10, 5 to 8, 11 to 14, 15 to 18, 13 to 16, 9 to 12, 7 to 10 and 11 to 14.

Repeat instructions from paragraph marked (*) until the design is the required length.

B: In this design, Cow Hitches are used for the Flats. To tie a Cow Hitch with one strand, pass it over the F to tie the first HH and under the F to tie the second HH. Alternate with first one and then the other strand.

Great importance should be attached to giving more than the necessary length required for the strands in a given article. Save all strands over 8 inches long after completing any square knot article. These strands can be used in making a tassel, dish mop or duster.

If a strand should break or become too short, open up knots to the spot where this particular strand is the filler. Then place a new strand through an opening in the previous row with an Overhand Knot on the end to hold it in place. Use this strand as a filler and continue as usual. This replacement does not show in the finished work.

Plate 7—SINGLE BAR DIAMOND DESIGN

For special instructions and abbreviations see Plate 4.

Fig. 12A: This Single Bar Diamond is tied differently along the border than any of the other designs.

Cut 10 strands 8 times the desired length. These strands are doubled, making 20 in all. Number strands 1 to 20 from left to right.

Work belt to a point in the usual manner.

(*) # 1 to right, HH with 2 to 10.
20 " left, " " 19 to 11.

Tie SK with 1 to 4, 3 to 6.
Tie 2 SK with each of 5 to 8 and 1 to 4.
Tie SK with 3 to 6, 1 to 4, 17 to 20 and 15 to 18.
Tie 2 SK with each of 13 to 16 and 17 to 20.
Tie SK with 15 to 18 and 17 to 20.

11 to left, HH with 10 to 1.
11 " right, " " 12 to 20.

The middle of this design is left open.

Repeat instructions from paragraph marked (*) until the design is the required length.

B: Shows a Twenty-four-Strand Belt with a Single Bar Diamond Design.

Plate 8—SAW TOOTH DESIGN

Fig. 13: This Saw Tooth Design is attractive and easy to form.

For abbreviations see Plate 4.

Cut 10 strands 10 times the desired length. These strands are doubled, making 20. Number the strands 1 to 20 from left to right.

Work the belt to a point in the usual manner. Then tie 3 SK from the edge on the left toward the middle.

Tie SK with 17 to 20, 15 to 18, 13 to 16, 11 to 14, 17 to 20, 15 to 18, 13 to 16, 17 to 20, 15 to 18 and 17 to 20.

(*) # 8 to right, HH with 9 to 14.
7 " " " " 8 to 13.

Tie SK with 13 to 16, 15 to 18, 17 to 20, 1 to 4, 3 to 6, 1 to 4, 3 to 6, 1 to 4 and 3 to 6.

#13 to left, HH with 12 to 7.
14 " " " " 13 to 8.

Tie SK with 5 to 8, 15 to 18, 17 to 20, 15 to 18 and 17 to 20.

Repeat instructions from paragraph marked (*) until the design is the required length.

Plate 9—OPEN DIAMOND DESIGN

Fig. 14A: Shows one Diamond in a Twenty-Strand belt.

B: This Diamond Design with opening in the middle is exceptionally attractive.

Cut 12 strands 10 times the desired length. These strands are doubled, making 24 in all. Number strands 1 to 24 from left to right.

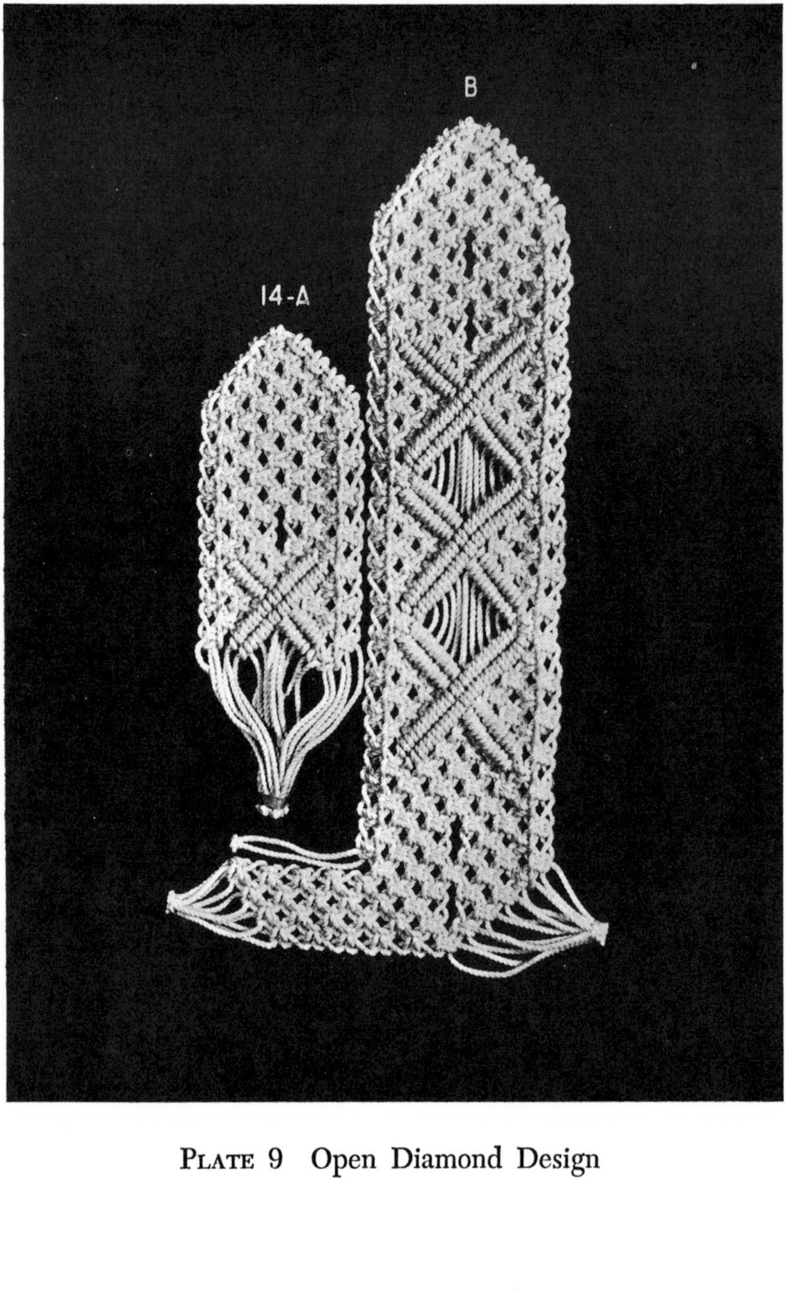

PLATE 9 Open Diamond Design

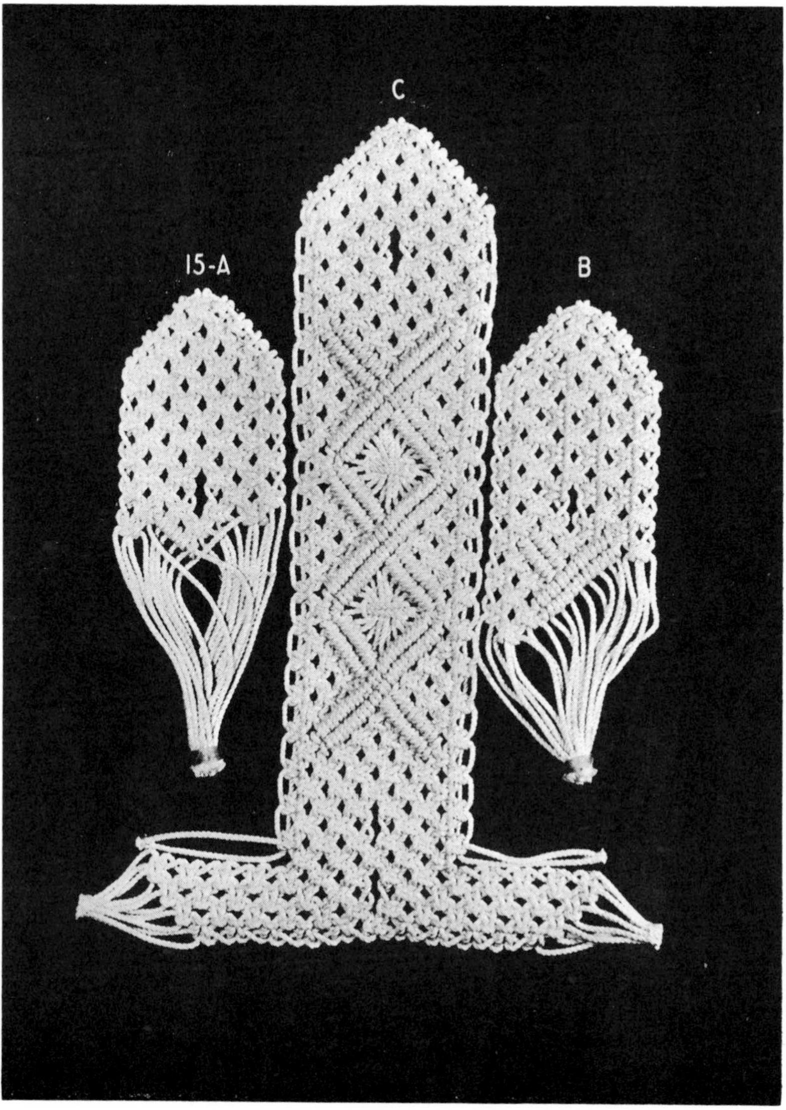

PLATE 10 Collection Knot Design

Work the belt to a point in the usual manner. Then tie 2 SK from each edge toward the middle.

(*) # 6 to right, HH with 7 to 12.
5 " " " " 6 to 11.

Tie SK with 1 to 4, 3 to 6, 5 to 8, 7 to 10, 1 to 4, 3 to 6, 5 to 8, 1 to 4, 3 to 6 and 1 to 4.

19 to left, HH with 18 to 5.
20 " " " " 19 to 6.

Tie SK with 3 to 6.

14 to right, HH with 15 to 20.
13 " " " " 14 to 19.

Tie SK with 19 to 22.

Repeat instructions from (*) until the design is the required length.

The edge of this belt is formed by using strands 1 and 3 as F, tying SK with strands 2 and 4. A smooth edge with a figure eight design is obtained.

The ridge effect in this belt is formed by pointing the Square Knots in one row to the left and in the next row to the right.

Plate 10—COLLECTION KNOT DESIGN

Fig. 15A: Shows the starting of this design with 20 strands.

B: Shows how the Half Hitches have been formed from the right to the left with twenty strands.

C: Cut 12 strands 10 times the desired length. These strands are doubled, making 24 in all. Number strands 1 to 24 from left to right.

Work the belt to a point in the usual manner. Then tie 2 SK from each edge toward the middle.

(*) # 6 to right, HH with 7 to 12.
5 " " " " 6 to 11.

Tie SK with 1 to 4, 3 to 6, 5 to 8, 7 to 10, 1 to 4, 3 to 6, 5 to 8, 1 to 4, 3 to 6 and 1 to 4.

19 to left, HH with 18 to 5.
20 " " " " 19 to 6.

Tie SK with 3 to 6.

14 to right, HH with 15 to 20.
13 " " " " 14 to 19.

Tie SK with 19 to 22.

Tie a Collection Knot by using strands 8 to 17 as F, and tying one SK with 7 and 18.

Repeat instructions from (*) until the design is the required length.

The openings in the tongue of the belt for the buckle tongue to go through are made by skipping SK in the middle every 1½ inches. When within 6 inches of the desired length, leave three more openings for the buckle tongue to go through for attaching to the belt. These openings are made about 2 inches apart in order to adjust the belt to the required length.

The edge of this belt is formed by using strands 2 and 3 as filler, tying SK with strands 1 and 4. A picot or lace effect is given to the edges.

PLATE 11—DIAMOND DESIGN

Fig. 16A: Shows a Twenty-four-Strand Diamond with an open middle design. The instructions are similar to those mentioned in Plate 10.

B: Shows a Twenty-four-Strand Diamond with Collection Knot in the middle of the design.

C: A complete belt.

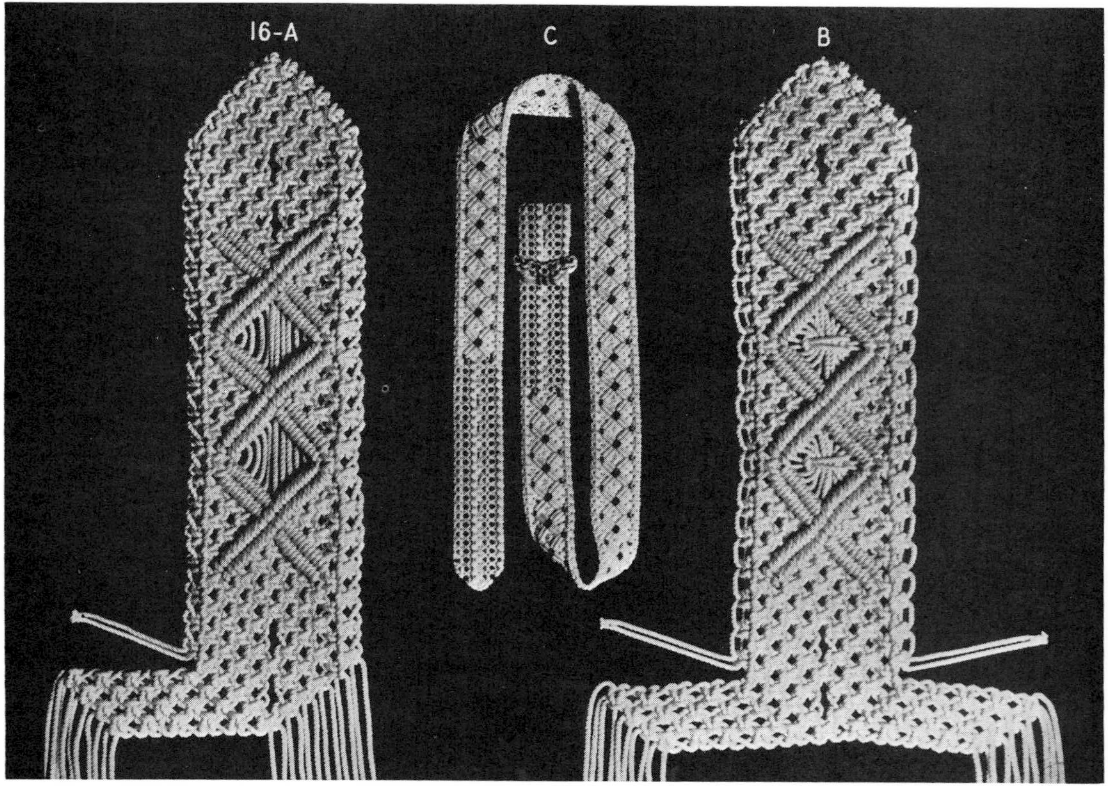
16-A
C
B

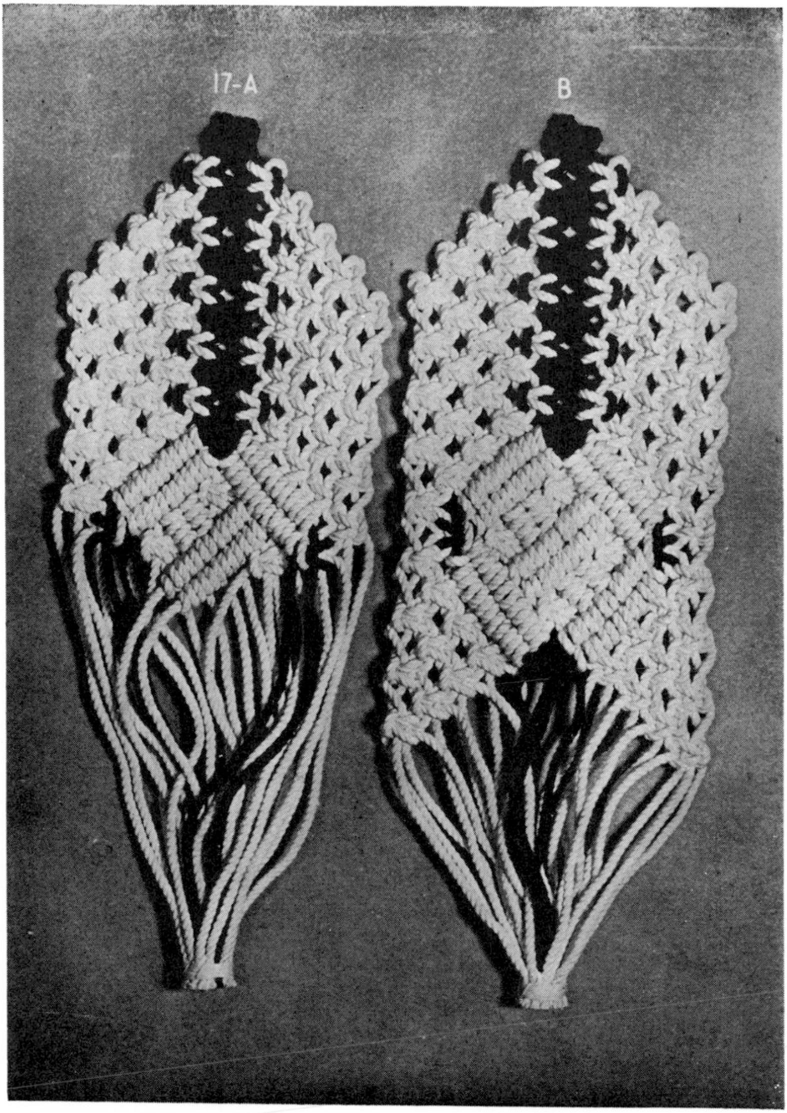

PLATE 12 Five Diamond Design

Plate 12—FIVE DIAMOND DESIGN

Fig. 17A and B: This Attractive Design has 5 Diamonds with a Square Knot in the middle of each diamond. See Plate 13 for instructions.

Plate 13—FIVE DIAMOND DESIGN

Fig. 18: This Attractive Design has 5 Diamonds with the middle open.

Cut 12 strands 10 times the desired length. These strands are doubled, making 24 in all.

Work belt to a point in the usual manner. Then tie 10 SK on the left side in the following order: 1 to 4, 3 to 6, 5 to 8, 7 to 10, 1 to 4, 3 to 6, 5 to 8, 1 to 4, 3 to 6 and 1 to 4. Similarly tie 10 corresponding SK on the right side.

(*) #11 to left, HH with 10 to 5.	14 to right, HH with 15 to 20.
12 “ “ “ “ 11 to 6.	13 “ “ “ “ 14 to 19.

Tie SK with 3 to 6 and 19 to 22.

10 to right, HH with 11, 12.	13 to right, HH with 14, 15.
9 “ “ “ “ 10, 11.	6 “ “ “ “ 7 to 12.
15 “ left, “ “ 14 to 9.	5 “ “ “ “ 6 to 11.
16 “ “ “ “ 15 to 10.	19 “ left, “ “ 18 to 13.
14 “ right, “ “ 15, 16.	20 “ “ “ “ 19 to 14.

Tie SK with 11 to 14. Fill the right and left side in with 10 SK on each side, as indicated above.

Repeat instructions from paragraph marked (*) until the design is the required length.

Plate 14—WAVE DESIGN

Fig. 19: In order to get the 4 colored strands in the middle, it is necessary to use 2 white strands as a filler. See method 5, Plate 4, which explains this idea thoroughly. This belt may also be started from brads.

Cut 12 strands ten times the desired length. After working the belt to a point, tie 3 SK from each edge toward the middle.

(*) #	8 to right, HH with 9 to 12.	17 to left, HH with 16 to 13.
	7 " " " " 8 to 11.	18 " " " " 17 to 14.

Tie SK with 1 to 4, 3 to 6, 5 to 8, 7 to 10, 1 to 4, 3 to 6, 5 to 8, 1 to 4, 3 to 6, 21 to 24, 19 to 22, 17 to 20, 15 to 18, 21 to 24, 19 to 22, 17 to 20, 21 to 24 and 19 to 22.

11 to left, HH with 10 to 7.	14 to right, HH with 15 to 18.
12 " " " " 11 to 8.	13 " " " " 14 to 17.

Tie SK with 11 to 14, 9 to 12, 13 to 16 and 11 to 14.

Repeat instructions from (*).

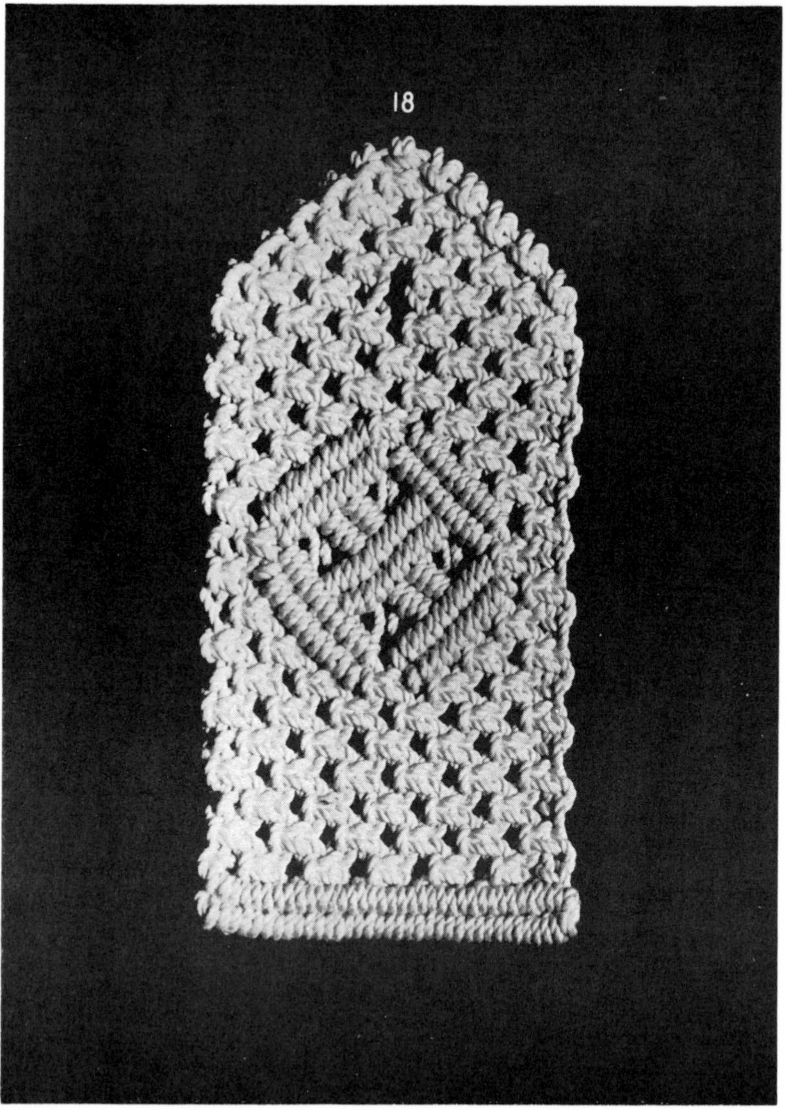

PLATE 13 Five Diamond Design

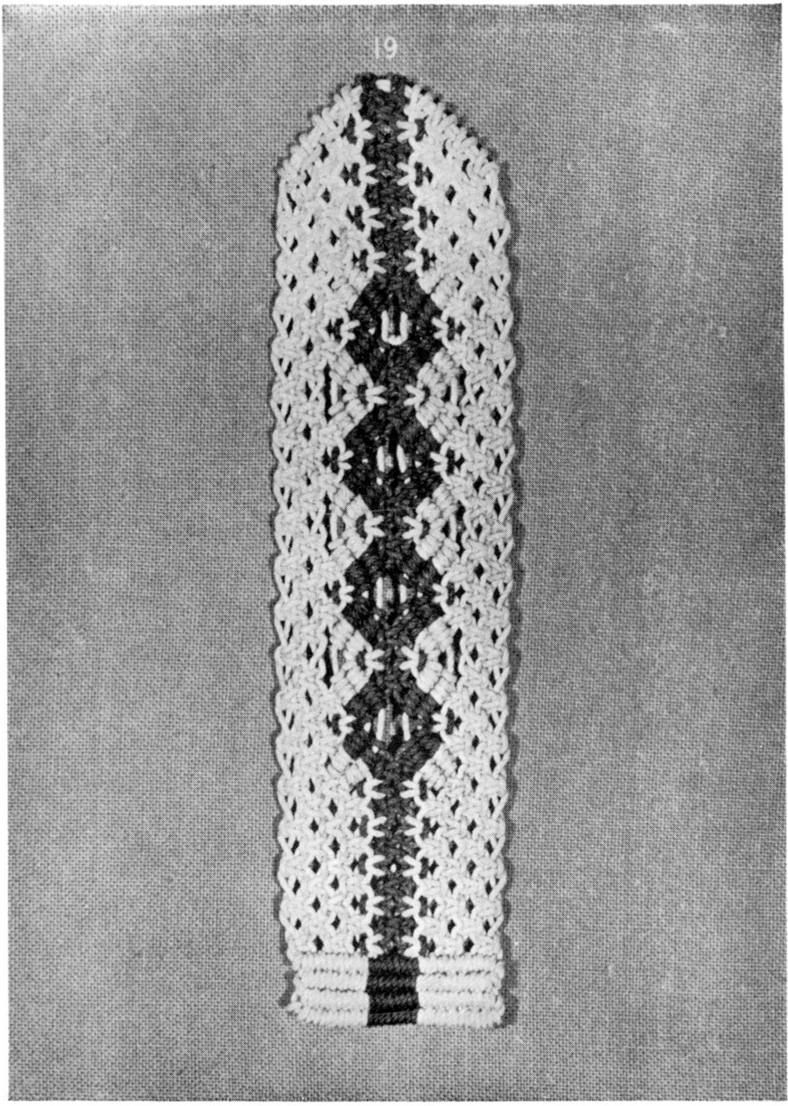

Plate 14 Wave Design

Plate 15—FULL DIAMOND DESIGN

Fig. 20: This Design is an old favorite among the majority of advanced Square Knotters. It takes a little more time to make than some of the others, but is well worth the effort.

Cut 12 strands 10 times the desired length. These strands are doubled, making 24 in all.

Work the belt to a point in the usual manner. Tie 3 SK from each edge toward the middle.

	# 8	to right,	HH	with	9 to 12.
	7	" "	"	"	8 to 11.
	17	" left,	"	"	16 to 13.
	18	" "	"	"	17 to 14.
(*)	5	" "	"	"	4 to 1.
	6	" "	"	"	5 to 1.
	20	" right,	"	"	21 to 24.
	19	" "	"	"	20 to 24.
	12	" "	"	"	13 to 18.
	11	" "	"	"	12 to 17.
	11	" left,	"	"	10 to 7.
	12	" "	"	"	11 to 8.
	2	" right,	"	"	3 to 12.

1	to right,	HH	with	2 to 11.
23	" left,	"	"	22 to 7.
24	" "	"	"	23 to 8.
5	" "	"	"	4 to 1.
6	" "	"	"	5 to 1.
20	" right,	"	"	21 to 24.
19	" "	"	"	20 to 24.
14	" "	"	"	15 to 18.
13	" "	"	"	14 to 17.
2	" "	"	"	3 to 12.
1	" "	"	"	2 to 11.
23	" left,	"	"	22 to 13.
24	" "	"	"	23 to 14.

Repeat from (*) until the design is the required length.

This design can be made with 4 Square Knots in the middle and 1 on the sides. In fact, the diamonds are likely to be more regular if formed in this manner.

Plate 16—THE VICTORY DESIGN

Fig. 21A and B: This design with a Square Knot border and "V" shaped bars in two colors is not difficult to duplicate. Study the directions to the end before attempting the design.

Cut 6 strands 6 times the desired length for the outside, and cut 6 strands (3 white and 3 black) ten times the desired length for the middle. These strands are doubled, making 24 in all. The black strands are in the middle.

(*) # 9	to	left,	HH	with	8, 7.
10	"	"	"	"	9 to 7.
11	"	"	"	"	10 to 7.
12	"	"	"	"	11 to 7.
16	"	right,	"	"	17, 18.
15	"	"	"	"	16 to 18.
14	"	"	"	"	15 to 18.
13	"	"	"	"	14 to 18.
13	"	left,	"	"	12 to 7.

14	to	left,	HH	with	13 to 8.
15	"	"	"	"	14 to 9.
15	"	right,	"	"	16 to 18.
14	"	"	"	"	15 to 17.
13	"	"	"	"	14 to 16.
13	"	left,	"	"	12 to 10.
14	"	"	"	"	13 to 11.
15	"	"	"	"	14 to 12.

These strands are now in their original sequence, 9 white, 6 black and 9 white.

The border is now formed by tying 8 SK in 2 columns on the left, alternating strands 1 to 4 and 3 to 6. Next, tie a SK with strands 5 to 8 in order to join the border to the design. Tie 8 SK in 2 columns on the right, alternating strands 20 to 24 and 19 to 22. Using strands 17 to 20, tie SK to join the border to the design. Repeat instructions from paragraph marked (*).

Fig. 22: Shows a complete belt with the above design.

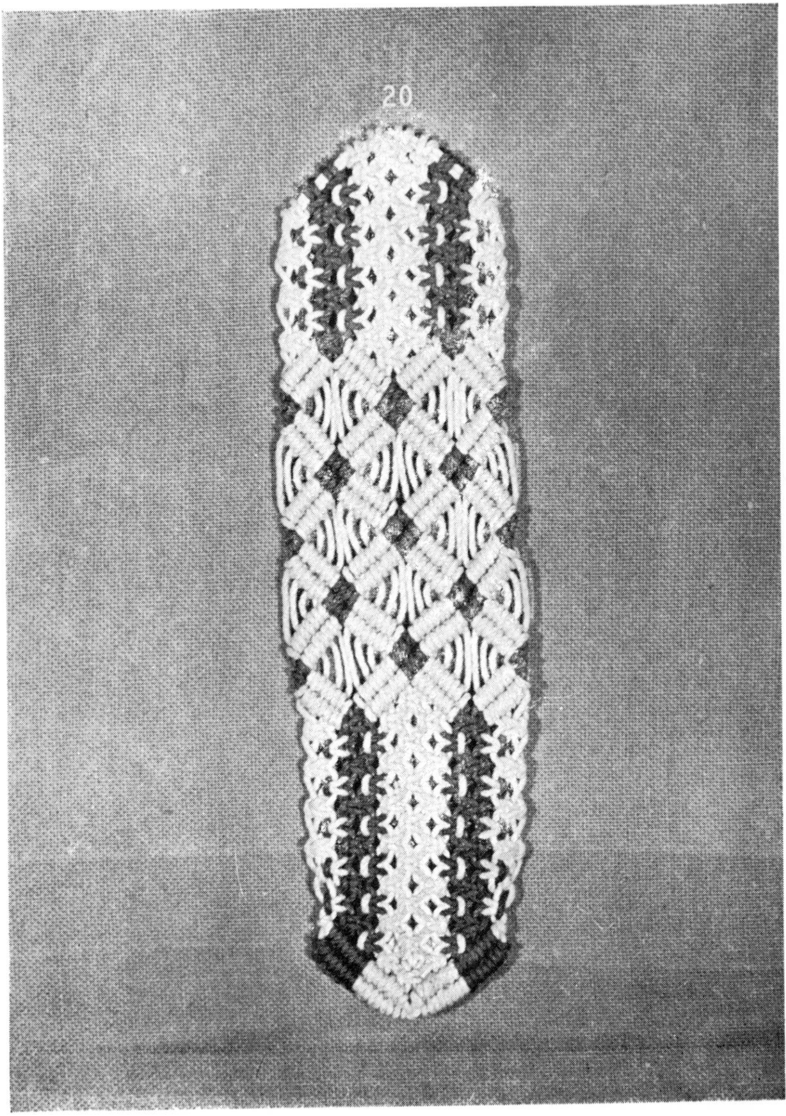

PLATE 15 Full Diamond Design

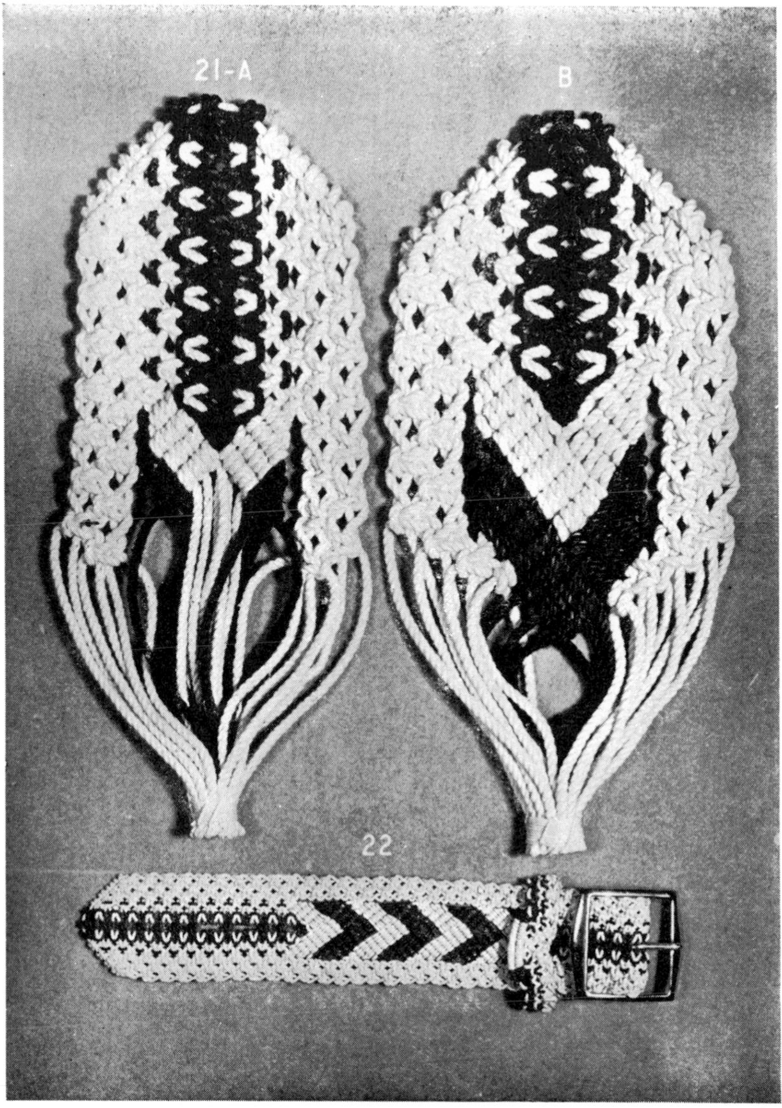

PLATE 16 Victory Design

Plate 17—SLANTING BAR DESIGN

Fig. 23: This Design with a Square Knot Border, Half Hitch Slanting Bars in two colors is started the same as the one shown in Plate 16.

#	9	to	left,	HH	with	8, 7.
	10	“	“	“	“	9 to 7.
	11	“	“	“	“	10 to 7.
	12	“	“	“	“	11 to 7.
	16	“	right,	“	“	17, 18.
	15	“	“	“	“	16 to 18.
	14	“	“	“	“	15 to 18.

13	to	left,	HH	with	12 to 7.
14	“	“	“	“	13 to 8.
15	“	“	“	“	14 to 9.
16	“	“	“	“	15 to 10.
17	“	“	“	“	16 to 11.
18	“	“	“	“	17 to 12.

These strands are now in their original sequence, 9 white, 6 black and 9 white.

The border is now formed by tying 8 SK in 2 columns on the left, alternating strands 1 to 4 and 3 to 6. Next, tie SK with strands 5 to 8 in order to join the border to the design. Tie 8 SK in 2 columns on the right, alternating 20 to 24 and 19 to 22. Using strands 17 to 20, tie SK to join the border to the design. If at any time the border and the design should get a little out of line, stretch them to make them even. This irregularity is sometimes caused by the cord stretching or by more strain being applied to some knots than others during the formation of the work.

(*)	17	to	left,	HH	with	16 to 13.
	18	“	“	“	“	17 to 14.
	18	“	“	“	“	17 to 15.
	18	“	“	“	“	17, 16.
	18	“	“	“	“	17.
	9	“	“	“	“	8, 7.
	10	“	“	“	“	9 to 7.
	11	to	left,	HH	with	10 to 7.

12	to	left,	HH	with	11 to 7.
13	“	“	“	“	12 to 7.
14	“	“	“	“	13 to 8.
15	“	“	“	“	14 to 9.
16	“	“	“	“	15 to 10.
17	“	“	“	“	16 to 11.
18	“	“	“	“	17 to 12.

For the border as instructed previously.

Repeat instructions from the paragraph marked (*) until the design is the required length.

If in the process of making a belt the strands are too long to handle, a good way to shorten a working strand is to start from the end, and wind it in “S” turns around the thumb and little finger.

Then remove and add a frapping around the middle, thus forming a hank. An easily adjustable hitch can be made around the middle by holding the hank in the right hand. The left hand grasps the working strand, turning it over and forming a loop which is placed over the hank. See illustration (a).

A commercial bobbin or a meshing needle may also be used. To make a bobbin, first wind ends, then the middle, and don't run back over ends in winding. See illustration (b).

A Single Chain Sennit is begun at the bottom of each strand by forming a slip bit in an Overhand Knot. Then continue the braid by passing each additional bit through the eye of the last bit. See illustration (c).

Plate 18—SNAKE DESIGN

Fig. 24A: Shows This Design Open, how the Flats are attached to the sides, and how they are attached in the middle.

Cut 8 white strands 10 times the desired length. Then cut 4 colored strands 15 times the desired length. These strands are doubled, making 24 in all.

Work the belt to a point in the usual manner. Then tie 4 SK with 11 to 14, thus making a Flat of five SK in the middle.

Tie SK with 5 to 8, 7 to 10, 5 to 8, 7 to 10, 5 to 8, 7 to 10, 17 to 20, 15 to 18, 17 to 20, 15 to 18, 17 to 20 and 15 to 18.

(*) Tie 2 Flats of 6 SK in each with 1 to 4 and 21 to 24.

Then lift up the Flat in the middle so as to be able to tie the outside Flats together underneath. Using strands 4 and 21 as F, tie SK with 3 and 22.

Tie 2 Flats of 7 SK in each with 1 to 4 and 21 to 24.

Tie SK with 9 to 12, 13 to 16, 11 to 14, 5 to 8, 7 to 10, 5 to 8, 17 to 20, 15 to 18 and 17 to 20.

11 to left, HH with 10 to 7.	14 to right, HH with 15 to 18.
12 " " " " 11 to 8.	13 " " " " 14 to 17.

Tie SK with 5 to 8, 17 to 20, 3 to 6 and 19 to 22. Notice that the last 2 Square Knots join the Flats to the sides.

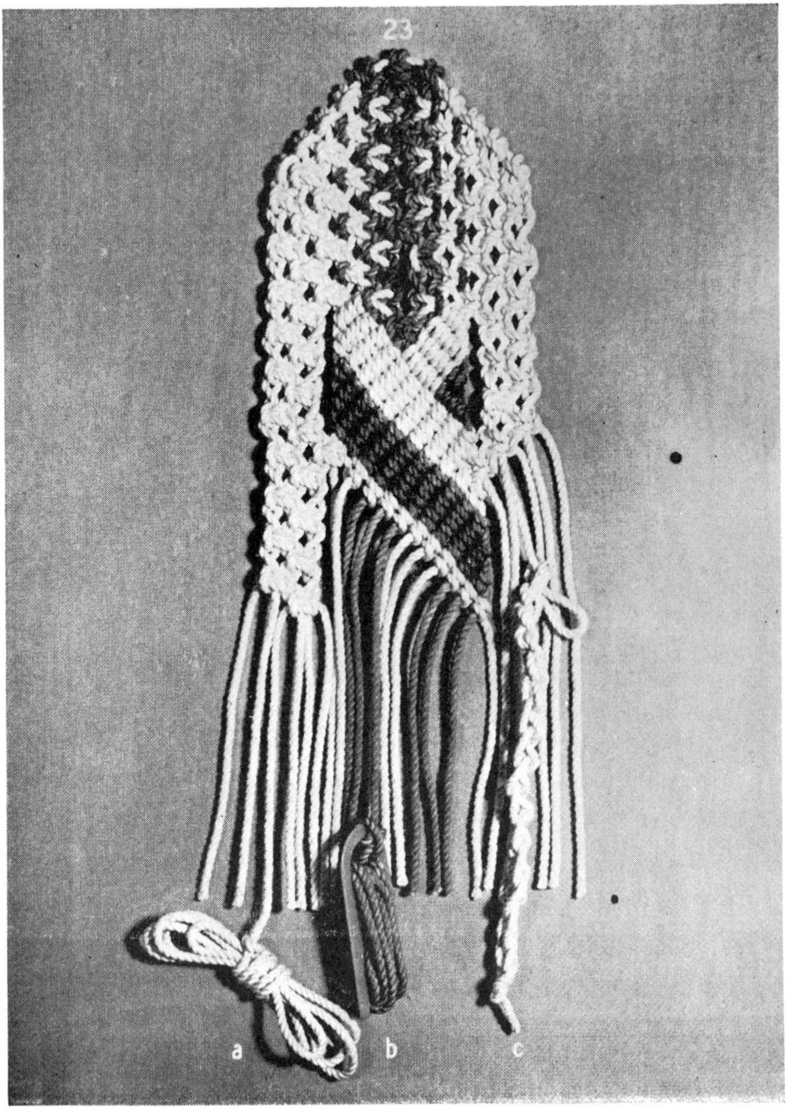

PLATE 17 Slanting Bar Design

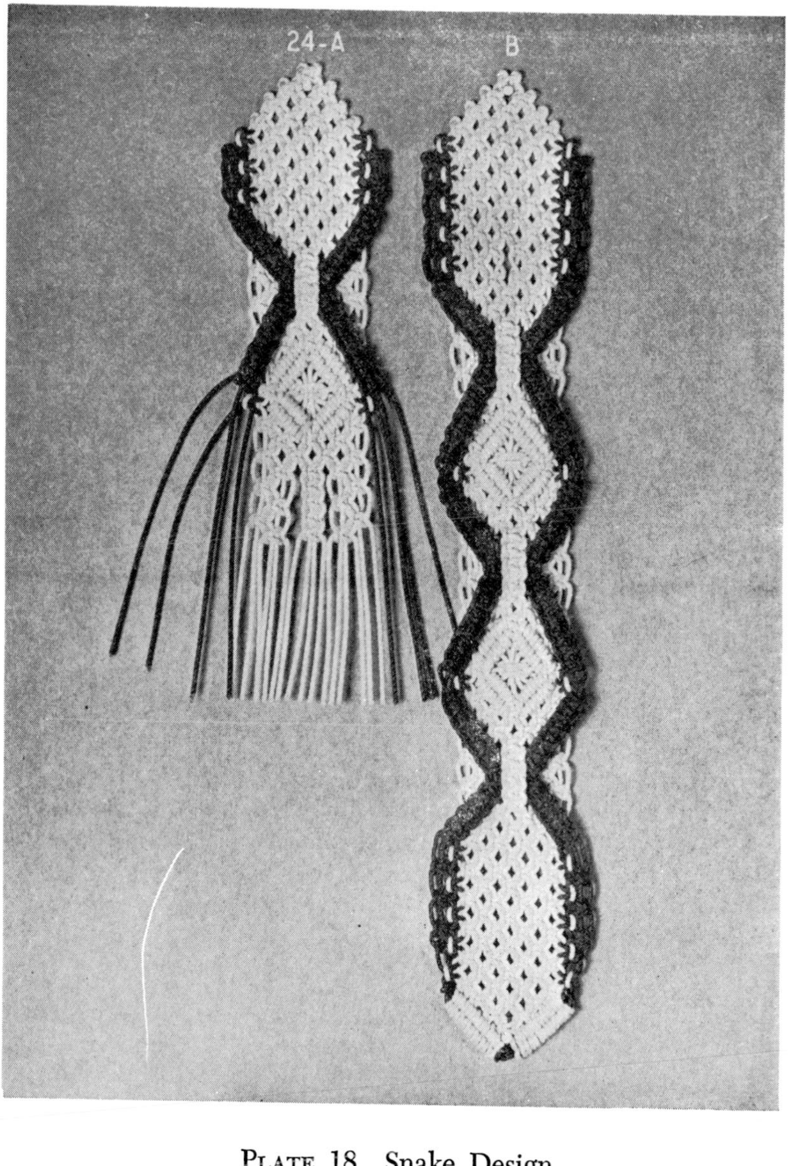

PLATE 18 Snake Design

Form a Collection Knot by using strands 10 to 15 as Filler and tying 2 identical Half Knots with 9 and 16.

8 to right, HH with	9 to 12.	17 to left, HH with	16 to 13.
7 " " " "	8 to 11.	18 " " " "	17 to 14.

Tie SK with 11 to 14, 5 to 8, 7 to 10, 9 to 12, 5 to 8, 7 to 10, 5 to 8, 7 to 10, 5 to 8, 7 to 10, 17 to 20, 15 to 18, 13 to 16, 17 to 20, 15 to 18, 17 to 20, 15 to 18, 17 to 20 and 15 to 18.

Tie a Flat of 5 SK with strands 11 to 14.

Repeat instructions from paragraph marked (*) until the design is the required length.

B: This Snake Design is rather unusual and attractive.

A Twenty-four-Strand Belt finished to a point with two rows of HH, cut strands 2, 4, 21 and 24. There are now 20 working strands.

2 to left, tie one HH with 1.

Tie SK in 4th row with strands 1 to 4.

19 to right, tie one HH with 20.

Tie SK in 4th row with strands 17 to 20.

1 to right, tie HH with	2 to 10.
1 " " " " "	2 to 9.

While tying the second part with 3, tuck 2 through before making the knot taut. Then tuck 3 through 4; etc.

20 to left, tie HH with	19 to 11.
20 " " " " "	19 to 10.

While tying the second part of 18, tuck through 19 before making the knot taut. Then tuck 18 through 17; etc. Tie SK with strands 9 to 12. Turn the belt over and pull taut all strands that were tucked through HH loops. Then bury strands 9 to 12.

Plate 19—SNAKE DESIGN

Fig. 25A: The Outside Flats consist of 21 Square Knots, using strands 1 to 4 and 21 to 24. Then make 2 more Flats, using strands 5 to 8 and 17 to 20. This design is similar to the one explained in Plate 18.

B: Shows a complete belt with the above design.

Note that the belt loop has been formed on the right side of the belt, which, of course, makes it a woman's belt. Snap fasteners may be attached to keep the belt in place.

Plate 20—THE WHEELMAN DESIGN

Fig. 26: This design is very striking in a woman's sports belt.

Cut 10 strands 9 times the desired length.

Start the belt in the usual manner, and work to a point at each side. Then tie SK with 1 to 4, 3 to 6, 5 to 8, 1 to 4, 3 to 6, 1 to 4, 17 to 20, 15 to 18, 13 to 16, 17 to 20, 15 to 18 and 17 to 20.

#	9	to	left,	HH with	8 to 1.
	10	"	"	" "	9 to 1.
	12	"	right,	" "	13 to 20.
	11	"	"	" "	12 to 20.
(*)	2	"	"	" "	3 to 10.
	1	"	"	" "	2 to 9.
	19	"	left,	" "	18 to 9.
	20	"	"	" "	19 to 10.
	8	"	"	horizontally and back, HH with 7 to 1 and 1 to 7.	
	9	"	"	HH with	8 to 1.
	10	"	"	" "	9 to 1.
	13	"	right horizontally and back, HH with 14 to 20 and 20 to 14.		
	12	"	"	HH with	13 to 20.
	11	"	"	" "	12 to 20.

Repeat instructions from (*) to continue the design.

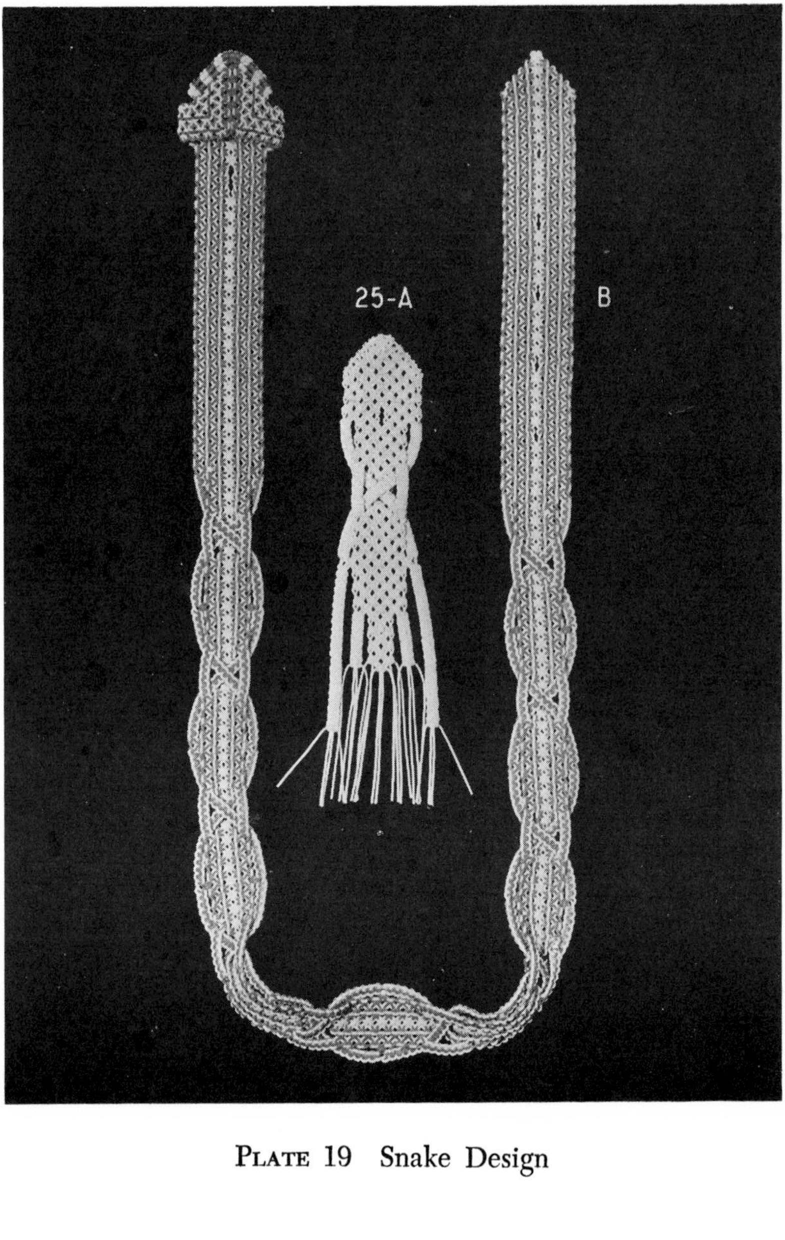

PLATE 19 Snake Design

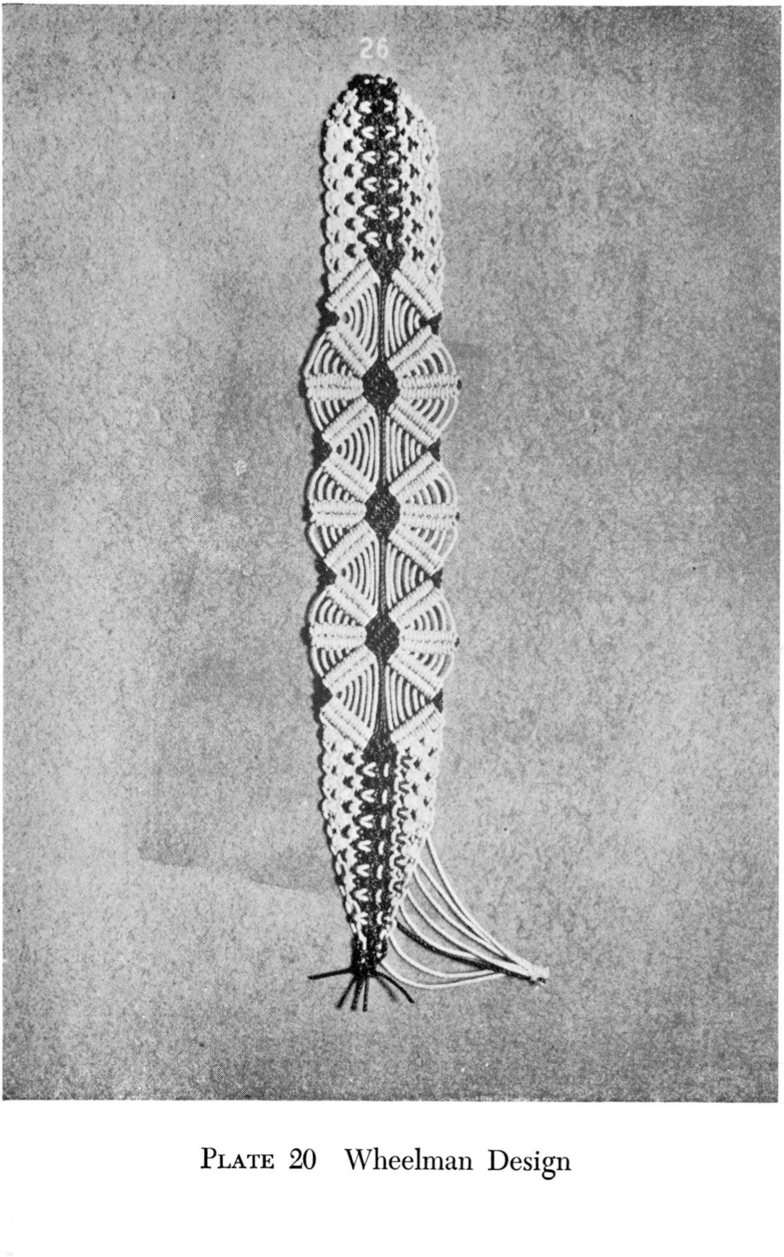

Plate 20 Wheelman Design

Plate 21—SHELL KNOT DESIGN

This Attractive Design, with a Square Knot border and slanting quadruple bar, has a Shell Knot in the middle. It is not difficult to make, but the instructions must be closely followed, as the design is made very nearly like several others.

Cut the 6 outside strands (3 for each side) 6 times the desired length, and cut the 6 middle strands 10 times the desired length. These strands are doubled, making 24 in all. Work the belt to a point in the usual manner. Then tie 3 SK from each edge toward the middle.

Fig. 27A.

(*) # 8 to right, HH with 9 to 12.	7 to right, HH with 8 to 12.
7 “ “ “ “ 8 to 12.	7 “ “ “ “ 8 to 12.

Tie SK with 1 to 4, 3 to 6, 1 to 4, 3 to 6 and 5 to 8.

17 to left, HH with 16 to 13.	18 to left, HH with 17 to 13.
18 “ “ “ “ 17 to 13.	18 “ “ “ “ 17 to 13.

Tie SK with 21 to 24, 19 to 22, 21 to 24, 19 to 22, and 17 to 20.

B: To make the Shell Knot, use the 2 middle strands (12 and 13) as a filler, and 11 and 14 for tying. Tie a single Half Hitch with 11, then one with 14, then 11 again, thus alternating until there are 10 single Half Hitches. Pass the 2 filler strands down through the opening between the 2 quadruple bars of Half Hitches and bring them out in front. Using these 2 strands as a filler, tie SK in front of the Shell Knot with 11 and 14. Continue as follows:

11 to left, HH with 10 to 7.	14 to right, HH with 15 to 18.
12 “ “ “ “ 11 to 7.	13 “ “ “ “ 14 to 18.
12 “ “ “ “ 11 to 7.	13 “ “ “ “ 14 to 18.
12 “ “ “ “ 11 to 7.	13 “ “ “ “ 14 to 18.

The border is now formed by tying 8 SK in 2 columns on the left, alternating strands 1 to 4 and 3 to 6. Next, tie SK with strands 5 to 8 in order to join the border to the design. Tie 8 SK in 2 columns on the right, alternating strands 20 to 24, and 19 to 22. Using strands 17 to 20, tie SK to join the border to the design. The middle of this is left open.

Repeat instructions from paragraph marked (*) until the design is the required length.

C: Shows two complete designs in a belt that is made with Square Knot cord.

Fig. 28: Shows the same type of belt with four designs utilizing a Square Knot instead of a Shell Knot.

Plate 22—MACRAMÉ KNOTS

Fig. 29: The French or Grapevine Bar shows how the Half Hitches are formed around a two-cord core. This procedure is the same as for a whipping or seizing of the same nature. See Plate 3, Fig. 6A for Half Knot designs of a similar style. See Plate 4 for special instructions, abbreviations and the proper sequence of lettering strands, which in the following case have imaginary numbers.

Fig. 30: The Lark's Head Tatting Bar may be worked on a double core, and is pulled up snugly as the work proceeds.

Fig. 31: The Single Chain Design is formed by using a Lark's Head to begin with. Proceed by half hitching one strand around the other, as illustrated.

Fig. 32: The Double Chain Design is formed in the same manner as the single, except that the strands are doubled. In some cases 3 or 4 strands may be used for this operation. This type of chain work is used in many kinds of Macramé designs, where color schemes are employed to give the patterns added effect.

Fig. 33: A succession of Square Knots formed on a filler in this manner is known as a Flat.

Fig. 34: A Spiral of Half Knots may be formed in this manner. When tied the same way repeatedly they will automatically twist into spiral form.

Fig. 35: The Half Knot Loop Design is often used to obtain a novel effect in Square Knot work.

Fig. 36A and B: The Constrictor Knot Loop Design is another way

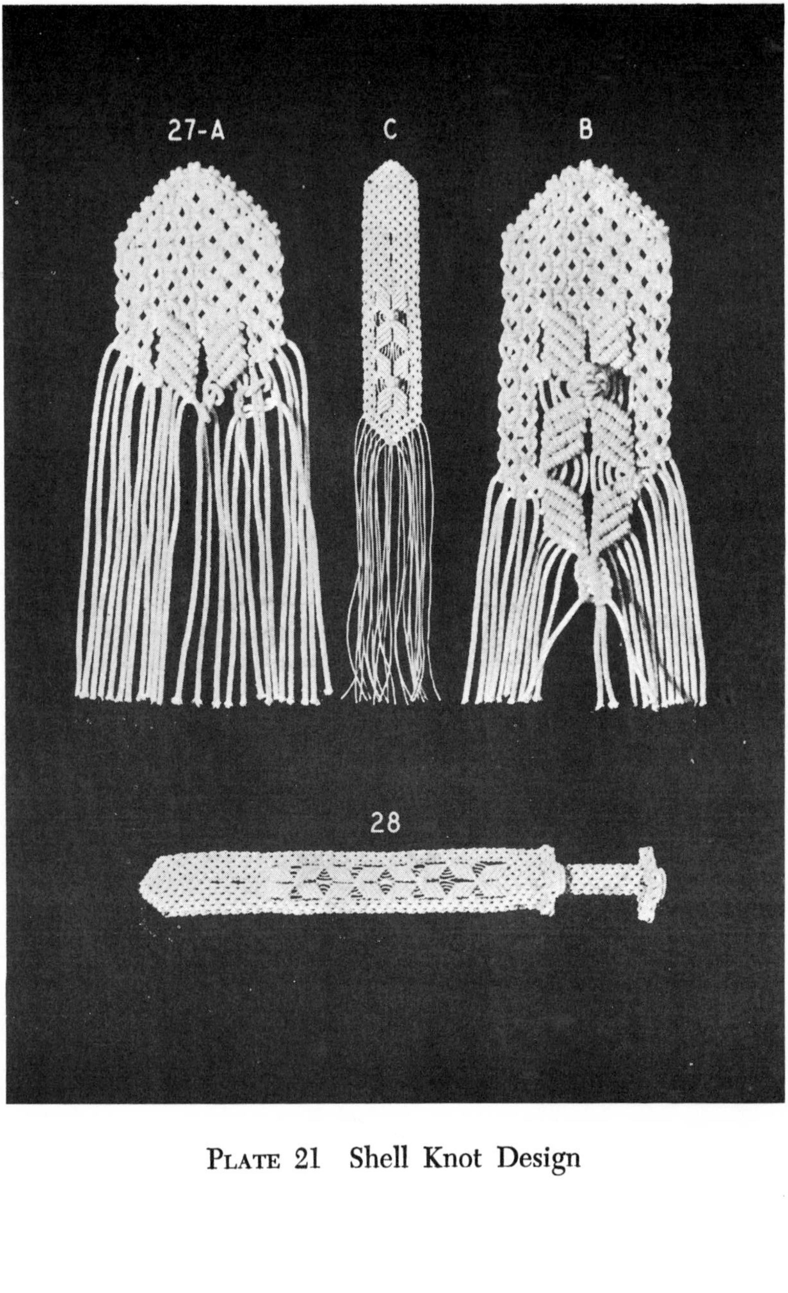

PLATE 21 Shell Knot Design

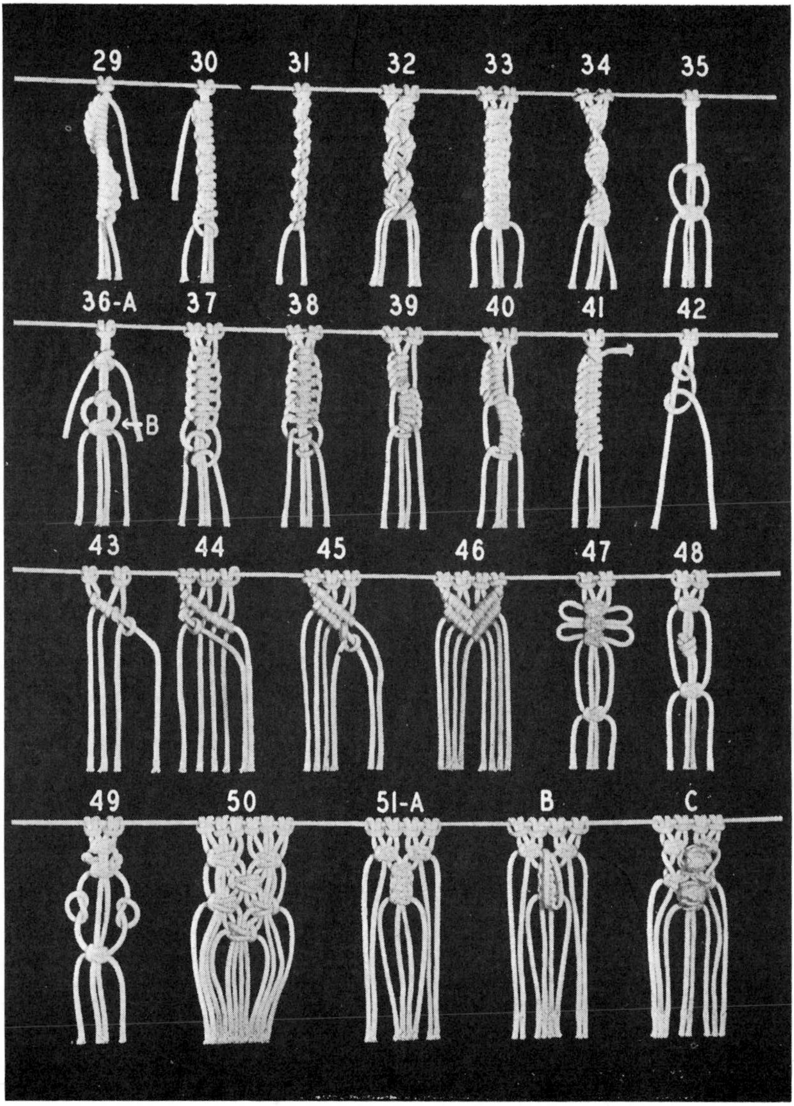

PLATE 22 Macramé Knots

of presenting a similar pattern. The Constrictor Knot is shown opened up in Fig. A.

Fig. 37: The Genoese Bar illustrates a method of alternately hitching left and right Half Hitches around a double core.

Fig. 38: The Alternating Genoese Bar is similar to Fig. 37; except that the hitches are made the opposite way instead of both being made in the same manner as for the previous method.

Fig. 39: The Shell Bar consists of a series of 5 Half Hitches that are tied alternately with the cord from the right side and then from the left side.

Fig. 40: The Shell Bar shown here embraces the same principle of construction as shown in Fig. 39, except that a series of 7 Half Hitches are tied each time instead of 5.

Fig. 41: The Buttonhole Bar embraces a series of Half Hitches that are formed in a rigid manner to prevent the cord from twisting before the work is made fast.

Fig. 42: The Half Hitch represents the most practical knot in Macramé work for obtaining variations in designs. Its construction can easily be followed from this illustration.

Fig. 43: A Series of Half Hitched Cords are formed in the manner shown.

Fig. 44: In beginning a new row of diagonally hitched cords, strand 1 is used as a filler while forming successive Half Hitches with strands 2 to 6 in their proper sequence.

Fig. 45: Two rows of diagonally Half Hitched Cords are brought down with the hitches formed in the manner shown here to finish off.

Fig. 46: When forming 2 rows of Half Hitches—one slanting diagonally to the right and the other diagonally to the left—they are brought together in the middle by joining the 2 filler strands 1 and 6 with Half Hitches in the manner shown.

Fig. 47: The Centipede Knots are formed with a series of Looped Square Knots which are spaced far enough apart to insure the formation of a loop when the knots are pushed together.

Fig. 48: The Small Shell Knot represents another variation of this type of knot work. It is made by first forming a Square Knot which is followed with an Overhand Knot in the filler cords in the manner shown. Another Square Knot is then tied underneath this knot with the working strands.

Fig. 49: The Knotted Loop Square Knot is of similar construction to the Centipede design in Fig. 47; except that the Overhand Knots are formed in the loops before proceeding to the next series of knots.

Fig. 50: The Collecting Knot represents a number of cords brought together in the middle of a Square Knot. In order to execute certain designs, it is necessary to collect a number of cords in this manner.

Fig. 51A: The Beaded or Shell Knot is formed in the following manner: Double 4 strands over a core and tie 4 Lark's Head Knots. Then tie a Square Knot with strands 1 to 4 and 5 to 8. Using strands 4 and 5 as a filler, tie 3 Square Knots with strands 3 and 6.

B: Pass the two middle strands 4 and 5 down through the opening between the 2 Square Knots.

C: Using strands 4 and 5 as a filler, tie a Square Knot in front of the Bead or a Shell Knot with strands 3 and 6.

Plate 23—POPULAR BELT DESIGNS

Fig. 52: The Sport Belt shown here portrays a double row of crossed Half Hitches with a single chain on the outer edges, which forms a unique pattern of open work. (See Plate 22, Fig. 31.)

Fig. 53: A belt such as this consists of 4 rows of Half Hitches with double rows of crossed Half Hitches in the middle. Various color combinations may be utilized for all types of belts, which can best be determined by the patterns involved, using any number of suitable strands from 24, 28, 32, etc.

Fig. 54: Represents a Full Diamond Design as illustrated in Plate 15.

Fig. 55: Shows a Single Cross Bar Design with open work in the middle.

Fig. 56: This Type of Belt represents one of the most interesting and popular of all belt designs. It consists of the following patterns: The Full Diamond is followed in sequence by the Braided Carrick, the Half Diamond, and a double row of Hitching that is formed in the shape of a square with a Spiral in the middle.

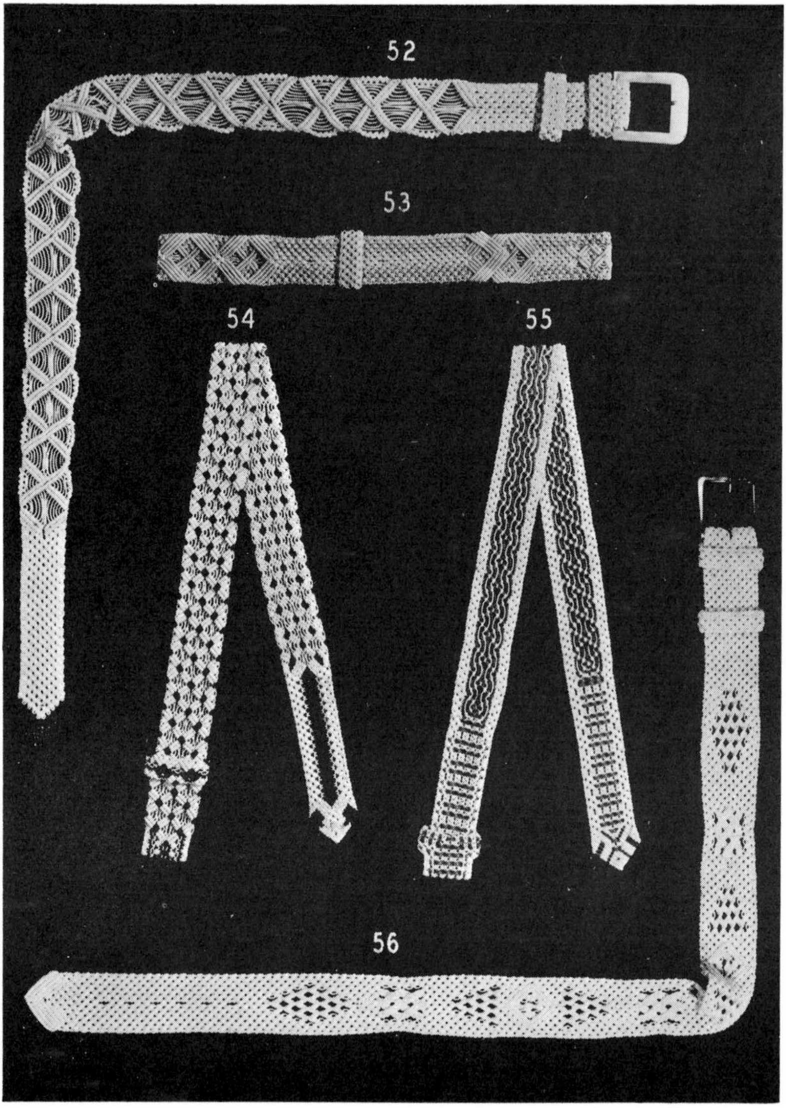

PLATE 23 Popular Belt Designs

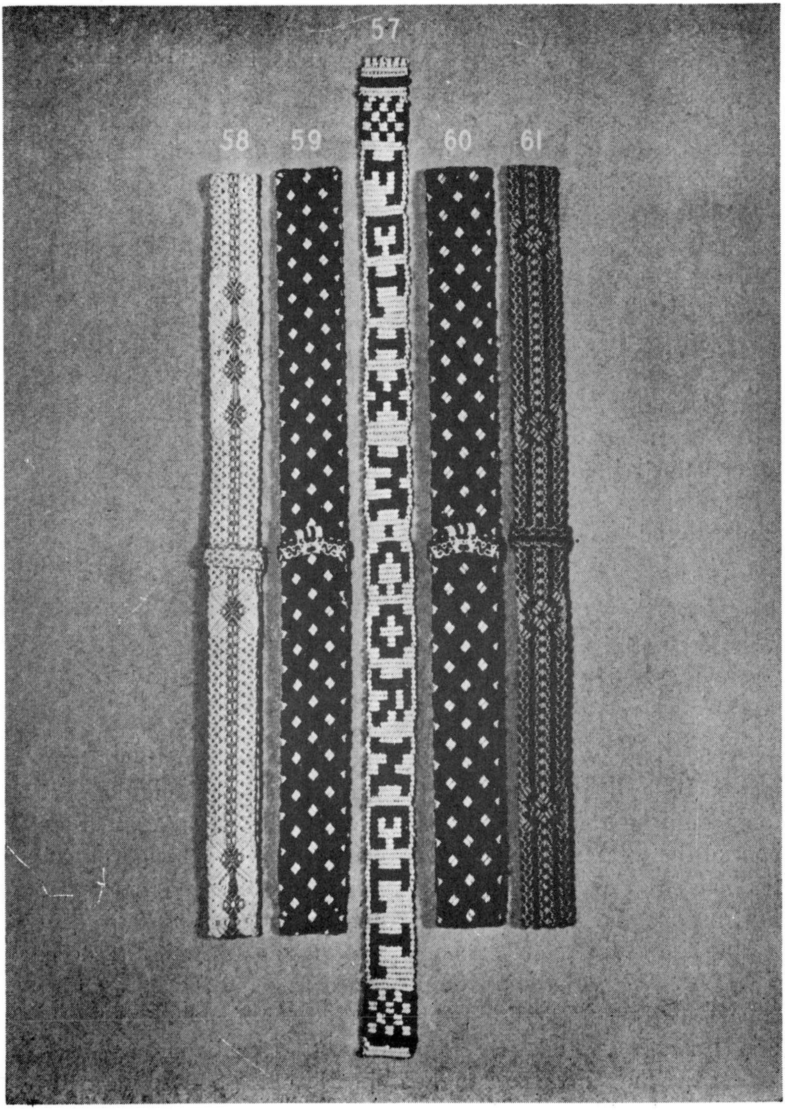

PLATE 24 Forming Letters and Other Designs

Plate 24—FORMING LETTERS AND OTHER DESIGNS

Fig. 57: Illustrates for the first time this practical, simple way of putting a name in a belt. Lettering in a belt has been done before but in a more difficult way. This belt consists of 12 white strands and 1 colored strand. The white Half Hitches are made vertically and the lettering is made with the colored strand horizontally. See Plate 34 for the complete alphabet. This lettering can also be made with 6 strands.

Fig. 58: This Twenty-Strand Belt with a Double Bar Half Hitched Design was started from the point and finished off at the belt loop. (See Plate 9.)

Fig. 59 and 60: These Twenty-four-Strand Full Diamond Designs are explained in Plate 15.

Fig. 61: This Twenty-Strand Double Bar Half Hitched Design is similar to the one explained in Plate 9.

Plate 25—WOMEN'S TIE BELTS

Fig. 62: This Woman's Tie Belt combines Square Knotting, Braiding and Half Hitching, but is not difficult to make. The middle portion should be about 2 inches shorter than the waistline measurement of the wearer, and each end is about 12 inches long. To make this belt, cut 6 strands 8 times the desired length of the middle section plus one and a half times the combined length of the two ends. Double and fasten them to a hook, thus making 12 strands. Proceed as follows: With 4 strands, tie 1 Square Knot 18 inches from the loops. Using these 4 strands and 2 more to the left and 2 to the right, tie 2 Square Knots. Then tie 3 Square Knots, using 2 more strands to the left and the remaining 2 to the right. Next tie 2 Square Knots and follow this with 3 lines of Spirals of any desired length. Using Square Knots again, join the Spirals and bring the work to point.

Using the first strand on the left as a filler, make 2 Half Hitches around it with each of the next 5 strands to the right. Using the first strand on the right as a filler, make 2 Half Hitches around it with each of the 11 strands on the left. Keep the Half Hitches on a diagonal line, especially when tying with the last 3 or 4 strands. Now select the sixth strand from the right, and using it as a filler, make 2 Half Hitches around it with each of the 5 strands to the right, taking care to keep the Half Hitching on a diagonal line. Repeat the directions in this paragraph until the half hitched design is of the desired length. When half hitching away from the middle, tie the Half Hitches with each of the 2 outside strands about an eighth of an inch away from the last Half Hitches, then draw up taut. In this way the strands are kept curved, thus producing an attractive, scalloped edge.

When the end of the Half Hitch work is reached, tie the same Square Knots and Spirals as at the beginning but in reverse order. Next, divide the 12 strands into 4 groups of 3 strands each and braid them together, using the Four-Strand Round Sennit. This Sennit is formed by bringing the outside strand on either side around in back toward the opposite side, then under the outside strand and over the next strand toward its own side. Repeat same procedure from each side until braid is finished. (See Plate 51, Fig. 170.) Tie the ends into a small tassel. Cut the loops in the strands at the beginning of the belt and braid in the same manner.

The finished belt is tied about the waist by using a Square Knot or a Double Carrick Bend. Do not use a Granny Knot.

Fig. 63: Another variation of a Woman's Tie Belt. (For abbreviations see Plate 4.)

Tie 3 Flats of 3 SK with 1 to 4, 5 to 8 and 9 to 12.

Tie SK with 3 to 6, 7 to 10, 1 to 4, 5 to 8, 9 to 12, 3 to 6, 7 to 10, 5 to 8, 9 to 12, 7 to 10 and 9 to 12.

Holding strand 12 diagonally to the right and using it as F, make 2 HH around it with each of strands 11 to 1. Using the same strand as F, hold it diagonally to the left and make 2 HH around it with each of strands 2 to 12. Keep the HH on a diagonal line, especially when tying with the last 3 or 4 strands. Repeat the directions in this paragraph until the half hitched design is of the desired length.

Tie SK with 9 to 12, 7 to 10, 5 to 8, 3 to 6, 1 to 4, 9 to 12, 7 to 10, 5 to 8, 3 to 6, 9 to 12 and 7 to 10.

Tie 3 Flats of 3 SK with 1 to 4, 5 to 8 and 9 to 12. Cut 1 strand out of each Flat. There are now 9 working strands.

Using strand 5 as F, make a Four-Strand Double Round Sennit. This Sennit is made the same as the Four-Strand Single Round

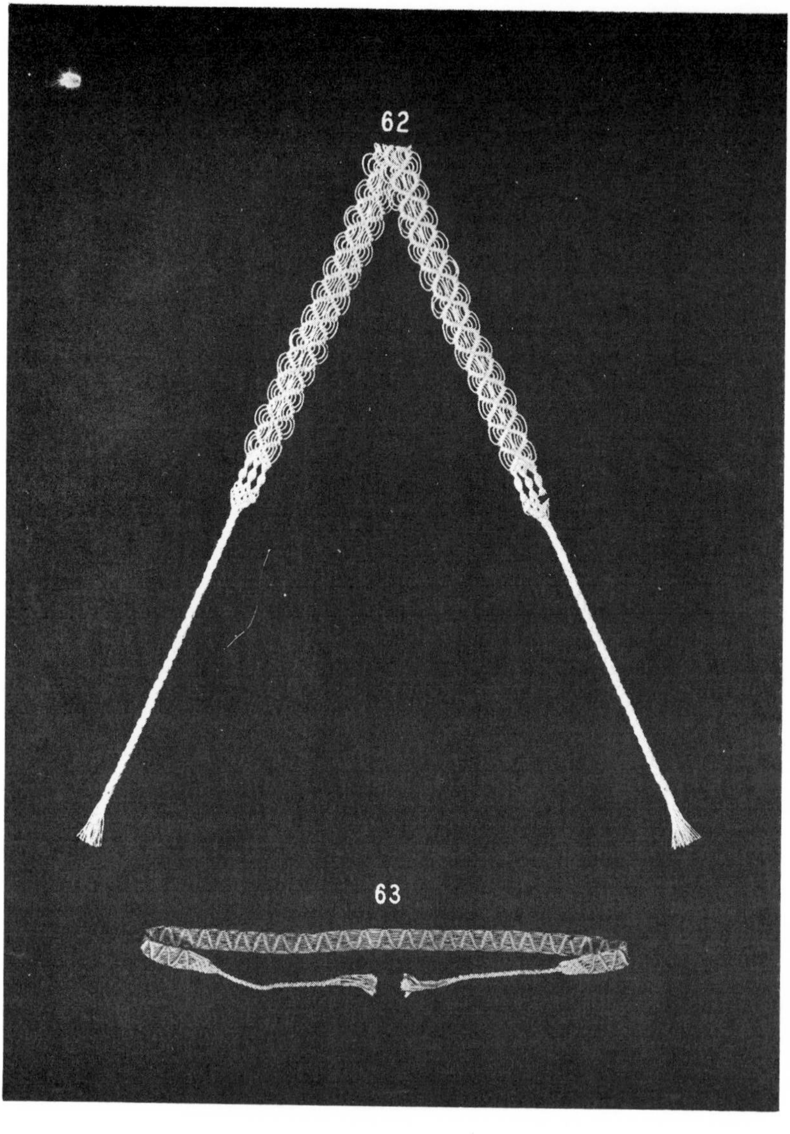

PLATE 25 Ladies' Tie Belts

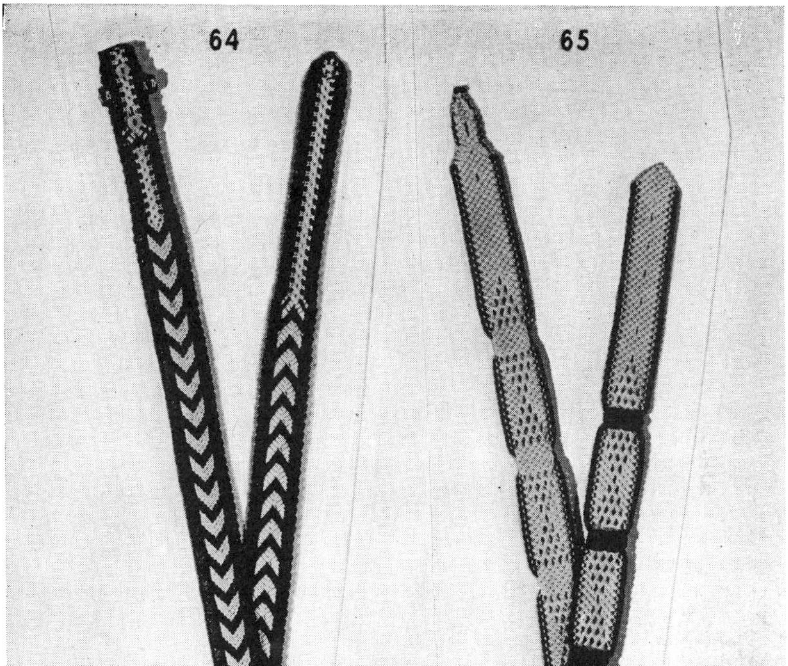

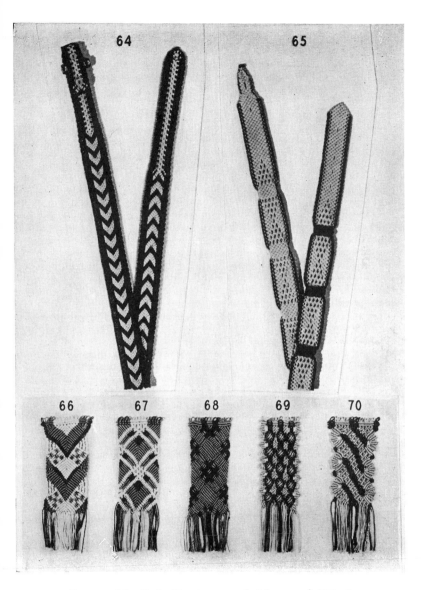

PLATE 26 Belt Designs and Macramé Work

Sennit, with the double instead of single strands. (See Plate 51.) Bring the outside pair of strands on the left side around in back toward the right side, then under the outside right pair of strands and over the next pair toward the left. Follow the same procedure with the right pair of strands, bringing them to the left side. Continue in this manner from each side until the braid is finished. Seize the strands at the end of the braids using a needle and thread, and leave a 2 or 3 inch tassel. Cover place where strands were seized with a whipping or Turk's Head Knot.

Plate 26—BELT DESIGNS AND MACRAMÉ WORK

Fig. 64: The Victory Design embraces 4 rows of Half Hitches in white, and 2 rows in color, in the middle of a Square Knot Border. (See Plate 16.)

Fig. 65: The Carrick Bend Design has the Carrick Bends formed across the body by utilizing four outside strands on each side, which are joined across the top in the manner referred to. Spirals in the form of Half Diamonds are used between each Carrick design.

Figs. 66 to 70: Blended Macramé Designs may be formed by using a variety of many contrasting colors. Artistic designs such as these are used in the construction of belts, book marks and other similar objects.

Plate 27—MACRAMÉ DESIGNS

Fig. 71: This Thirty-six-Strand Macramé Pattern may be used in belt work, or as a book mark. It is begun by placing 16 brads ¼ inch apart on a board and looping 16 doubled strands over each brad. At this point a double strand is added, which is used as a filler. The work is continued by tying 64 Half Hitches on the filler. Proceed by adding another doubled strand, which is used as a filler. At this point tie 68 Half Hitches on it with 34 strands. There are now 36 working strands. These designs are made with French D. M. C. #1 cord.

Fig. 72: This Macramé Pattern in two colors, which is made with 36 strands, is worked in the same manner as in the previous examples.

Plate 28—FORMING WAMPUM BELT DESIGN

Fig. 73A: Decorative beaded effects can skillfully be made by using Half Hitches. For a 36″ belt, cut 4 white strands 30 feet long and one colored strand 50 feet long. These strands are doubled over a buckle, with the colored strands in the middle. Then tie 5 Lark's Head Knots. There are now 10 working strands. (For abbreviations see Plate 4.)

B:	# 1	to right,	HH	with	2 to 5.
	1	"	"	"	2 to 4.
	1	"	"	"	2, 3.
	1	"	"	"	2.
C:	10	" left,	"	"	9 to 1.
	10	"	"	"	9 to 1.
	10	"	"	"	9 to 1.
	10	"	"	"	9 to 1.
D:	(*)9	to 1 right,	HH	with	10.
E:	10	to left,	HH	with	9 to 1.
	10	"	"	"	9 to 1.
	10	"	"	"	9 to 1.
	10	"	"	"	9 to 1.
F:	Repeat from paragraph marked (*).				

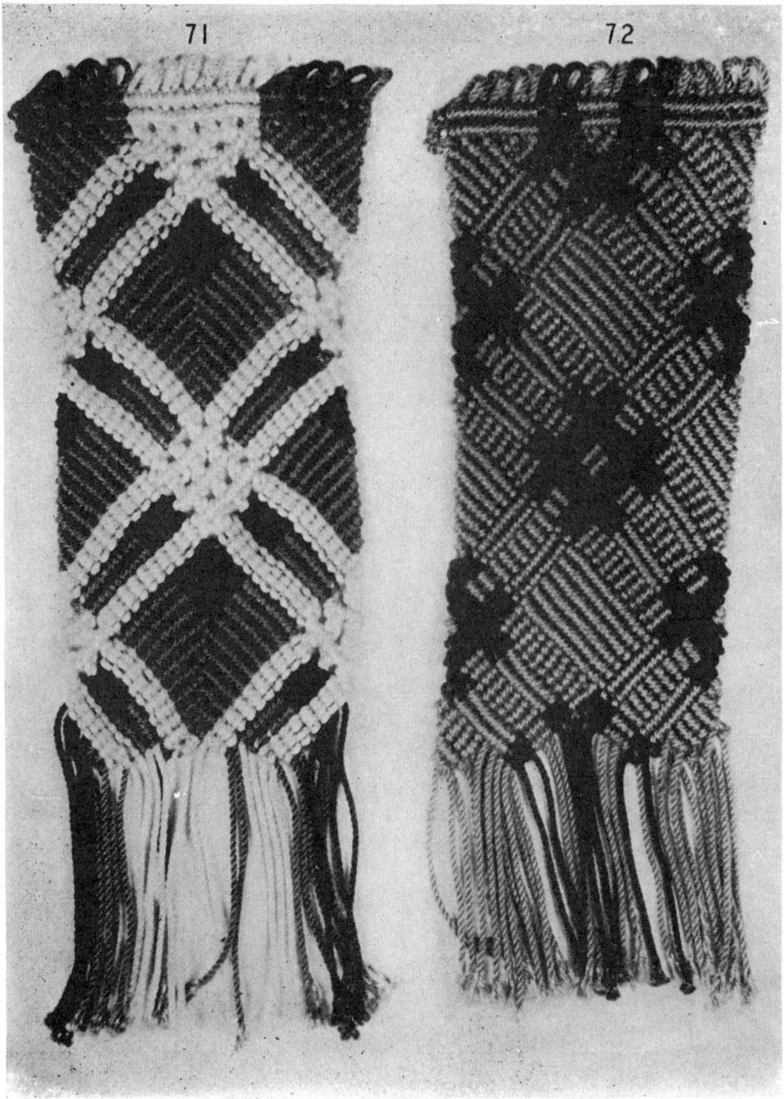

PLATE 27 Macramé Designs

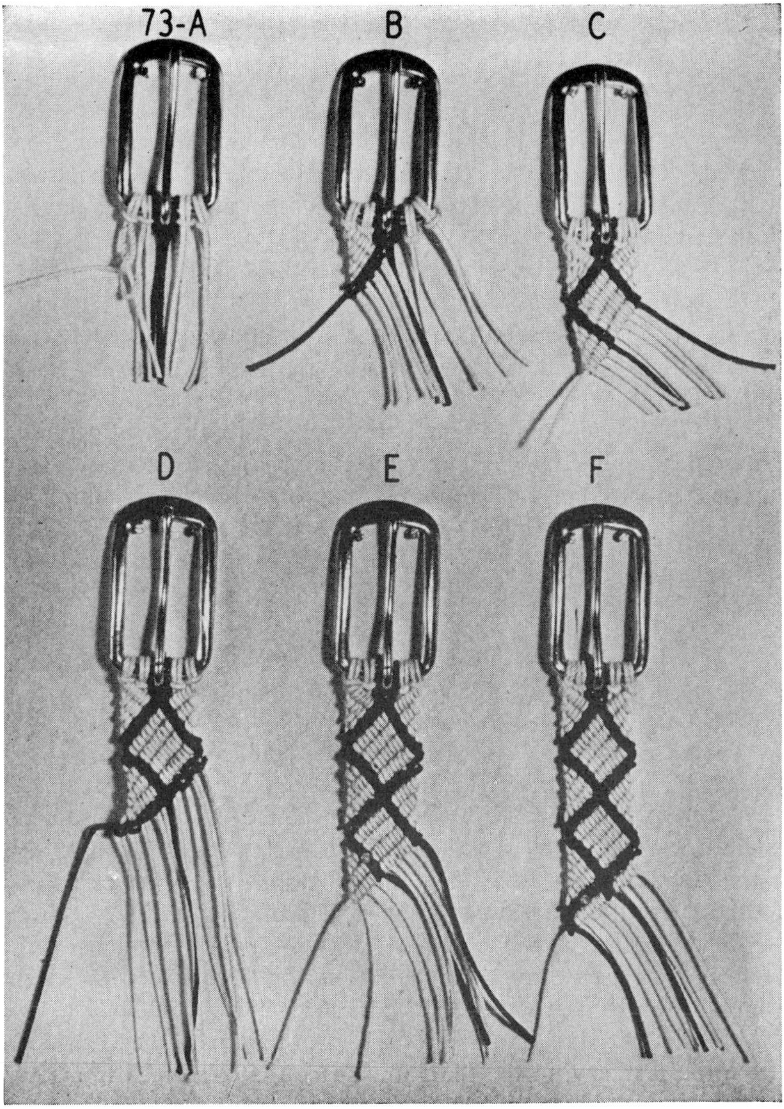

PLATE 28 Forming Wampum Belt Designs

Plate 29—WAMPUM BELTS

Fig. 74: A wampum belt in which the colors are blended as illustrated, forms an attractive design for this type of belt work.

Fig. 75: This represents a different wampum pattern, which is woven in the usual manner. It is another example of the many possibilities in color blending and open work design as explained and illustrated in Plate 28.

Fig. 76: The Wampum Belt shown here is of similar construction to the pattern in Fig. 77.

Fig. 77: The Wampum Belt Design with buckle attached shows an attractive pattern which is woven with Half Hitch work and colored cord.

Fig. 78: A Wampum Design which makes an interesting pattern. These illustrations show a few of the many varied designs that may be used to make beautiful work of a novel and practical nature.

Plate 30—A SQUARE KNOT DOILY

Fig. 79A: One inch bone ring.

B: Shows how the 24 strands have been doubled and looped over the ring, and 24 Lark's Head Knots tied.

C: Shows 3 rows of SK, 1 row of Flats, and a Flat of 7 SK added at 12 o'clock, 3 o'clock, 6 o'clock and 9 o'clock.

D: Cut 24 strands 4 feet long. The length is ascertained by measuring the length of the strands 6 times, which will give the length of a strand doubled. Drive a nail part way into a board, near the edge. Place the bone ring over this nail; then double and loop these 24 strands through the ring, tying 24 Lark's Head Knots. In the first row tie 12 SK taut round the ring; in the second row space the SK ⅛ inch from the first row; in the third row space the SK ½ inch from the second row; and in the fourth row, tie 12 Flats of 7 SK.

Cut 24 strands 4 feet long, double and loop 2 strands between the 12 Flats, tie 12 Flats of 7 SK, thus bringing them even with the other Flats. Form 3 more rows of SK, and in the fourth row, tie 24 Flats of 7 SK.

Cut 48 strands 3 feet long, double and loop 2 strands between the 24 Flats, tie 24 Flats of 7 SK, thus bringing them even with the other Flats. Tie one more row of SK ½ inch from the 48 Flats. Then, using 4 strands as a filler, tie SK with 4 strands. Do this 23 more times. Read special instructions for the Compass Doily in the following plate.

Plate 31—A DOILY COMPASS

Fig. 80: The amount of cord needed to form this artistic doily is 176 yards. The linen material used in forming this doily is 12 thread, and of natural color. The doily shows 32 points of a compass, each representing 11¼ degrees.

Cut 24 strands, each 4 feet long. This will make a doily measuring 8 inches from the center to the outer edge. If a larger doily or a tablecloth is desired, the length of the strands are determined by measuring the distance from the center of such a doily to the outer edge. Each strand should measure 6 times this distance, which will give the length of a doubled strand. Near the edge in a board place a nail, over which to fit a bone or metal ring 1 inch in diameter. Double and loop these 24 strands over the ring. Tie 24 Lark's Head Knots. Then tie 12 SK tautly round the ring. In the second row, space the SK ⅛ inch from the first row; in the third row space the SK ½ inch from the second row; and in the fourth row tie 12 Flats of 3 SK.

Cut 24 strands 4 feet long. Double and loop 2 strands between the 12 Flats, and tie 12 Flats of 3 SK thus bringing them even with the other Flats. Form 3 more rows of SK, and in the fourth row, tie 24 Flats of 3 SK.

Cut 48 strands 3 feet long. Double and loop 2 strands between the 24 Flats, and tie 24 Flats of 3 SK. Form 3 more rows of 3 SK, and in the fourth row tie 48 Flats of 3 SK.

Cut 96 strands 2 feet long. Double and loop 2 strands between the 48 Flats, and tie 48 Flats of 3 SK. There are now 96 Flats with 384 strands.

Tie 6 SK, using strands 1 to 4, 5 to 8, 9 to 12, 3 to 6, 7 to 10 and 5 to 8. Do the same with the next 12 strands; etc. forming 32 triangles all around.

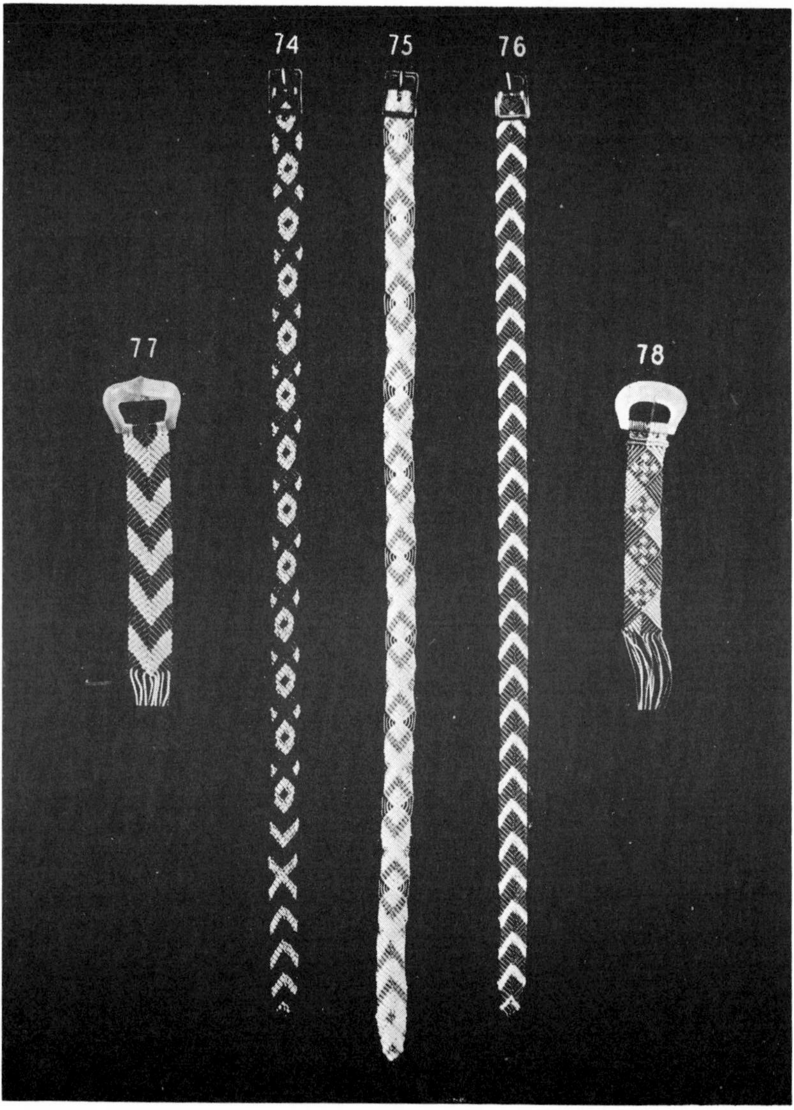

PLATE 29 Wampum Belts

PLATE 30 A Square Knot Doily

Upon completion the doily should be washed and, while wet, placed on a board in order to stretch it to form. A practical way to do this is to place four nails in the center of the ring. Using a cord as a plumb line, measure and mark it at 5 inches. First, place one brad at 12 o'clock 5 inches from the center, then place another brad at 6 o'clock 5 inches from the center, a third at 3 o'clock, and a fourth at 9 o'clock. Continue placing a brad 5 inches from the center at all the points of the compass. Stretch the wet doily over the brads so that a brad comes through the middle of each of the 32 triangles. After the doily has dried, cut a cardboard 2″ x 3″ and punch a hole near the end so that it will fit over a brad. Cut 12 strands at a time for the fringe, using the cardboard as a guide. Comb the fringe, and remove the doily from the board.

Plate 32—CROSS CLOVE HITCHED DOILY

Fig. 81A: A Wooden Frame is made to the exact size (inside dimensions) of the desired pillow-top or doily. The horizontal top and bottom rows of brads are placed 1 inch apart and numbered from 1 to 7. The vertical, left and right side rows of brads are placed 1 inch apart and numbered from 8 to 14.

Using 12-thread shoemaker's linen cord, make 4 passes, vertically and horizontally, for the bottom, and four passes for the top. The passes are made from brad #1 at the top to brad 1 at the bottom and across to brad 7, and from brad 8 on the right side and across to brad 14.

B: The frame is now turned over. Wind as much good strong thread as possible on a meshing needle. Then start making Clove Hitches at each intersection diagonally across the frame as shown, in vertical rows 1, 2, 3, 4 and 5. Rows 6 and 7 show how the Clove Hitches can be made vertically. To make a Clove Hitch, take the end or standing part in one hand and pass the needle or moving part across the intersection, down through the near square and up through the square on the far side. In other words, the thread is placed around the intersection. Then make another turn around the intersection, bringing the thread up on the other side of the standing part and pass it through the loop made in its own part. For illustration of a Clove Hitch see Plate 45. It is necessary to tie 98 Clove Hitches on this frame.

C: The frame is now turned right side up. Insert a small stick about ½″ x 5″ in the middle of one square and cut the horizontal strands against the stick halfway between the intersections. Repeat in this manner, cutting the vertical and horizontal strands. Do not cut any diagonal cords. After the cuts have been made, soak the frame in water and let it dry. Then pinch and brush the clusters to give them a tufted effect. Cut the strands close to the nails and comb the fringe. Using a piece of cardboard as a guide, trim each tassel evenly.

D: Shows a doily which was made on the same size frame as in the previous illustrations, except that the brads were placed ½ inch apart.

Plate 33—AMERICAN FLAG

Fig. 82: The colors in our flag have the following significance: Red symbolizes Courage; White, Liberty; Blue, Loyalty.

Before starting to make this beautiful Cross Clove Hitched American Flag, it is advisable to make a pattern drawing of the complete job. This will give a thorough understanding of just what is to be Cross Clove Hitched and what is not. Study the picture in detail, and follow the directions closely.

Make a wooden frame 3″ x 13½″ x 25″ inside dimensions. Place ¾ inch brads ½ inch from corners, all around the frame ½ inch apart. The horizontal brads along the top are numbered from 1 to 49, and the corresponding brads along the bottom are also numbered 1 to 49. The vertical brads on the left are numbered from 50 to 75, beginning at the top, and the corresponding brads on the right are also numbered 50 to 75. If a gold fringe is desired, put an extra row of brads all around near the outside of the frame.

With six-thread cord, which is used for the base, make about 6 passes from brad 1 at the top to brad 1 at the bottom, continuing across to include brad 49. Do the same, beginning with brad 50 at the left to brad 50 at the right, and continue downward to include brad 75. This will provide a base with 6 strands in each row, vertically and horizontally.

Rope silk, #3 Silkine Pearl cotton, or #3 DMC may be used in

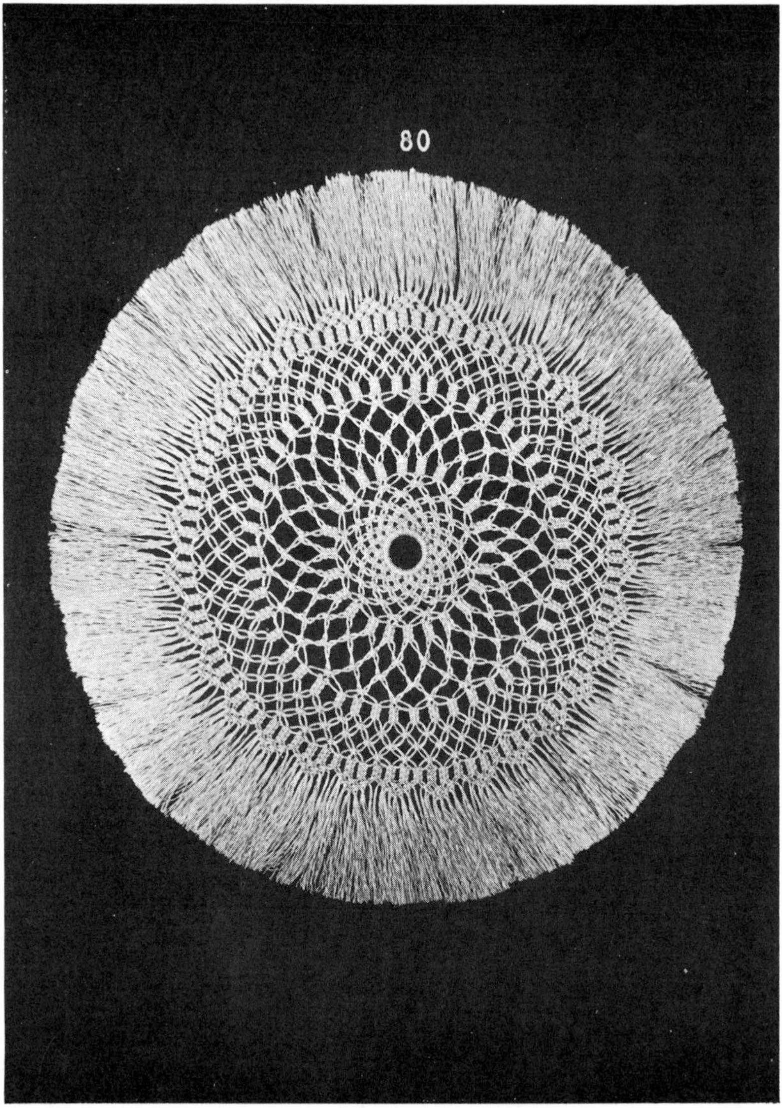

PLATE 31 A Doily Compass

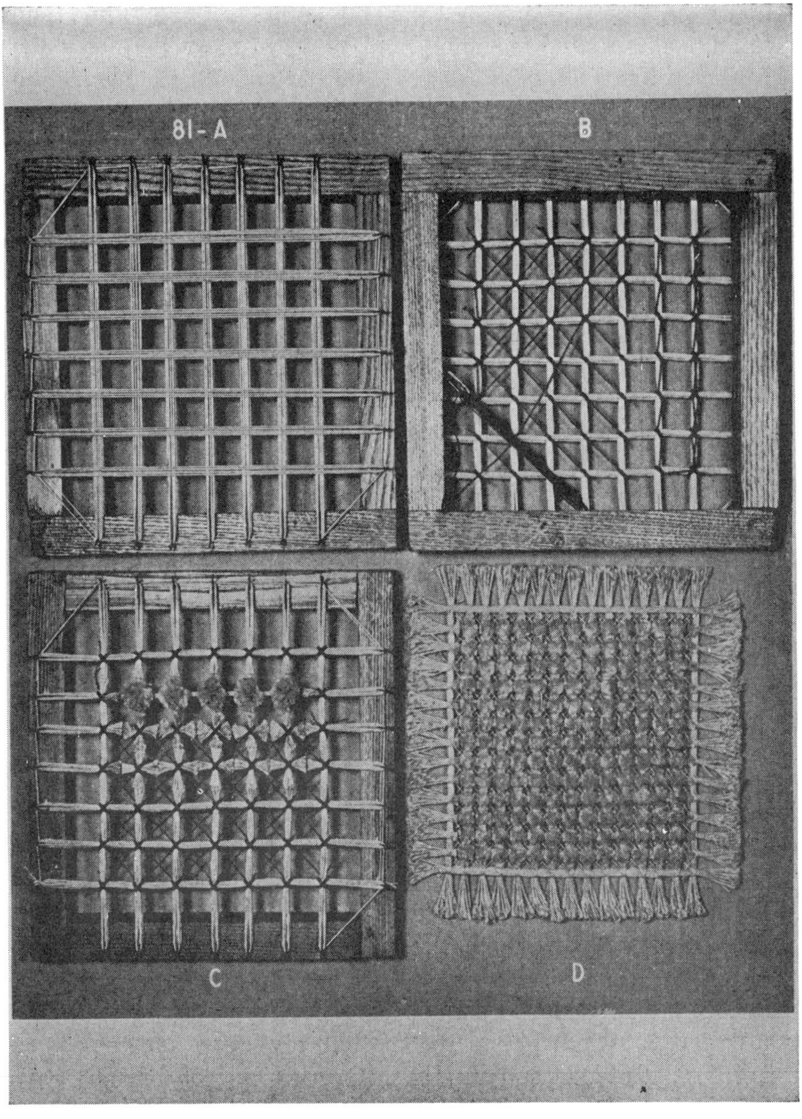

PLATE 32 Cross Clove Hitched Doily

making this flag. Next, using red rope silk, make eight passes from brad 1 at the top to brad 1 at the bottom; brads 2 to 2; 3 to 3; and so on, across to and including brad 49. Then make the horizontal passes on brads 50 to 50; 51 to 51; skip 52 and 53; include 54 and 55; skip 56 and 57; include 58 and 59; skip 60 and 61; include 62 and 63; skip 64 and 65; include 66 and 67; skip 68 and 69; include 70 and 71; skip 72 and 73; include 74 and 75. There are now 8 strands of red in each row, vertically and horizontally.

Make something similar to a meshing needle of wood, brass or steel aboot ¼″ x 6″, with a notch in both ends. This tool is used for winding on the thread that will make the Cross Clove Hitches on the back or reverse side. (See Plate 45.) The thread used to Cross Clove Hitch is Button and Carpet, #24 Silk thread, or three-cord Superior linen thread. Clove Hitches may be made horizontally if desired. Turn the frame over and start to Clove Hitch diagonally, making the first Clove Hitch at the intersection of rows 50 and 18; make the second Clove Hitch at the intersection of rows 51 and 19; skip 52 at 20 and 53 at 21; Clove Hitch 54 at 22 and 55 at 23; skip 56 at 24 and 57 at 25; etc. Clove Hitch diagonally from right to left. Turn the frame over and cut out all the horizontal and vertical rows of red that are not needed. There should be 7 double rows of red exactly where the stripes belong. Use a plumb line and check the vertical and horizontal rows of red to make sure they are in line; sometimes they pull out of line.

Using white rope silk make 8 passes from brad 1 at the top to brad 1 at the bottom; brads 2 to 2; 3 to 3; and so on, across to and including brad 49. Then make the horizontal passes on brads 52, 53, 54, 56, 57, 58, 60, 61, 62, 64, 65, 68, 69, 72 and 73. Turn the frame over and start to Clove Hitch all the stars with white thread. The first row of stars comes off brad 52 at 2, 4, 6, 8, 10, 12, 14 and 16. This provides 8 stars in the first row. The second row comes off brad 54 at 2, 4, 6, 8, 10, 12, 14 and 16. The third row comes off brad 56 at 2, 4, 6, 8, 10, 12, 14 and 16. The fourth row comes off brad 58 at 2, 4, 6, 8, 10, 12, 14 and 16. The fifth row comes off brad 60 at 2, 4, 6, 8, 10, 12, 14 and 16. The sixth row comes off brad 62 at 2, 4, 6, 8, 10, 12, 14 and 16. After the 48 stars have been Cross Clove Hitched, turn the frame over and make a thorough check. Cut out the horizontal rows coming off brads 54, 58 and 62 at 18. Turn the frame over and Cross Clove Hitch the six white stripes. Now, cut out all the white threads, vertical and horizontal, that are not needed.

Using Blue rope silk, make 8 passes vertically from brad 1 at the top to brad 1 at the bottom; brads 2 to 2; 3 to 3; and so on, over to and including brad 17. Then make 8 passes horizontally on brads 50, 51, 52, 53, 54, 55, 56, 57, 58, 59, 60, 61, 62 and 63. Turn the frame over and Cross Clove Hitch all the blue. Turn the frame back again, and cut out all the blue cord that is not needed. The red and white thread that was used for Cross Clove Hitching, which crosses the white and red stripes, may also be cut out.

A piece of wood, pointed at both ends, ¼″ x ½″ x 6″, is also needed for inserting between the base of the article and the work itself, in order to cut the threads on the front side in the middle of each square, with a razor blade or sharp scissors. From the top of the frame, between the base—which is six-thread cord—and the rope silk, insert this piece of wood in the middle of each square. Then cut the rope silk with a razor blade halfway between the Clove Hitches. When all the cuts have been made, brush out, or place the frame over a steaming kettle of water. This produces a small ball or tuft effect in the form of squares.

To remove the flag from the frame cut the thread close to the edge, including the base, and the job is finished.

Plate 34—MAKING INITIALS IN PILLOW-TOP WORK

Fig. 83: These Initials are made by using 5 vertical squares for each letter after first forming a complete foundation of pillow-top work in one color as previously described in Plates 32 and 33. Proceed by cutting the respective squares which form each kind of initial. This operation will have to be determined according to the type of letter that is used. The open spaces which were originally cut are next filled in by proceeding in the usual manner with colored cords. It is finished in the same way as explained in the two preceding plates.

82

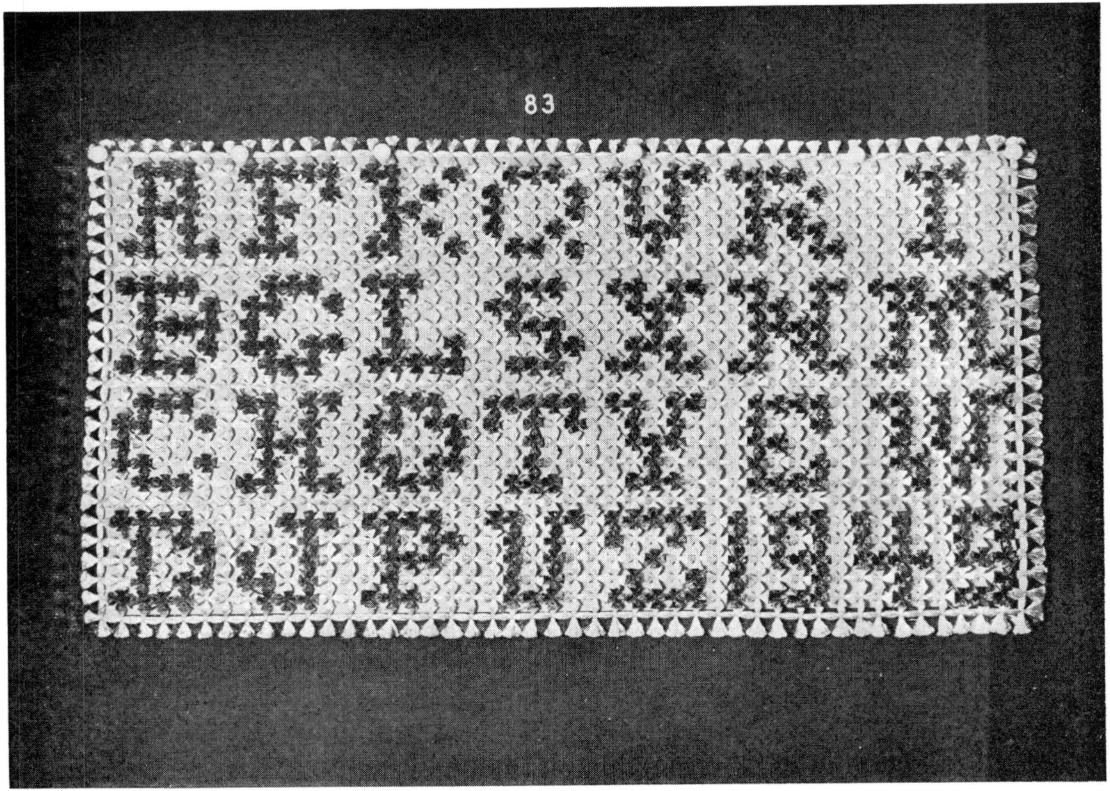

PLATE 34 Making Initials in Pillow Top Work

Plate 35—MATS

Figs. 84 to 86: Mats such as these are made in the same manner as the example which is explained and illustrated in Plate 32, except that the intersections are not cut, thus forming a more solid, compact body. These mats make ideal pads for use underneath hot plates.

Plate 36—PARACHUTE CORD MAT

Fig. 87: This Attractive Mat is also formed in the same manner as explained in Plate 32, except that parachute cord has been used in its construction, which adds lustre and body to the completed design.

Fig. 88: A Square Knot Mat which embraces the same principle of construction as Square Knot Belts, and is also finished off the same way. Any required number of strands may be used in order to obtain the desired size.

Plate 37—MAT DESIGN WITH LETTERING

Fig. 89: Represents a unique method of producing letter work in Mat Designs. Any problem of this nature may be arranged and worked out to suit the individual taste. See Plate 34 for explanatory text and illustrated letters.

Plate 38—WOMEN'S FOUR-STRAND METALLIC TUBULAR BELTS

In the illustrations and instructions in the next 4 plates, the authors are bringing to the public for the first time a novel and unique way of making a woman's belt with 4, 6 or 8 strands. These belts are made with braided gold, silver and many other colors in metallic tubular. This tubular is about ¼ inch in diameter. A belt fashioned from it is serviceable and attractive. The youngest to the oldest can make this style of belt.

Fig. 90A: For a 36″ belt, cut 2 cords 10 feet long. The point is a four-strand flat braid. To make it, place one doubled cord around the other doubled cord, making 4 strands. Of the 2 inside strands, cross the left over the right. The strands are now numbered from left to right 1 to 4. Strand 1 is passed under strand 2. Strand 4 is passed over strand 3. Strand 1 is next passed over strand 4 in the middle. When braiding with an even number of strands in a flat braid, remember that one outside strand must be brought under, and the other outside strand must be brought over. Continue with this key to the required length of the braid. (See Plate 51, Fig. 165.)

B: Hold strand 1 in the left hand, slanting it toward the left. Using this strand as a filler, tie 1 Half Hitch with the right hand with strand 2. Hold strand 4 in the right hand, slanting it toward the right. Using this strand as a filler, tie one Half Hitch with the left hand, using strand 3.

C: Using strands 2 and 3 as a filler, tie a SK with strands 1 and 4. Continue to tie a SK every two or three inches on the filler strands 2 and 3 to the required length. Then pass strand 1 under strand 2. Pass strand 4 over strand 3, then strand 1 over strand 4, and so on. To form the belt loop, pass strand 1 under and over the braid and bring it back to its original position. Then make a few more passes in the braid. Sew the strands together flat. Then pass them over the center bar of the buckle with the tongue going through the middle of the braid. Allow a sufficient amount of the braid to come over and under the center bar so as to be able to sew the top and bottom of the braid together. For additional effect, Coxcombing may be utilized on the buckle. Coxcombing is a series of Half Hitches.

Fig. 91: Shows the belt for which the directions have just been given.

Fig. 92: Shows the same type of belt, except that strands 1 and 4 are used as the filler, and strands 2 and 3 are used to tie the Square Knot.

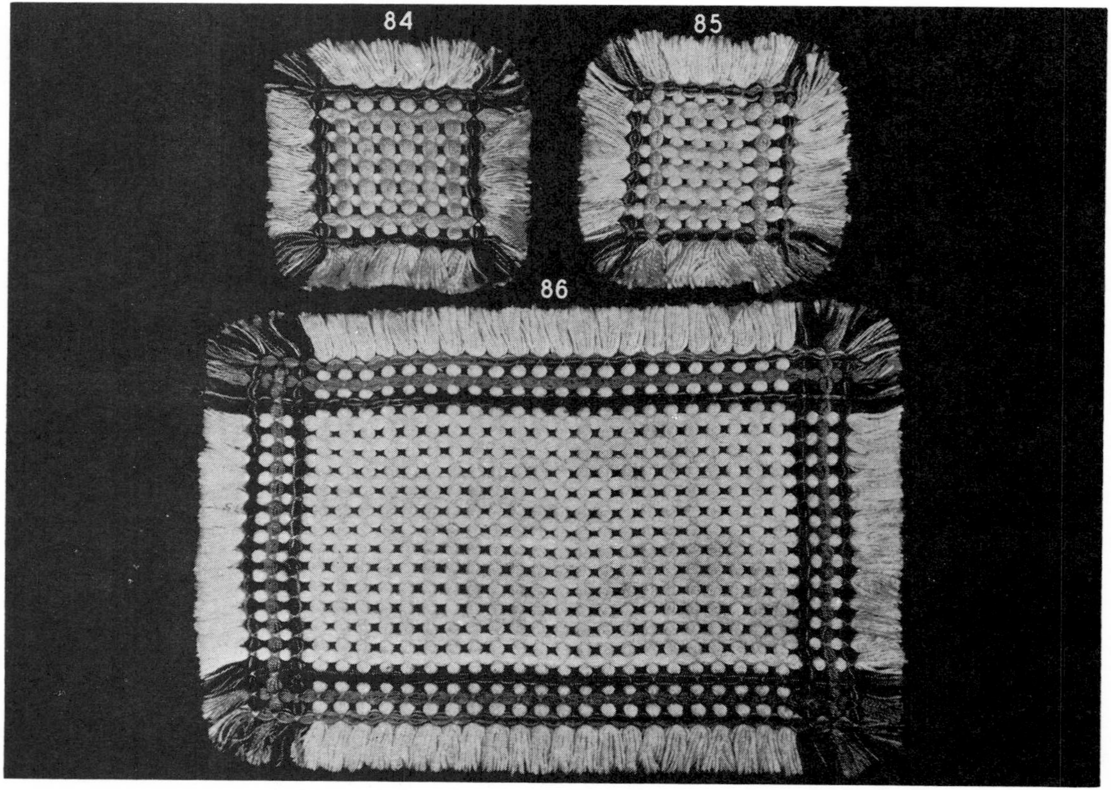
84
85
86

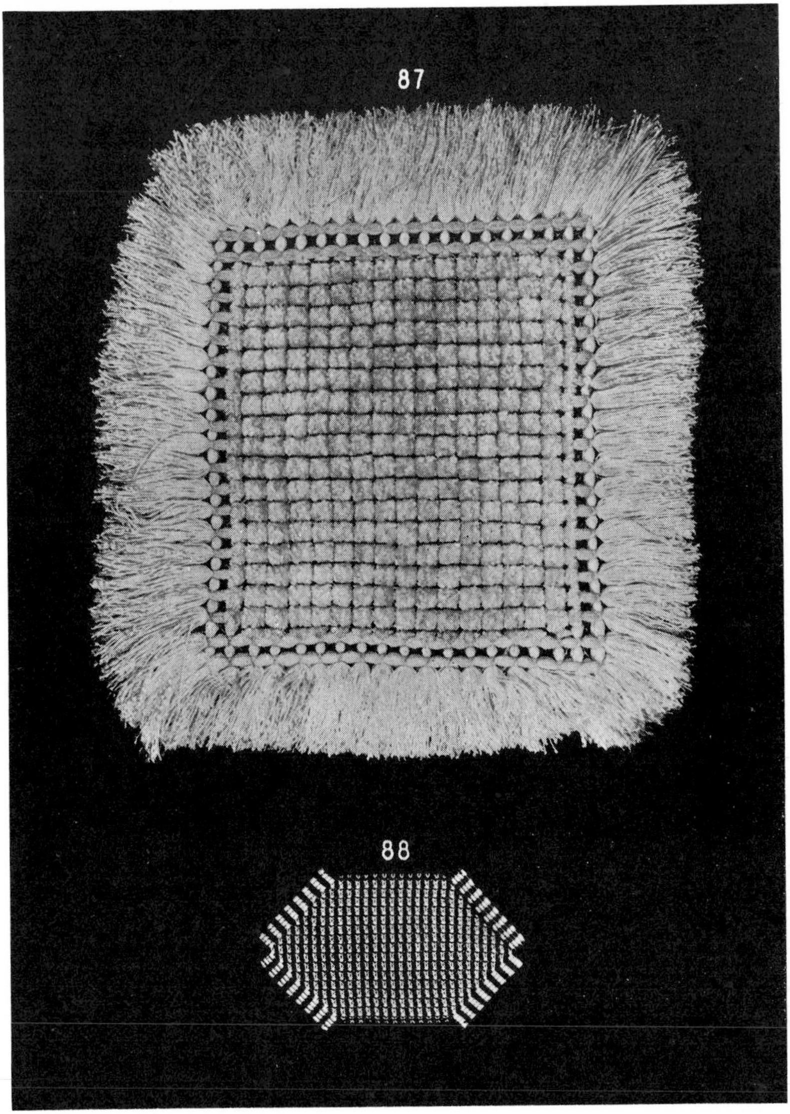

PLATE 36 Parachute Cord Mat

Plate 39—ARTISTIC BELT DESIGNS WITH METALLIC CORD

Fig. 93: Represents an Openwork Design. Cut 3 cords 12 feet long for a 36 inch belt of this nature.

This work is begun with a Combination Flat Sennit of 6 strands that is actually started by doubling 3 strands, with one pair used in one group, thus forming 2 doubled and a single strand which is doubled to form 2 strands in the other group. This combination is braided down the required distance to form the tongue of the belt. At the base of the tongue an inside HH is formed on each side. (For abbreviations see Plate 4.)

The work is formed so that the doubled strands remain on the outside with the single strands in the middle. At this point the single strand on the left is used to form an inside HH on the double strands that are on the same side. This procedure is then repeated by using the single strand on the right or opposite side which is likewise used to form an inside HH on the double strands at the right side.

2 as F, tie SK with 1 and 3. *5 as F, tie SK with 4 and 6. 3 and 4 as F, tie SK with 2 and 5. 2 as F, tie SK with 1 and 3. 3 as F, tie SK with 2 and 4. 4 as F, SK with 3 and 5. 5 as F, tie SK with 4 and 6. 4 as F, tie SK with 3 and 5. 3 as F, tie SK with 2 and 4. 2 as F, tie SK with 1 and 3. Repeat from the (*) mark until the design is the required length, and finish as previously explained.

Fig. 94: Another Unique Design which is started in a manner similar to Fig. 93. Strands 3 and 4 are used as a filler throughout the preparation of this pattern with Square Knots formed at certain intervals as illustrated.

Fig. 95: An Attractive Design, which may be followed by closely observing the picture.

Plate 40—WOMEN'S METALLIC TUBULAR BELT DESIGNS

Fig. 96: These Eight-Strand Metallic Tubular Belt Designs which are shown in the same material as described in Plate 39, are started with a four-strand double Flat Sennit. (See Plate 38.)

Cut 4 strands 5 times the desired length.

After the braid has been made, tie an inside HH with strands 3 and 4 on strands 1 and 2. Then tie an inside HH with strands 5 and 6 on strands 7 and 8.

Tie SK with 1 to 4, 5 to 8, (*) 3 to 6, 5 to 8, 3 to 6, 1 to 4. Repeat from (*) until the desired length has been reached. Then tie SK with 3 to 6, 1 to 4 and 5 to 8.

The belt loop is formed by passing strand 1 over and down through the SK on the right. Add several SK and join the buckle as explained in Plate 38.

Fig. 97: Use the same instructions for the starting as described in Fig. 96.

Tie SK with 1 to 4, 5 to 8, 3 to 6, 5 to 8 and 1 to 4.

(*) 2 as F, tie SK with 1 and 3.

4 and 5 cross.

3 as F, tie SK with 2 and 4. 7 as F, tie SK with 6 and 8. 6 as F, tie SK with 5 and 7. Repeat from (*) until the design is the required length and finish as previously explained.

Fig. 98: Use the same instructions for the starting as described in Fig. 96.

Tie SK with 1 to 4, 5 to 8 and 3 to 6.

Using 4 and 5 as F, tie SK ½ inch down with 1 and 8, 3 and 6, 2 and 7. A Flat of 3 SK has thus been made. Continue ½ inch down, by using strands 4 and 5 as F, and tying a SK with the 2 strands alternating from the first, second and third SK.

Fig. 99: Use the same instructions for the starting as described in Fig. 96.

Tie SK with 1 to 4, 5 to 8, 3 to 6, 1 to 4, 5 to 8, 3 to 6, 1 to 4.

(*) 4 as F, tie SK with 3 and 8. 5 as F, tie SK with 4 and 7. 6 as F, tie SK with 5 and 8. 5 as F, tie SK with 1 and 6. 4 as F, tie SK with 2 and 5. Tie SK with 1 to 4.

Repeat from (*) to the desired length.

Plate 41—WOMEN'S EIGHT-STRAND METALLIC TUBULAR BELTS

Figs. 100 to 102: These Three Attractive Designs are started and finished off in the same manner as those described in Plate 40. The different patterns can be duplicated easily by observing the portrayed work.

68

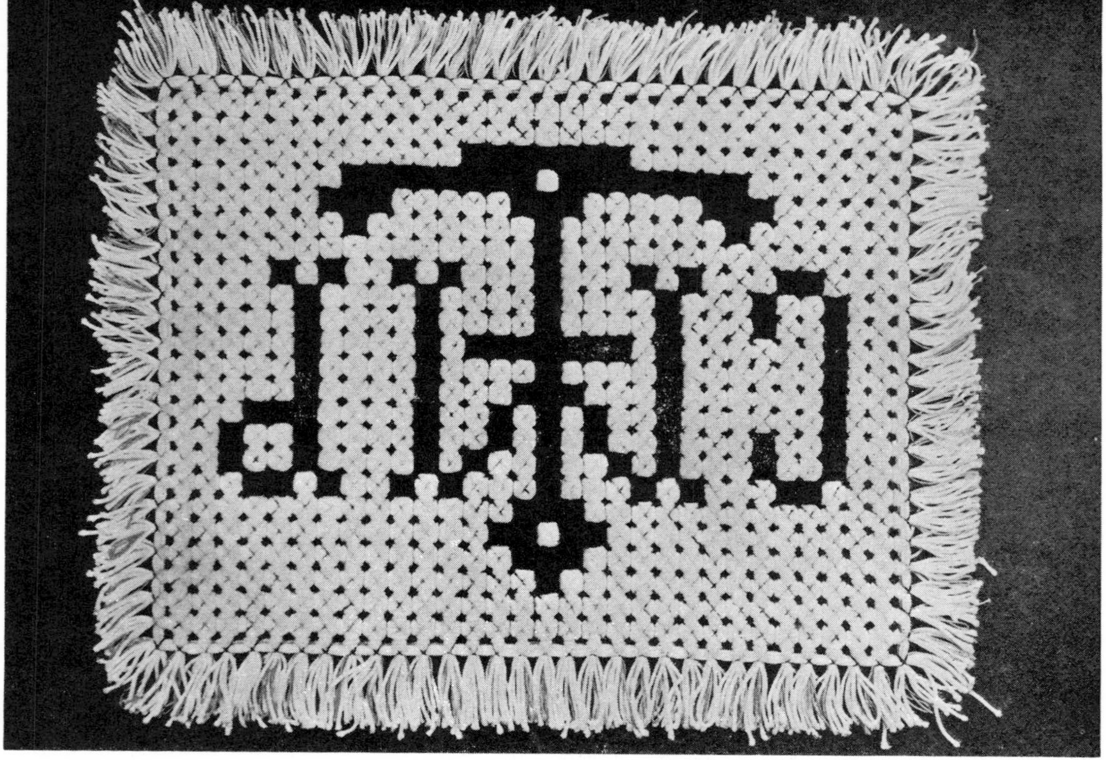

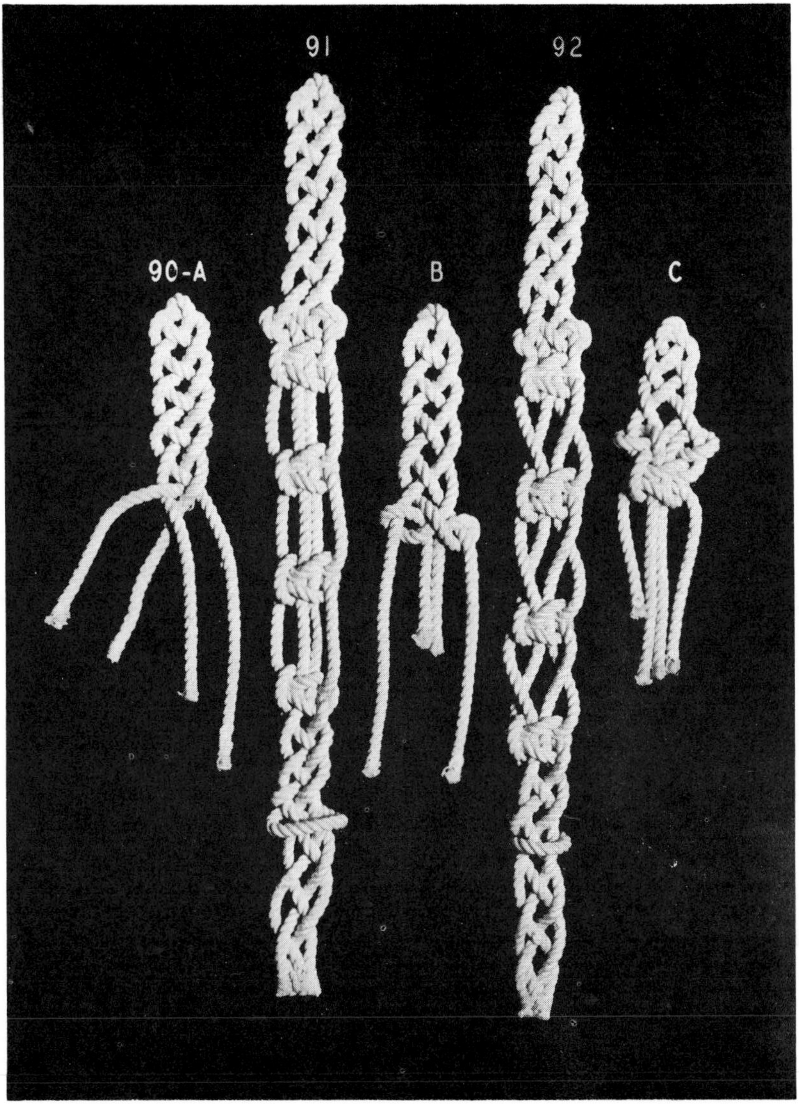

PLATE 38 Ladies' Four-Strand Metallic Tubular Belts

PLATE 42—WOMEN'S METALLIC TUBULAR BELT DESIGNS

Fig. 103: This Ten-Strand Sword Mat Belt Design is started with a four-strand double Flat Sennit.

A Sword Mat is formed by first middling the strands over a lashing. Proceed by taking every other strand up across the weave, with alternate strands lying down, then pass the warp from each side. Next bring the bottom strands up, with the top strands lying down and again pass the warp between the strands, and so on.

Fig. 104: This Four-Strand Centipede Knot Belt Design is started with a Four-Strand Flat Sennit.

This design is made along a series of Square Knots placed a short distance apart. The cord that is left between the knots forms a loop when they are pushed together.

Fig. 105: This Eight-Strand Portuguese Square Sennit Belt Design is started with a Four-Strand double Flat Sennit.

This Sennit is made by forming a Square Knot Flat, using 2 strands as a filler in the middle throughout. The strands are braided over and under to and from the Square Knot. The buckle is attached as explained in previous text. These examples are presented with white line to help clarify their method of construction.

PLATE 43—TWO-STRAND KNOTS

Fig. 106A: Shows a Two-Strand Wall Knot opened up to illustrate how the strands are walled around the standing part, then tucked under their own parts. Basic knot work of 2 and 3 strands should be mastered thoroughly by Square Knot students, since this type of knotting enlarges the scope of fancy ornamental designs.

B: The finished knot as it appears after each strand has been pulled up snug and in its proper place.

Fig. 107A: This is an open illustration of the Two-Strand Lanyard

Knot, that shows the additional tuck which is necessary to transform the Two-Strand Wall Knot in Fig. 106B into a Lanyard Knot.

B: Pictures the knot as it appears after being pulled up neatly. This type of knot forms a very good base for more intricate types of knot work.

Fig. 108A: The Two-Strand Elongated Matthew Walker Knot may look confusing at first glance but each step in its construction is rather simple after the strands are traced. Each strand is brought around the standing part twice and then tucked under its own part as shown.

B: The knot will then appear as shown here after the strands have been pulled up carefully, with each turn in its proper place around the standing part.

Fig. 109A: A Two-Strand Diamond Knot fully describes its method of construction.

B: Shows the same knot doubled. It can be followed around and doubled easily after observing how the first tucks are made in Fig. 110A.

Fig. 110A: The Two-Strand Sennit Knot is continued from Fig. 109A in the manner shown.

B: After the first set of tucks have been made as shown in Fig. 110A, split the knot by tucking over the first 2 cross strands and then under the top 2 cross strands with each working part as indicated. The knot is then pulled up by working out the slack in a uniform manner.

Fig. 111: A Two-Strand Star Knot after the first set of tucks have been made.

B: Continue by passing the end of each working strand down through the opposite eye, then follow each parallel strand with the working end, up through the eyes. The work will then appear as shown here.

C: Proceed by following the parallel strands with each working end until the knot has two complete passes. The working ends are then tucked up through and out between the middle of the knot.

Fig. 112A: Shows a Two-Strand Manrope Knot opened up.

B: After the parallel strands of the bottom and top half have been doubled, the knot will then appear as shown here.

Fig. 113A: The Two-Strand Stopper Knot as it appears opened up.

B: The finished knot after the parallel strands of the top and bottom half have been doubled.

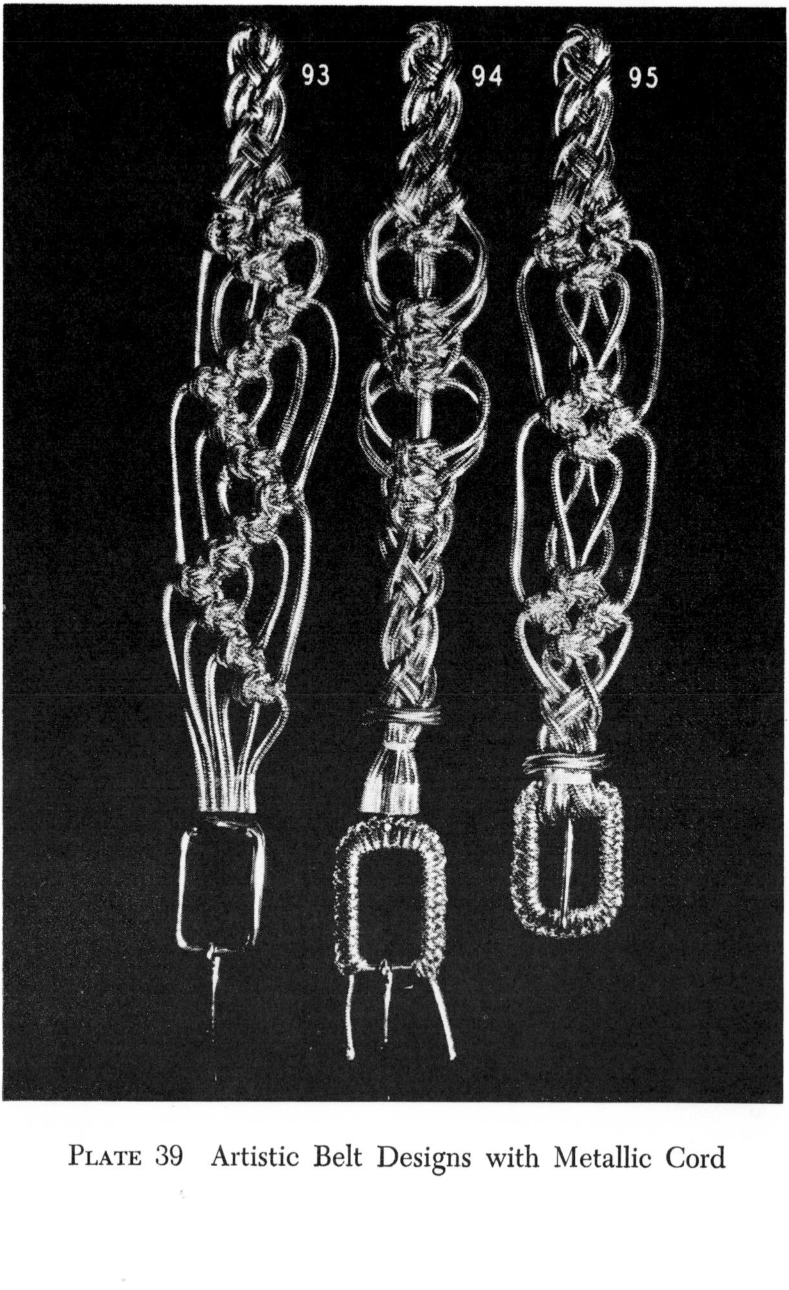

PLATE 39 Artistic Belt Designs with Metallic Cord

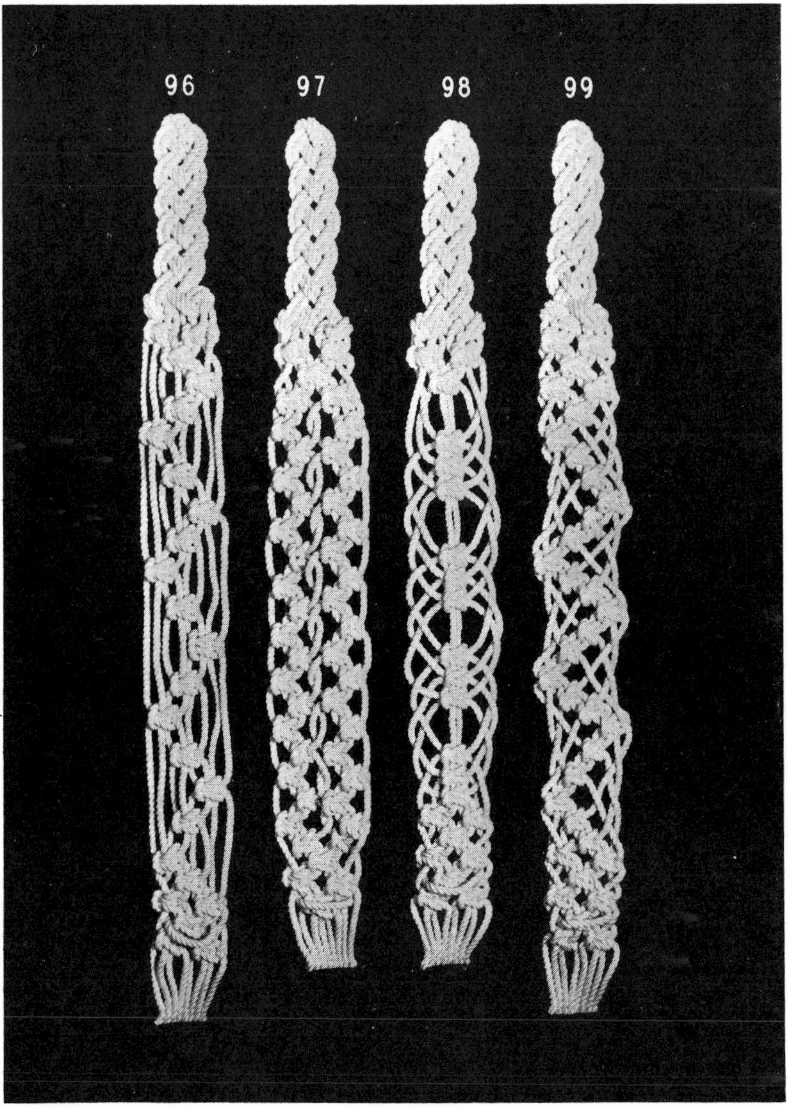

Plate 40 Ladies' Metallic Tubular Belt Designs

Plate 44--THREE-STRAND KNOTS

Fig. 114: An Open Illustration of a Three-Strand Crown that shows how each strand in turn is crowned over one strand, then tucked through the bight of the next strand. This, and the accompanying knots on this plate, are practical examples which are useful in many types of related Square Knot work.

Fig. 115: A Three-Strand Wall that is tied in the opposite way to the crown method or, in other words, walled up instead of being crowned down.

Fig. 116A: A Three-Strand Lanyard Knot is a continuation of the wall method, which requires an additional tuck with each strand as shown here with an open illustration.

B: As the same knot appears when closed up.

Fig. 117A: The Three-Strand Single Manrope Knot shown here is tied with a wall base and a crown top.

B: The same knot as it appears with the bottom part doubled.

C: This shows both top and bottom parts doubled which completes the Double Manrope.

Fig. 118A: The Three-Strand Single Stopper Knot shown here is tied with a crown base, and is then walled around the base of the crown.

B: The same knot as it appears with the top part doubled.

C: This shows both top and bottom parts doubled, which completes the Double Stopper.

Fig. 119A: An Open Illustration of a Three-Strand Matthew Walker Knot, showing how each strand is tucked under its own part after being passed around the body of the knot as indicated.

B: As the same knot appears after each strand is pulled up snugly and in its respective place.

Fig. 120A: An Open Illustration of an Outside Matthew Walker Knot. This knot differs from the ordinary form of Matthew Walker Knot, as the end of each line is passed around the body of the knot and over the other strands, instead of under to form the ordinary method.

B: As the same knot appears when completed and pulled up snug.

Fig. 121A: A Three-Strand Diamond Knot that is illustrated opened up to clarify its method of construction.

B: Shows the same knot pulled up with a single pass.

C: As it appears when doubled. It can be followed around and doubled easily after observing how the first tucks are made to parallel the proper strands as shown in Fig. 122A.

Fig. 122A: The Three-Strand Sennit Knot is continued from Fig. 121A in the manner shown.

B: After the first set of tucks has been made as shown in Fig. 122A, split the knot by tucking over the first 2 cross strands, and then under the top 2 cross strands with each working part as indicated. The knot is then pulled up by working out the slack in a uniform manner.

C: Shows the finished example.

Plate 45—MISCELLANEOUS KNOTS

Fig. 123A: Sailor's Breastplate. These figures portray a Double Carrick Bend formed in the end of a bight. It is begun by laying out the line in the manner shown.

B: The drawn-in line indicates how the end of the line is passed through to complete the design. This knot is an ornamental version of the Double Carrick Bend.

Fig. 124A: The True Shamrock Knot is tied by interlacing 2 Overhand Knots together as illustrated.

B: Each bight is then pulled through the opposite side in the manner illustrated. After it is pulled taut, the knot will appear as shown.

Fig. 125A: The Blood, Bullion, or Manifold Knot is used for shortening purposes, or where it is necessary to increase the diameter of a rope. The knot is formed with a series of turns through a loop as shown here.

B: Shows this knot pulled taut. This example is a Two-Fold Blood Knot.

Fig. 126: The Three-Fold Blood Knot is the same as the previous example, except that it is formed with 3 turns instead of 2.

Fig. 127: The Four-Fold Blood Knot is similar to the others, except that it has 4 turns.

Fig. 128A: The Two-Strand Carrick Diamond Knot is formed from a Sailor's Breastplate, which is used as a foundation for this type of knot, but in a slightly different manner from the usual method. Observe that one end of the working part comes out in the

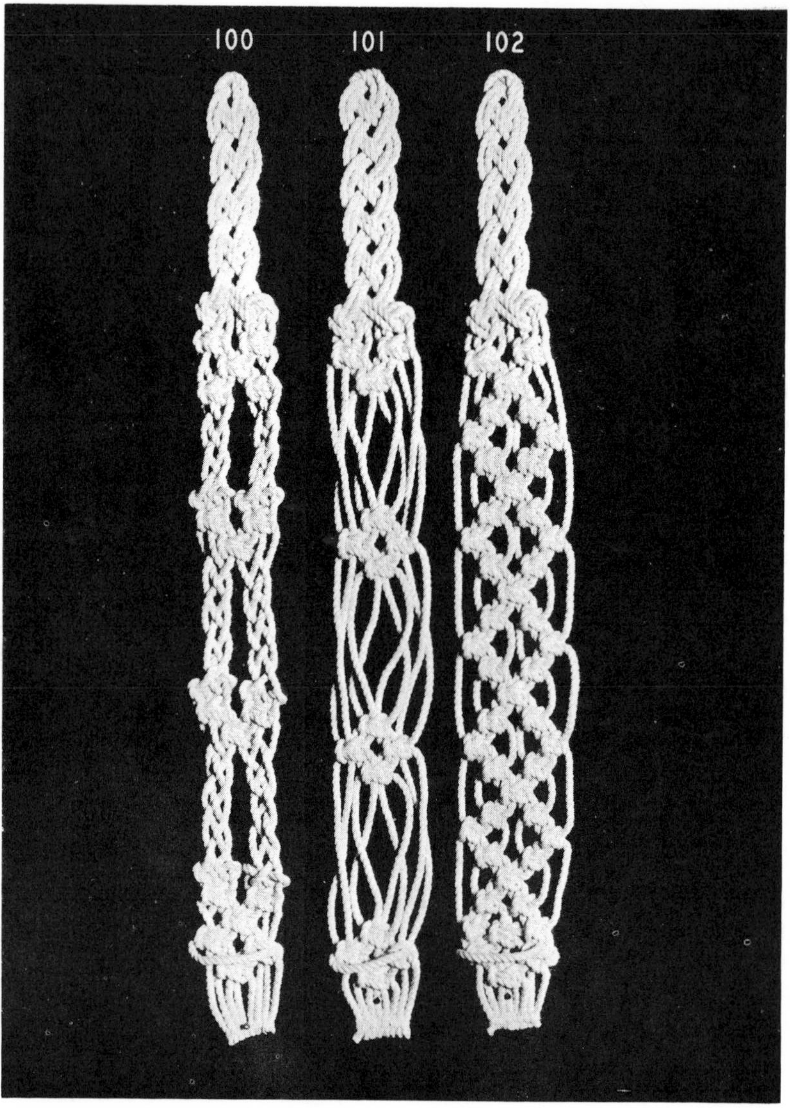

PLATE 41 Ladies' Eight-Strand Metallic Tubular Belts

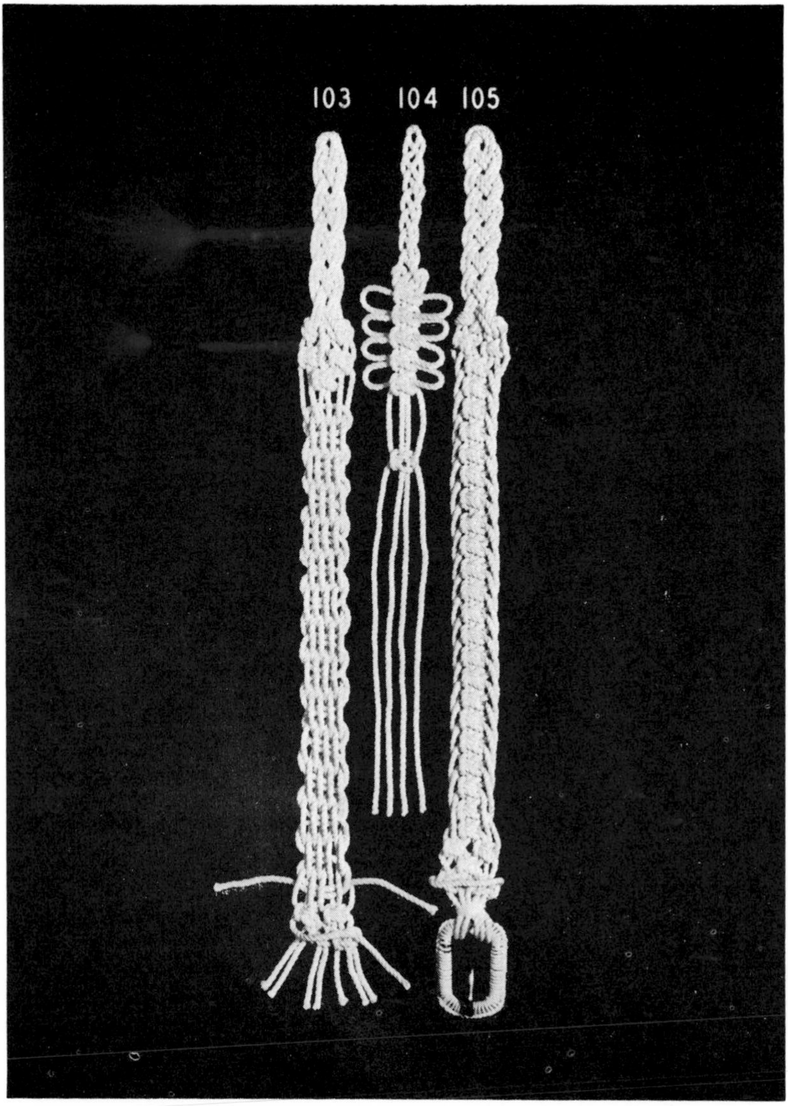

PLATE 42 Ladies' Metallic Tubular Belt Designs

middle or on the inside of the loop as shown. Follow the drawn-in lines for the proper way to pass each end through the body of the knot.

B: Shows the completed design when properly pulled up. This example makes a popular design for decorative purposes.

The Japanese Crown or Success Knot can be used in a variety of ways for ornamental designs.

Fig. 129A: Shows how the knot is begun.

B: Portrays the front side of the finished knot.

C: Shows the opposite or back side of the same example.

Fig. 130A: The Two-Leaf Dragonfly is begun in the manner shown. This is a decorative design. The end is passed over and around the 2 bottom parts with the drawn-in line which shows how the knot is closed.

B: Shows the knot as it looks when pulled up.

Fig. 131A: The Brief Knot is made as follows: Make a Reef Knot in the bottom of a loop, as shown in this illustration.

B: Now turn the work upside down and form another Reef Knot around the loop which is used as a filler.

C: At this stage the working ends are passed up through the Reef Knot which was tied to begin the operation.

D: After the previous step has been completed, the knot is again turned the opposite way, as it is pictured here, with the slack drawn out and worked up into a compact body.

Plate 46—HACKAMORE KNOT AND MONKEY'S FIST

Fig. 132A: A Hackamore Knot is tied by making 2 loops, with one overlapping the other in the manner shown. The lower part is pulled up under the inside part of the loop on the left, and then passed between the 2 overlapping parts in the middle going over and under as illustrated by the arrow.

B: The loops in front and in back of the bight are next capsized or inverted. This operation will automatically transform the shape of the knot to appear as it is illustrated here.

Formerly used as a decorative attachment on horsehair bridles, it is also a convenient knot to employ for slinging a bottle, jar or jug by means of passing the middle of the knot over the neck and pulling each side taut.

Fig. 133A: The Monkey's Fist is employed to give weight to the end of a heaving line. It is begun by forming 2 or 3 loops as illustrated. The work is continued by passing the end of the line around the first set of loops that were formed.

B: Now take the same number of turns that were made previously, and then reeve the end through the first set of loops and carry it around the second set of loops as pictured.

C: Then make the last set of turns the same as before and haul the knot taut, at the same time being careful to work it into its proper shape. This illustration shows the knot pulled taut with 2 passes.

Fig. 134: The Three-Strand Monkey's Fist is the same form of knot as previously described, except that 3 passes are made in this case.

Plate 47—STAR KNOTS

Fig. 135A: A Three-Strand Star Knot with the first operation completed.

B: The second stage of the same knot after each working strand has been brought across the front, then down through the following eye in the manner illustrated.

C: As the knot looks from the underneath or bottom part, after each parallel strand has been doubled by passing the working ends back up through the eyes.

D: As the knot appears from the top, after each part has been doubled the same as before.

E: Each eye is now followed around, and doubled. The ends are then passed out through the middle and the completed knot will appear as in this illustration.

Fig. 136A: The first step in making a six-strand Star Knot, with the line laid out in the manner indicated. The drawn-in line indicates how the next series of passes are started.

B: Shows how the knot looks after the second pass has been completed.

C: The third stage of the operation is shown here from the back

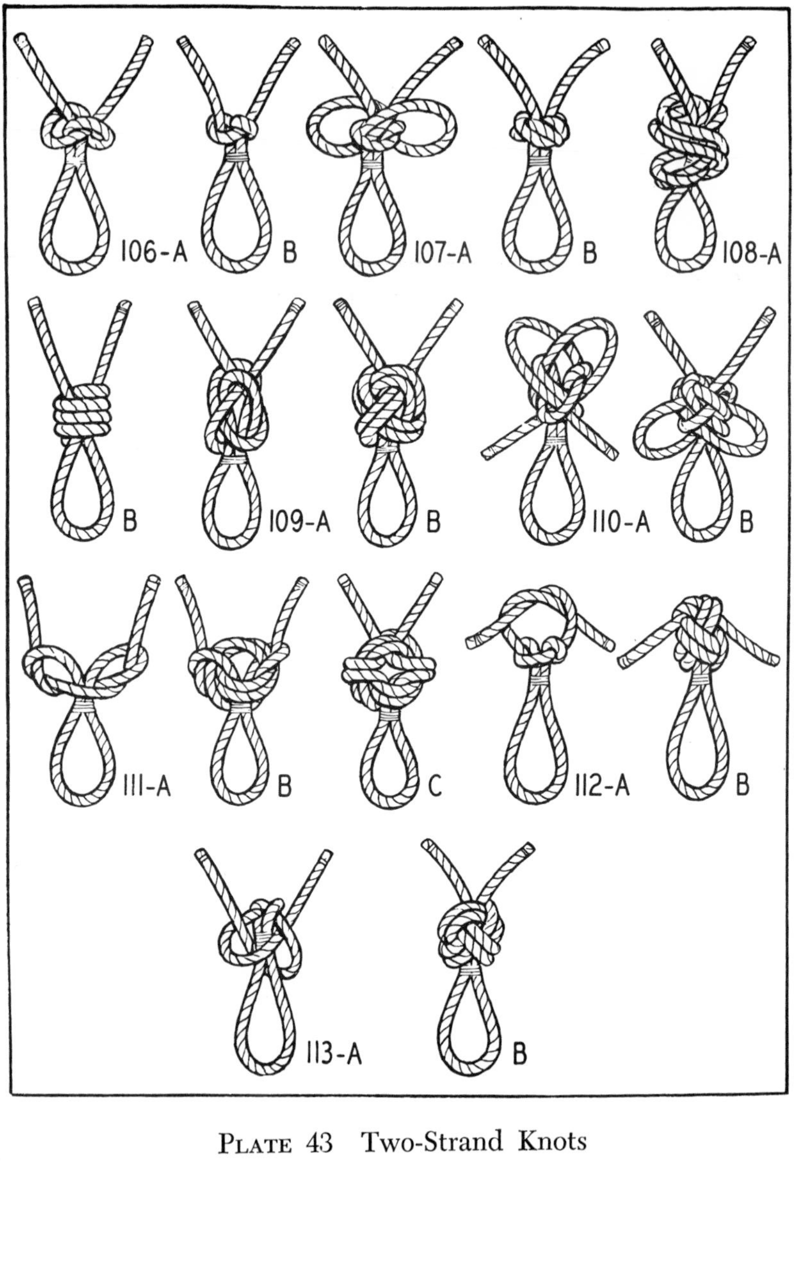

PLATE 43 Two-Strand Knots

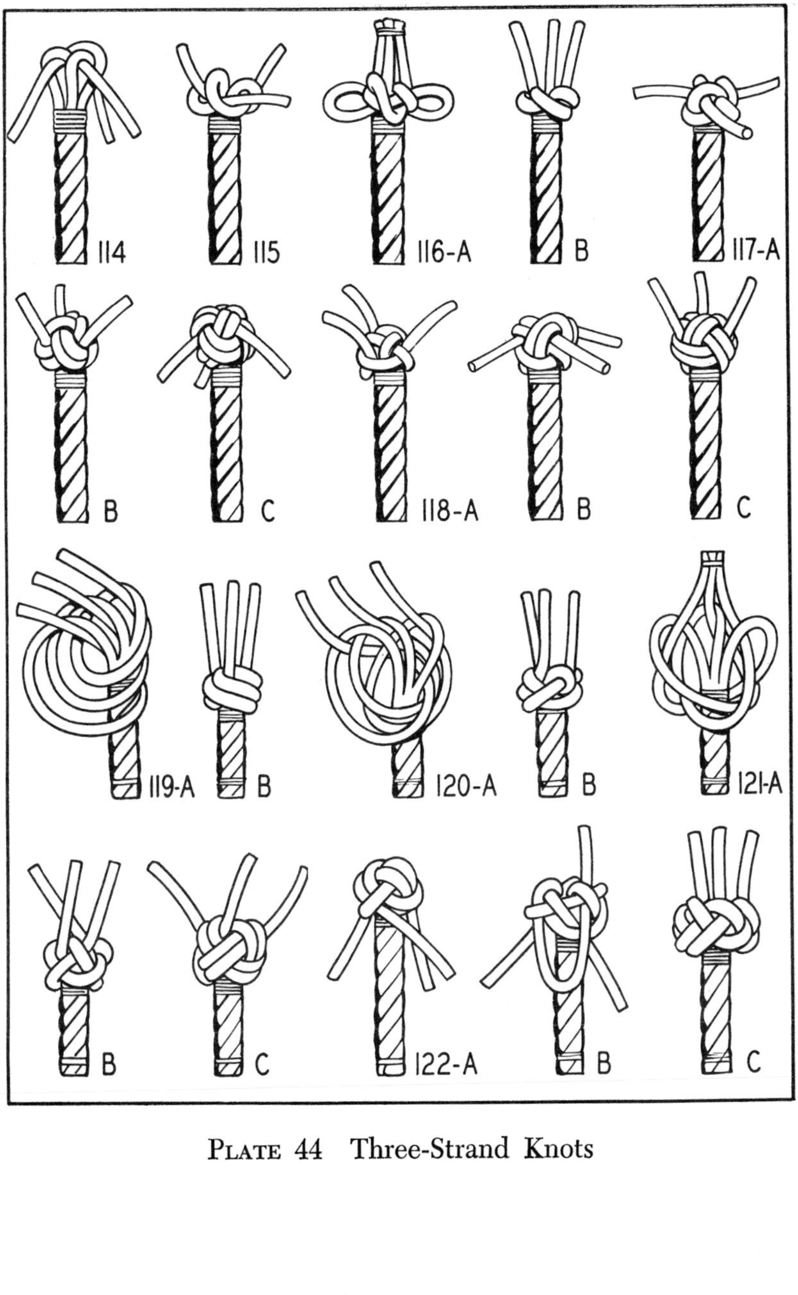

Plate 44 Three-Strand Knots

or underneath part of the knot after the working parts have followed the parallel strands up through the eyes again, making a double pass.

D: After the last operation has been completed, the knot will now appear as pictured here from the front or top part. The working ends are now passed under and out through each following eye as indicated by the drawn line. This operation doubles the top part of the knot.

E: Shows the top part with each pass completed. The eyes are now followed around and doubled with the end of each working part coming out in the middle and cut off or tucked out of sight down through the body of the knot.

F: As the completed knot appears. These knots may be used for ornamental purposes on women's handbags.

PLATE 48—BOATSWAIN'S CALLS AND HAMMOCK CLEWS

Fig. 137: This is an English Boatswain's Call with Lanyard. It is one of several different types that are used in the British Navy. The attached Lanyard can be made with Double Flat or English Sennit, using any number of strands suitable for the neck piece. Turk's Heads are applied as illustrated at intervals to serve as seizings and to give the work added distinction. Note the half hitch work on lower part of Lanyard.

A Boatswain's Call such as this is one of the oldest and most distinctive pieces of nautical equipment to be handed down from bygone centuries. In the days of antiquity a call pipe or flute was used by which the galley slaves of Greece and Rome kept stroke with their oars. According to history there is also a record that the call pipe was used in the Crusade of 1248 by the English Crossbowmen, who were called on deck to attack by its signal. It is further related that when the French, under the command of Chevalier Pregant de Bidoux, defeated the British in the naval action off Brest on April 25, 1513, the English Commander Lord High Admiral Sir Edward Howard, when certain the battle was lost, threw his gold boatswain whistle into the sea rather than see this badge of honor humiliated in surrender.

Fig. 138: The Hammock Clews as shown here are formed in the following way: First measure off the desired length for the twelve bights, which are attached to the canvas hammock by a jackstay after being inserted through the Grommet Eyelets. In order to get uniform length in each bight, space twelve nails or screws an equal distance apart and the same length from the hammock ring. The other end of the line is now run back and forth between the ring and the screws until all twelve screws are covered with bights. After this operation is completed, the working end of the line is run through the ring in the opposite manner, to the side where the operation was started. One end of the line will now be running through the ring from underneath, whereas the other end will be running through from the top. Continue by separating the stands with a rule which can be used as a spreader by passing it first over one strand and then under the next which will bring one strand up and the next strand down, as for a Sword Mat. After the spreader has been passed all the way through, the outside strands are used as a filler by running them through behind the spreader, and jamming them up snugly in place. This same operation is now continued until 6 passes of the filler strands have been made, taking care after each pass to drop a bight on each side until the end is reached. As the spreader is run through to separate the strands after each pass with the fillers has been made, caution should be used in picking up the proper strands, as the strands that are up should be dropped down, and the strands that are down should be picked up. A Square Knot is used to finish the operation which is tied between the 2 center bights in the manner indicated after the last pass has been made.

Fig. 139: An American Navy Regulation Boatswain's call with Lanyard and Sea Bean. Note Pineapple Knot on lower part of lanyard.

Fig. 140: Shows how the 12 bights are attached to the jackstay after having been passed through the Grommet Eyelets on the edge of the canvas. Heavy canvas is used for the construction of the hammock, which can be any length and breadth desired, with about two inches allowed for seams.

Fig. 141: Ripping Canvas is performed by picking up one yarn on the outside, and then, with the use of a sharp knife, cutting along-

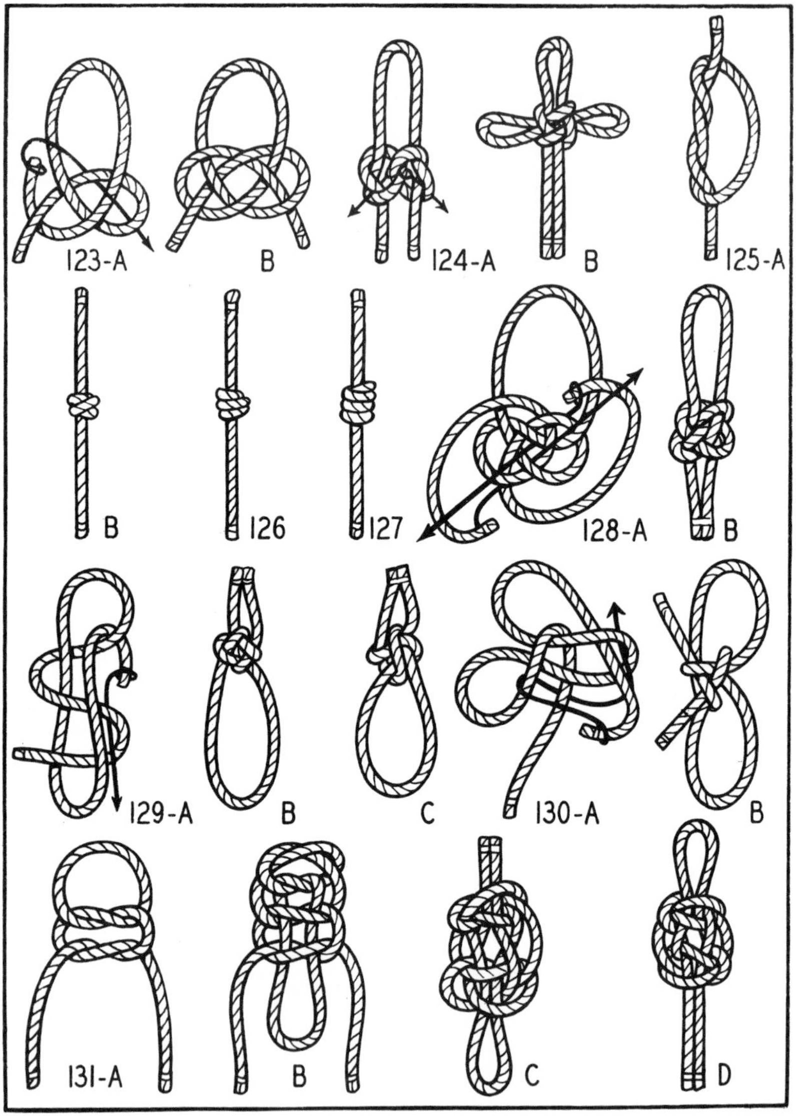

PLATE 45 Miscellaneous Knots

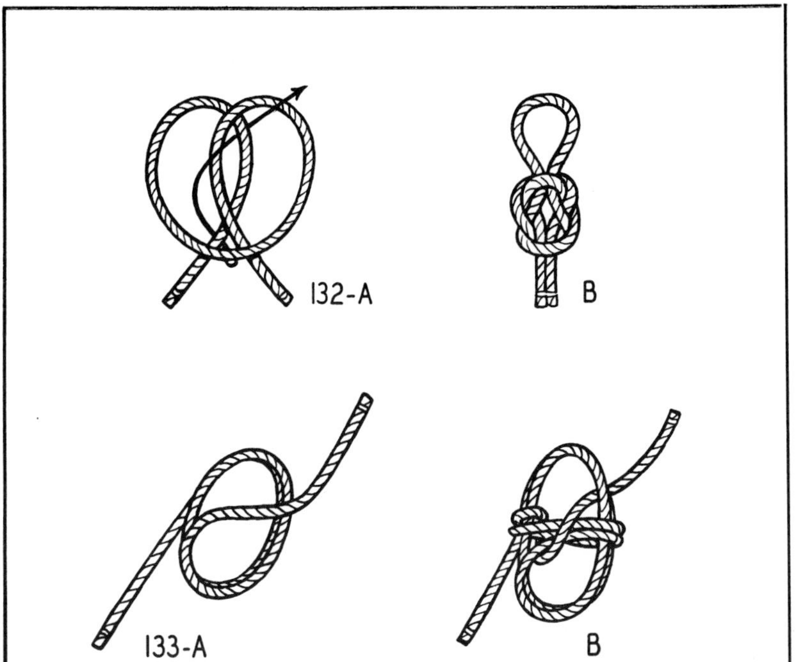

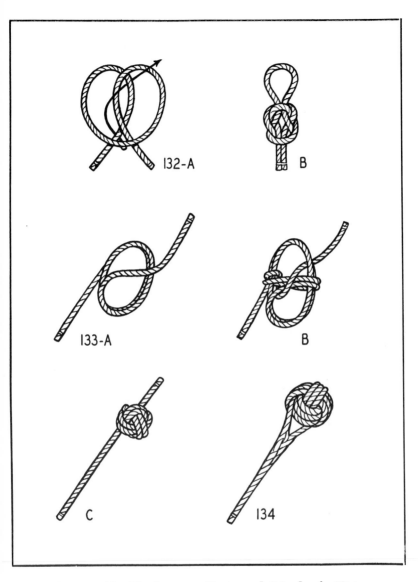

Plate 46 Hackamore Knot and Monkey's Fist

side of this yarn, which is kept under a slight strain as the operation is continued, on canvas that is hauled taut to simplify the work.

Fig. 142: Another Type of British Boatswain's Call.

Plate 49—KNOTS AND EQUIPMENT

Fig. 143: A Meshing Needle or Shuttle, loaded with line and ready for use.

Fig. 144: Shows a Square Knotter's Hook, Block and Tie Cord.

Fig. 145: A Square Knotter's Hook.

Fig. 146: Vice Clamp used in Square Knot Work.

Fig. 147A: Shows how to begin an Inverted Five Bight, Three-Strand Turk's Head. With the line laid out in this manner, the working end is passed through as indicated by the drawn-in line to complete the knot.

B: As the knot will appear after the previously explained pass has been completed, and the weave has been closed.

C: The knot is shown here after 3 passes have been made to fill in the body. Patterns such as this make good hot-plate holders. Use 120 thread white line, 10 feet long for this purpose.

Fig. 148A: The Constrictor Knot makes a firm and dependable tie. It can be cinched up hard and taut without slipping. This shows the initial stage of placing the line around a spar or other objects when starting this tie. Now follow the drawn-in line which indicates how the working strand is passed to complete the job.

B: As the finished knot will appear when pulled taut.

Fig. 149: A Clove Hitch such as this is one of the most familiar ties there is. It is used for many simple purposes and the Square Knotter will have numerous occasions to use it; such as in making pillow-tops, etc. It is begun by bringing the line from the top part down across the object to which it is being applied, and then around the object and over its own part and once again around the object, then passed out underneath its own part, with the working end of the line leading downward in this instance.

Fig. 150A: Shows the first stage of a Three-Ply Turk's Head Knot with 5 bights. The Turk's Head is generally used as a tubular knot.

It may also be used inverted for decorations on dresses and as a hot-plate holder (see Fig. 151). The Turk's Head is used in a variety of ways; such as on up-and-down spokes of ships' steering wheels, on footropes, handhold or manropes, yoke ropes, gym climbing ropes, guard rails, life lines, ditty bags, neckerchiefs, bridle reins, fishing rods, archery bows, vaulting poles, oars, paddles, tools, whips, lanyards, telescopes, leashes, chairs, bell ropes and tassels. With the application of varnish, shellac or clear varnish, it makes a nice napkin ring. In making a napkin ring, use 84 thread white line, 8 feet long. It is begun by placing the cord over the object on which the Turk's Head Knot is to be tied with the standing part (short end of strand) inside or near the worker. The moving part, or long end, is brought to the back. Then with the moving part, make 2 turns, one over and one under the standing part toward the right. Now place the moving part under the turn on the right and then over the turn on the left.

B: At this point place the moving part between the next crossed strands, going under and over toward the right. The work will then appear as pictured here.

C: Now take the turn on the left and push it under the turn on the right. The moving part is then passed between the crossed turns, under and over toward the left. This brings the work to the last tuck which is necessary to close the knot in order to make additional passes.

D: Pictures the knot ready for the final tuck with the moving part following the standing part at this point, to make a 2, 3, 4 or 5-ply knot.

Fig. 151: Shows a Three-Strand Five-Bight Inverted Turk's Head which is practically the same as Fig. 147, except that it fits up in a more compact and uniform appearance and is tied with larger line.

Fig. 152: Shows a Sailor's Breastplate Knot or Carrick Bend design, which is a common type of decorative design used in belts and women's handbags.

Fig. 153: A Three-Ply, Four-Bight Turk's Head. It can be started from the Sailor's Breastplate by pulling the slack out of the top part; then close the bottom part and double or triple pass the knot to make a complete job.

Figs. 154A and B: Show a Pair of Prickers which are very serviceable for different types of Square Knot work, etc.

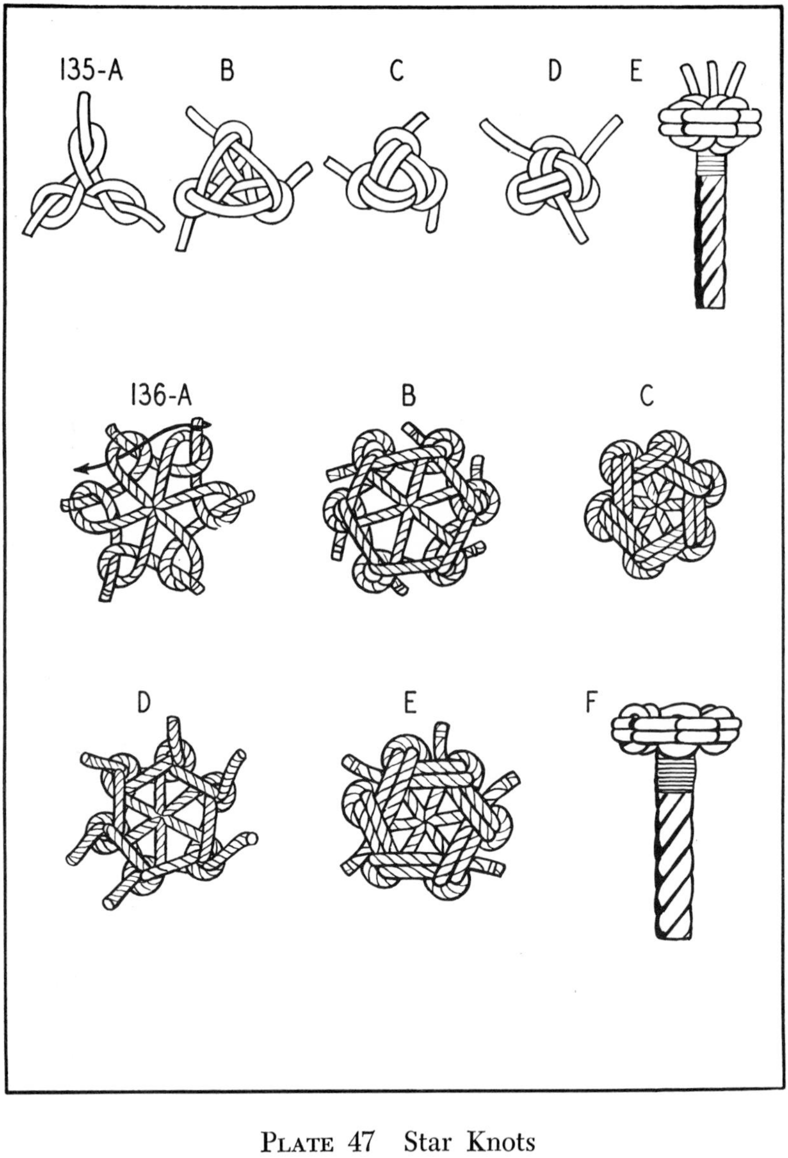

Plate 47 Star Knots

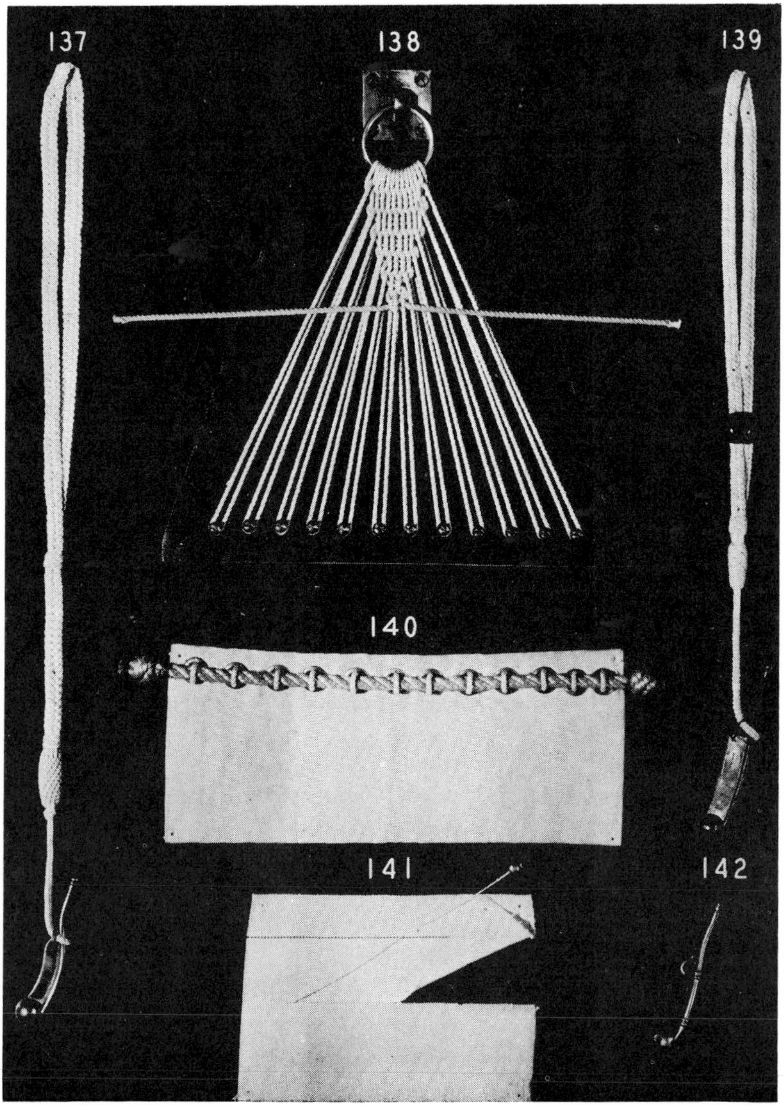

PLATE 48 Boatswains' Calls and Hammock Clews

Fig. 155: A needle that is used for winding thread on while making a Cross Clove Hitched doily.

Figs. 156 to 159: Show various sizes of Triangle Sailmakers' or Furriers' Needles.

Fig. 160: Another type of needle on which to wind small material while working designs.

Plate 50—TURK'S HEADS

Fig. 161A: The beginning of a Three-Strand Turk's Head with the first tuck completed as indicated.

B: Shows the second tuck after the line on the right side has been pulled under the line on the left side. Now continue by pulling the line on the left side under the line on the right side, or in the opposite direction from the previous operation; then tuck the working end under it as before.

C: Shows the step that completes the Turk's Head, which is now ready for doubling. This is done by following the parallel line around the knot that lies beside the working end after being closed up.

D: As it appears after 2 passes have been made.

Fig. 162A: A Four-Strand Turk's Head after the first pass has been made with the first tuck under both parts of the line as indicated.

B: Shows the second stage of the operation, after the working end of the line has been passed around and over the line on the left side in back, then out over the cross strand and under the previous tuck that was made to begin the operation.

C: As it appears after the cross strand in the middle has been picked up in the back and passed underneath. The working end is then carried over the next strand on the side, and out under the strand that is indicated, to close up the knot, which brings it alongside the opposite end of the line. It is now ready to be doubled.

D: Shows the finished Turk's Head after 2 complete passes have been made. To complete the operation the ends should be cut off short to hide them from view.

Fig. 163A: The beginning of a Five-Strand Turk's Head after the first tuck is made in exactly the same manner as for a Three-Strand Turk's Head in Fig. 161A. The line is then carried over the outside strand on the left in back, then out under the next cross strand which brings it alongside the opposite end of the line. Now follow the opposite end with the working end by making a parallel pass to the opposite side of the knot; then pick up the middle cross strand and tuck the working end underneath it in the manner indicated.

B: The operation is continued by passing the working end of the line out over the line on the left side. Next, split the 2 parallel strands of the last operation, then go over the outside and under the middle strand between the 2 parallel strands in the manner indicated.

C: After completing the last operation, the weaving is continued by tucking underneath the outside strand on the right, then crossing toward the opposite side of the knot by going over the next strand, then under the second strand, and over the outside strand. The weaving is now closed up as indicated to complete the knot.

D: Shows two complete passes. Any number of passes can be made, depending on the desired width of the weave. Turk's Heads such as these are useful as ornamental decorations on stanchions, handbag handles, handrails, shade pulls and various other objects.

Plate 51—SENNIT BRAIDING

Fig. 164: The Three-Strand Sennit is begun with strands 1 and 2 on the left, and 3 on the right. Start with strand 1, bring it down under strand 2 and across to the right side; then bring strand 3 down under strand 1 and across to the left side in the same manner. This method is repeated until the desired length of braid has been finished. The beginner will find it easier to learn the knack of braiding if he letters the strands the same as they are in this and the following illustrations. Sennit work should be thoroughly mastered as it forms the foundation for many types of Square Knot patterns, such as, dog leashes, whistle lanyards, knife lanyards and handbag handles.

Fig. 165: The Four-Strand Single Flat or English Sennit is formed in the following manner: Lead strand 1 down under strand 2 and across to the middle of the opposite side. Next lead strand 4 down over strand 3 and under strand 1 to the middle of the opposite side

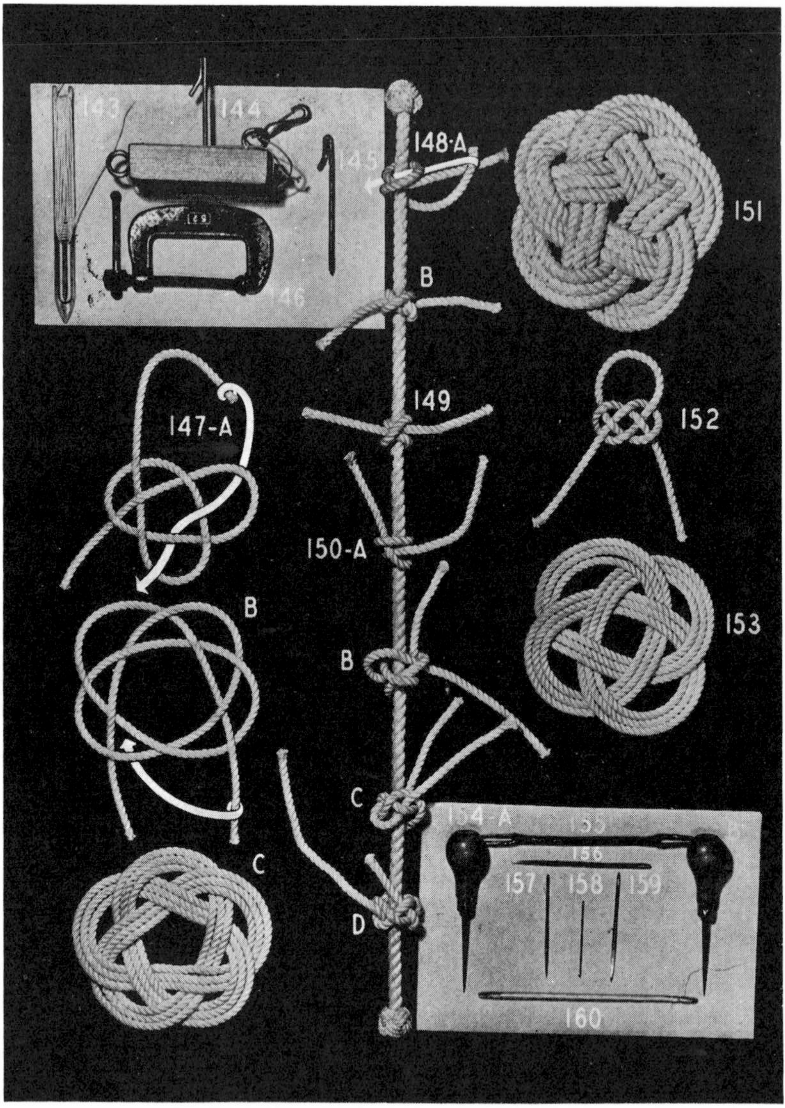

Plate 49 Knots and Equipment

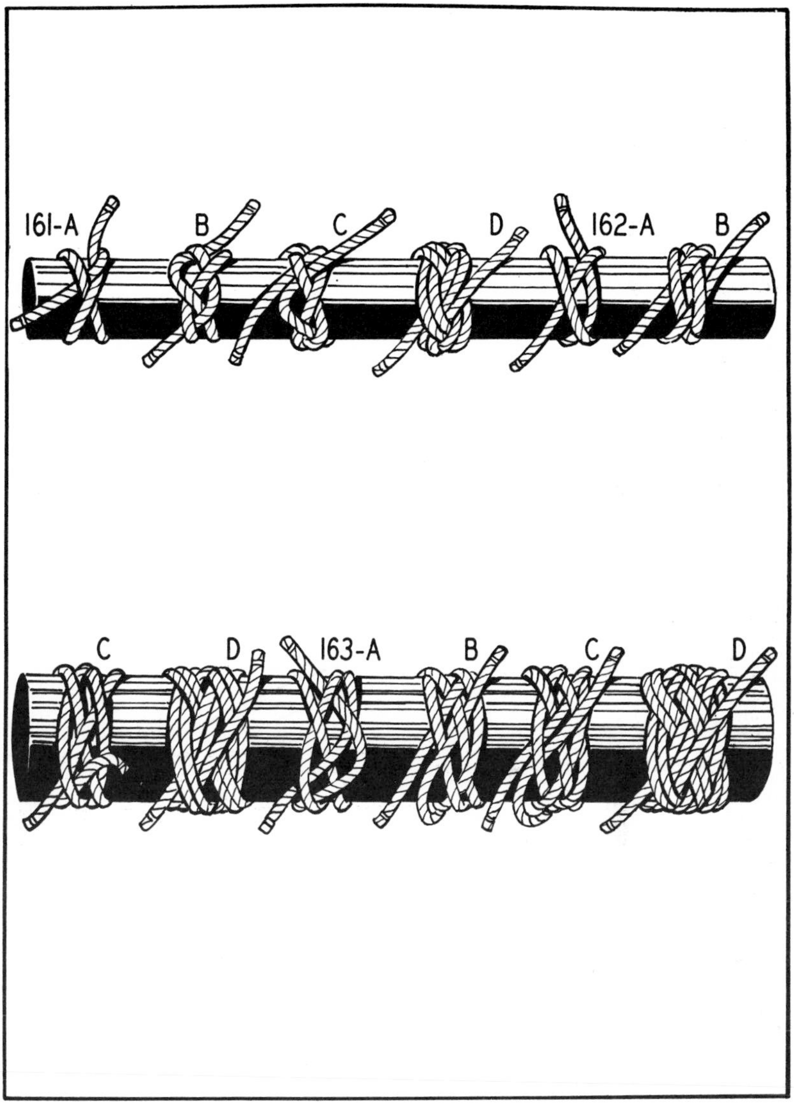

PLATE 50 Turk's Heads

the same as before. Continue with a repetition of the same key until the braid reaches the desired length.

Fig. 166: The Five-Strand Running Sennit is begun by bringing strand 1 down across the front, over strands 2 and 3 toward the opposite side. Now repeat the same procedure with strand 5, bringing it down across the front, over strand 4 and strand 1 toward the opposite side, etc. Repeat alternately from each opposite side in the foregoing manner until the braid is worked to the desired length.

Fig. 167: The Five-Strand Crabber's Eye Sennit is formed by dividing the strands 3-2. Strand 5 is brought around in back then passed between strands 2 and 3 and brought out toward the right on the inside of strand 4. Strand 1 is then led around in back to the opposite side in the same manner and passed between strands 4 and 5, then brought out toward the left on the inside of strand 3, etc. Repeat the same key as often as necessary to make the required length of braid. Remember at this point to visualize the strands in the position they should be after the last move, and not as they are shown in the illustration. This is very important to prevent confusion while braiding Sennits that are formed by leading the strands around and in back, then toward their own side again, as the descriptive text keeps pace with the imaginary braid and will not correspond with the illustration of the strands as they are lettered in the accompanying photograph after the first moves. The key to this braid is down under from right to left, then left to right, going under 2 and over 1 from one side, then under 1 and over 1 from the opposite side.

Fig. 168: The Six-Strand Single Flat or English Sennit. Strand 1 is brought down over strand 2 and to the inside of strand 3. Strand 6 is next brought under strand 5, over strand 4, under strand 3 and over strand 1 in the same manner. When using an even number of strands in the preparation of a Flat Sennit the outside strand on one side goes over to start the braid and then from the opposite side the outside strand goes under, whereas, in an odd number of strands, both outside strands are carried over from each side.

Fig. 169: The Seven-Strand Single Flat or English Sennit. Strand 1 is brought down over strand 2, under strand 3 and over strand 4 to the inside of strand 5. Now continue by bringing strand 7 down over strand 6, under strand 5 and over strand 1 to the inside of strand 4 in the same manner. Repeat the same moves alternately from each side to lengthen the braid.

Fig. 170: The Four-Strand Single Round Sennit is made as follows: Bring strand 4 around, in back up under strand 1 and over strand 2 toward its own or right side again. After this move is executed strand 4 will be lying on the inside of strand 3. Next bring strand 1 around in back in the same manner, then up under strand 3 and over strand 4 toward its own or left side. This move will bring strand 1 to the inside of strand 2 in similar fashion to the preceding move. Continue with the same key for any length of braid.

Fig. 171: The Four-Strand Double-Round Sennit (8 strands) is formed in the same manner as the single method except that the strands are doubled.

Fig. 172: The Six-Strand Half-Round Sennit is begun with its strands divided 3-3. Start with strand 6 down around and under from right to left, then under strand 2 and over strand 3 to the inside of strand 4. Next bring strand 1 in similar fashion down around and under from left to right, then under strand 4 and over strand 6 to the inside of strand 3. Key: Under 2 and over 1, alternately from each side.

Fig. 173: The Six-Strand Round Sennit is formed in the following manner: Divide the strands 3-3 and start with strand 6. Bring it around over strand 1 under strand 2 and over strand 3 to the inside of strand 4. Next lead strand 1 around over strand 5 under strand 4 to the inside of strand 3. The strands should be held in place very carefully for this braid, otherwise, the key will be lost and the braid will have to be started over again. The braiding is continued by repeating the key moves as often as desired.

Fig. 174: A Three-Strand Crown Sennit is tied with a series of crowns as illustrated. Strand 1 goes over strand 3 and under strand 2. Strand 2 goes over strand 1 and under strand 3. Strand 3 goes over strand 2 and under strand 1 in similar fashion to complete the crown.

Fig. 175: The Seven-Strand French Sennit has its strands divided 4-3. Start by bringing strand 1 down across the front, over strands 2 and 3 to the inside of strand 4. Next bring strand 7 down across the front, over strands 6 and 5 and under strand 4, then over strand 1 to the inside of strand 3. Key: Over 2 and under 1 across the front from one side, then over 2 under 1 and over 1 from the opposite side.

Fig. 176: The Eight-Strand Square Sennit has its strands divided 4-4. Start with strand 8. Bring it down around then under strand 2 and over strands 3 and 4 to the inside of strand 5. Now continue by

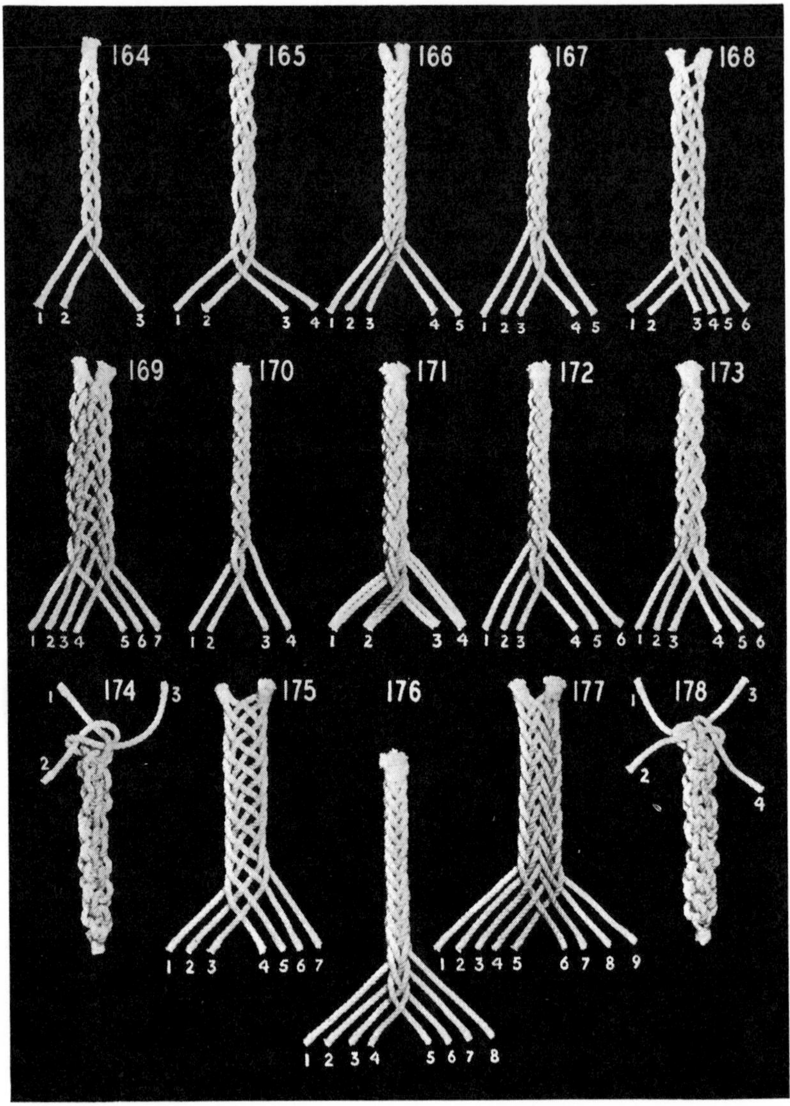

PLATE 51 Sennit Braiding

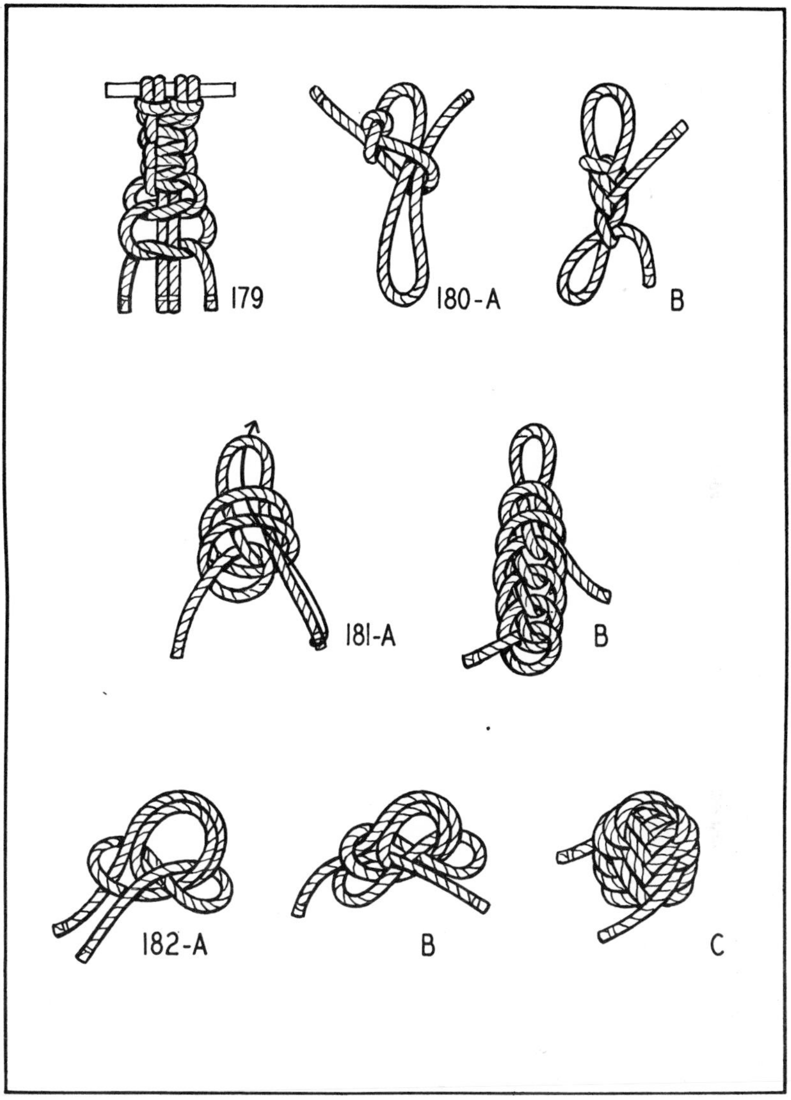

Plate 52 Sennit Braiding

bringing strand 1 down around, then under strand 6 and over strands 5 and 8 to the inside of strand 4. Key: Around in back, then under 2 and over 2, alternating from first one side and then the other.

Fig. 177: The Nine-Strand French Sennit is begun with its strands divided 5-4. Start by bringing strand 1 down across the front, over strands 2 and 3, then under strands 4 and 5 to the inside of strand 6. Now continue the same procedure from the opposite side by leading strand 9 down across the front, over strands 8 and 7, then under strands 6 and 1 to the inside of strand 5. Key: Over 2 and under 2 across the front from first one side and then the other.

Fig. 178: The Four-Strand Crown Sennit is formed with a series of Crowns as illustrated. Strand 1 is brought over strand 2 and under strand 3. Strand 2 is brought over strand 4 and under strand 1. Strand 3 is brought over strand 1 and under strand 4. Next bring strand 4 over strand 3 and under strand 2 to complete the Crown. Crown Sennits make distinctive designs when worked with leather strips, and are used in the making of attractive whistle lanyards, watch fobs and other things.

Plate 52—SENNIT BRAIDING

Fig. 179: A Continuous Row of Flat or Square Knots may be formed into a Sennit as illustrated. (See Plate 53, Fig. 185.)

Fig. 180A: A Triangle Sennit is begun by attaching the line to a ring or other object. Next, form a slip eye in an Overhand Knot with the opposite end of the line. Continue with the working end by forming another eye through the preceding one, in the form of a bight, as shown here.

B: The braid is continued by bringing the lower strand up after each pass has been completed, to form another pass in the same manner by carrying it over the braid and through the eye of the top or opposite strand which was used for the previous operation. Bights are formed with each alternate strand through the eye of the previous working strand in this manner until the braid reaches the required length. Care should be taken to draw the slack out of each bight in a uniform manner as the work proceeds.

Fig. 181A: The Bugler's Sennit is begun as follows: Make 2 round turns by folding each coil to the left, as shown in the illustration. Proceed to form the braid by passing an eye in the form of a bight under both round turns, which will automatically form another round turn of its own. The eye of each bight is pulled up and adjusted in a uniform manner before continuing to repeat the same process by passing the line over the first round turn, then under the next 2 round turns, which forms the last 2 coils on the braid.

B: This diagram portrays the braid after the fourth tuck has been completed. Any required length may be used for work of this type.

Fig. 182A: The Antique Sennit may be formed without difficulty by closely observing the accompanying illustrations. Begin with 2 round turns, which are made in a clockwise direction from left to right with the working end of the line encircling the 2 parts on the left side; then bring the line out through the middle. At this point, cross over and encircle the 2 parts on the right side the same as before, again bringing the line out through the middle and over the pass which was formed previously. This completes the first stage of the operation as shown here.

B: Next, encircle the line around the 2 bottom parts and lead it across through the middle, over the previous pass, then toward the opposite side again. This same procedure is repeated each time by picking up the 2 bottom strands with each alternating pass, which is then crossed over the previous pass and out through the middle of the weave again.

C: This illustrates the third stage of the operation, after the Sennit has been braided far enough to assume a neat uniform shape. Do not pull the work too taut during the process of forming the braid, as this type of Sennit has a tendency to assimilate considerable slack and to tighten up. For this reason care should be taken to allow plenty of slack when working it.

Plate 53—SENNIT BRAIDING

Fig. 183: The Interlocking Sennit. It is of simple construction and may be formed with nothing more than a series of Interlocking Hitches after first starting with an Overhand Knot for the base of

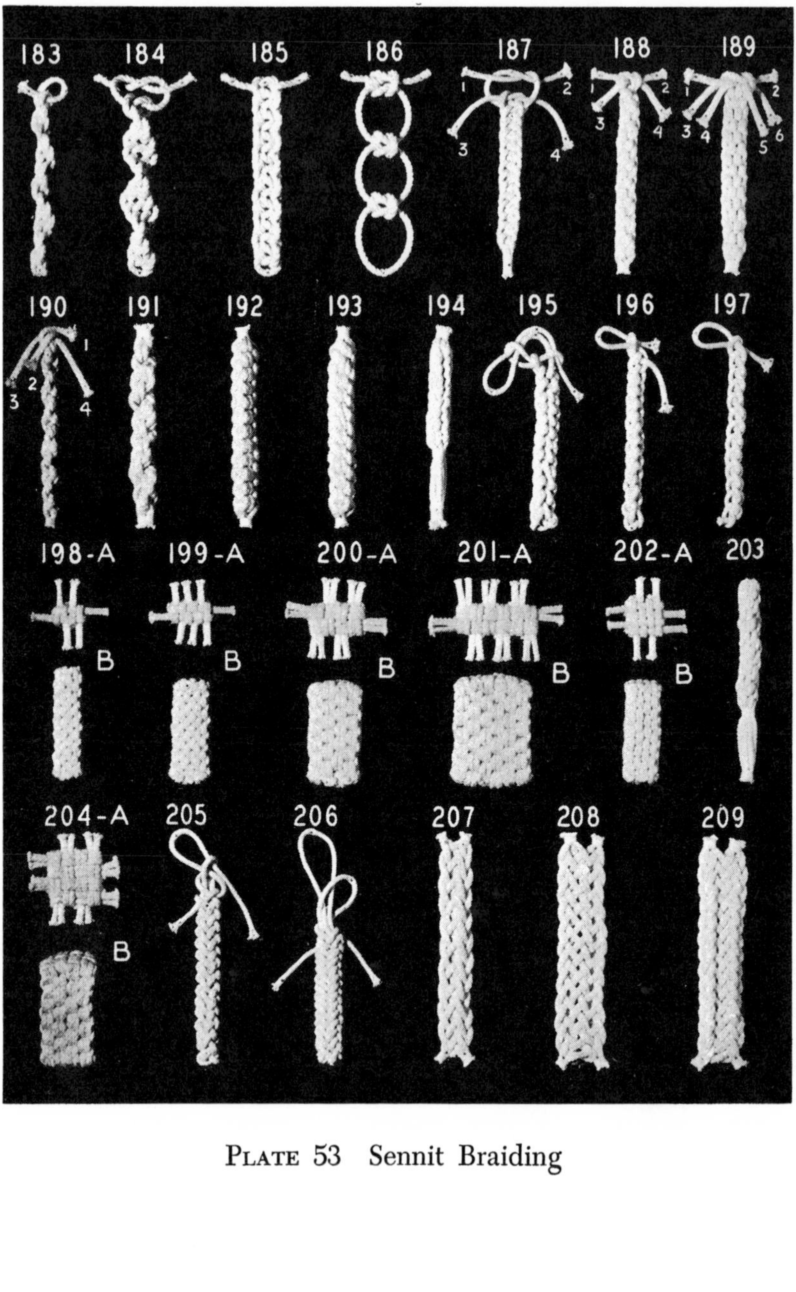

Plate 53 Sennit Braiding

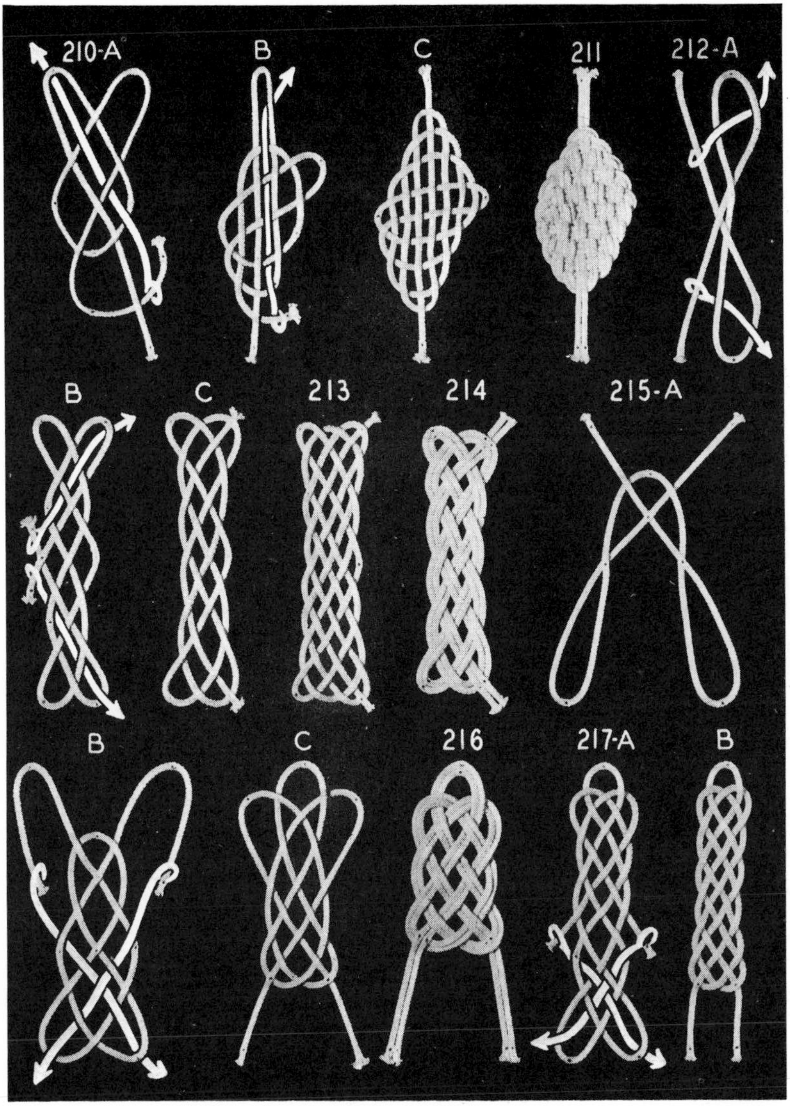

PLATE 54 Mats

the braid. Each succeeding pass is interlaced around and through the previous pass. This forms a Sennit of a slightly spiral nature.

Fig. 184: The Spiral Sennit. This design represents a series of Half Knots that are formed one on top of the other, which produces a spiral pattern. Spirals such as these are invaluable in numerous kinds of Square Knot work where they are used for creating variations in the pattern of the design. Each Half Knot is tied the same way every time a new knot is formed, thus creating a true spiral effect.

Fig. 185: The Square Knot Sennit shown here has the Square Knots pulled close together which produces a very neat uniform appearance. When tied around a core, this work, in Square Knot vernacular, is known as flats.

Fig. 186: The Square Knot Loop Sennit. It is tied by spacing each Square Knot an equal distance apart from the previous knot, thereby creating a loop effect in the general pattern.

Fig. 187: The Four-Strand Square Half Knot Sennit. By working the strands in alternating pairs with a succession of left and right Half Knots, the design will acquire a handsome square effect with twin edges. Strands 1 and 2 are tied on top of strands 3 and 4 in the manner shown, and vice versa.

Fig. 188: The Four-Strand Square Knot Folding Sennit. Form half a Square Knot with strands 1 and 2, then fold strands 3 and 4 alternately over the top from their respective sides. Now form the other half of the Square Knot with strands 1 and 2 again and then repeat the same procedure as before. The resulting Sennit will have a handsome, flat, symmetrical appearance.

Fig. 189: The Six-Strand Square Knot Folding Sennit. It is worked in similar manner to the four-strand method except for the additional strands. In this case, strands 1 and 2 are used for tying each half of the Square Knot, while strands 3, 4, 5 and 6 are alternately folded over the top from their respective sides after each half of the Square Knot is formed. The resulting Sennit has a more compact body than the previous example.

Fig. 190: The Four-Strand Single Folding Sennit. It is tied by first folding strands 1 and 2 over the top from each opposite side. Then repeat the same process with strands 3 and 4 from their respective sides. This Sennit builds very fast and has a most unusual and novel appearance.

Fig. 191: The Four-Strand Double Folding Sennit (8 strands). It is worked the same way as the single method, except that the strands are doubled.

Fig. 192: The Three-Strand Double Triangle Crown Sennit (6 strands). By reversing the crowns each time, the resulting Sennit will assume a perfect triangular shape. It is a Sennit of unusual distinction and beauty.

Fig. 193: The Three-Strand Double Helixed Round Crown Sennit (6 strands). By tying the crowns the same way each time, the Sennit will adopt a perfect helix with a handsome round surface. In this case the crowns revolve the same way each time.

Fig. 194: The Eight-Strand Half Knot Round Sennit. Seize the strands together, then begin by tying a right Half Knot with each set of opposite strands. Next, tie 2 left Half Knots on top of the previous knots with the other 2 sets of opposite strands in the same manner as before. Continue to alternate by tying first one pair of opposing strands and then the other with right Half Knots from one side, then with left Half Knots from the other side, etc., until the braid has reached a sufficient length. This operation will build into one of the oddest Sennits in existence. It forms a basically round braid, yet there are actually four individual weaves in its make-up, each of which resembles an ordinary Three-Strand Sennit.

Fig. 195: The Double Foundation Crocheting Stitch Sennit. It comes from *Caulfield and Saward's Dictionary of Needlework*. Start by tying a Tom Fool's Knot, then form a bight through the left end with the right end of the Tom Fool's Knot. Continue forming eyes with each additional bight which in this case is worked from the right to left in the manner illustrated. Note that after each bight is formed through the previous eye, the line is run through the middle of its own two parts before being inserted through the eye of the last bight. It is then brought up to form another eye for each succeeding bight as the work proceeds. This Sennit can also be worked in the opposite way, from left to right.

Fig. 196: The Two-Strand Triangle Spool Sennit is taken from *Bocher's Cordes, Tresses et Noeuds*. Each one of the three sides represents a different type of braid. By forming a bight in a Slip Overhand Knot and then leading first one bight and then the other through the eye of the bight from the opposite end, the result will automatically assume a three-sided braid when each part is worked as pictured here.

Fig. 197: The One-Strand Triangle Spool Sennit. This braid was

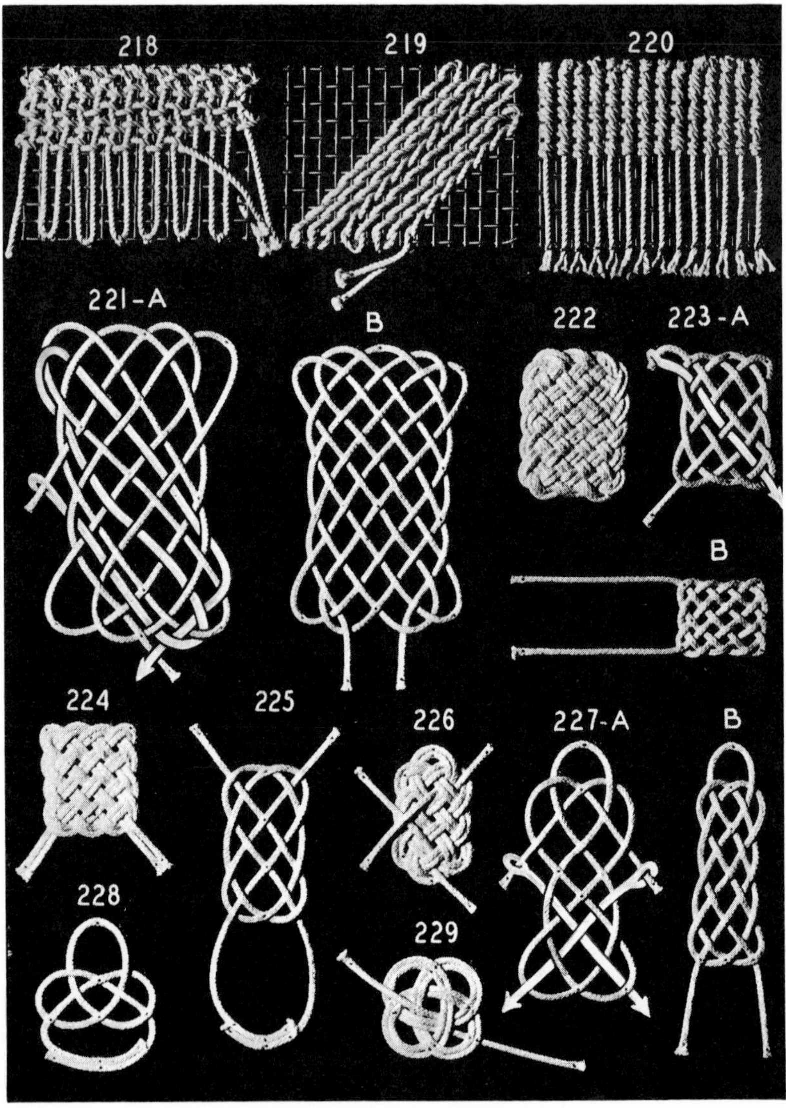

PLATE 55 Mats

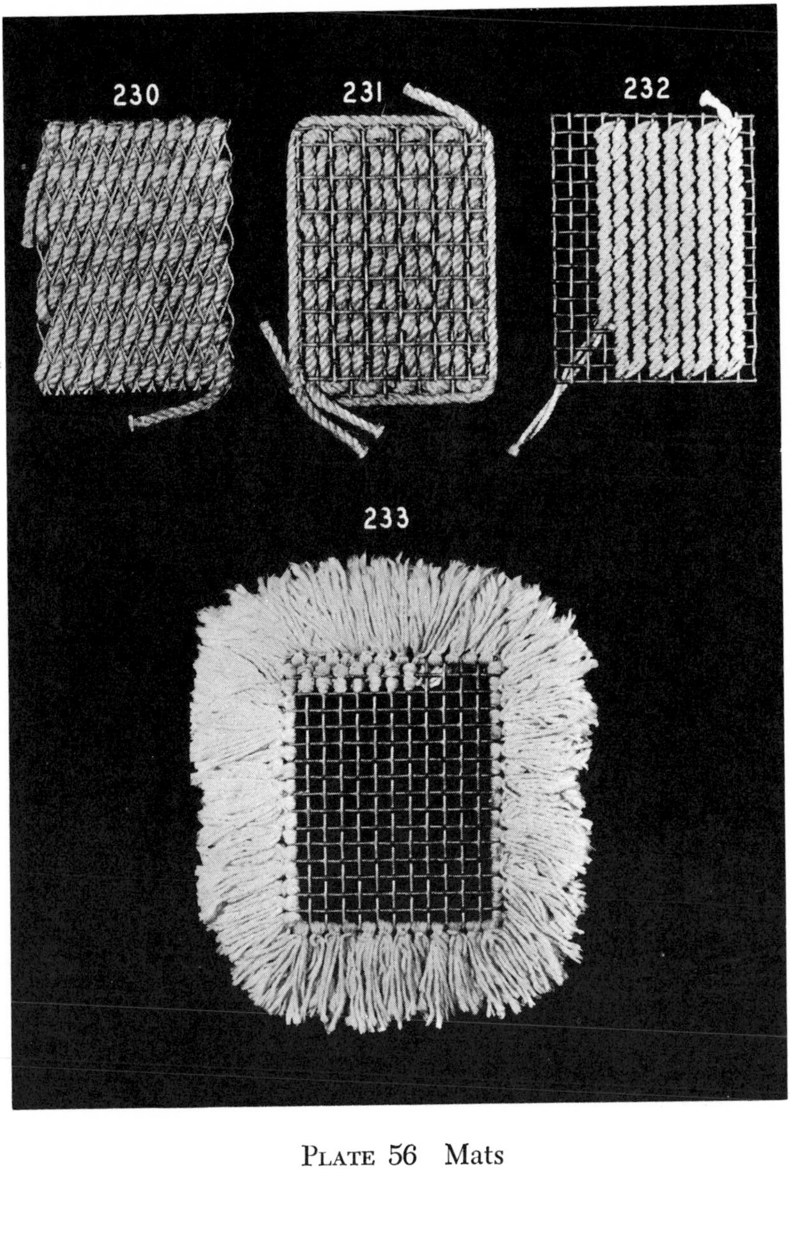

Plate 56 Mats

developed from the preceding example. Two of its sides are alike. Otherwise, as can be noted, it is worked in the same general way as its predecessor, except that only 1 strand is used in this case.

Fig. 198A: The Six-Strand Single Oblong Sennit. It is worked in Spritsail Sheet fashion by leading the end strands parallel to each other across the body of the weave to the opposite side. These 2 strands are then crowned by alternately working from first one side and then the other, with the side strands. This method can readily be grasped by observing the illustration at this point.

B: The body of the Sennit is shown here after it has been worked down a short way. This example makes an excellent handle for handbags when worked with small material.

Fig. 199A: The Eight-Strand Single Oblong Sennit is formed in the same way as the preceding example except that it has 2 additional strands, which give added bulk to the braid.

B: The same example when braided into a short length.

Fig. 200A: The Six-Strand Double Oblong Sennit (12 strands) makes an impressive design when worked into Sennit form.

B: As it appears in final shape.

Fig. 201A: The Eight-Strand Double Oblong Sennit (16 strands). It represents a very pleasing type of Sennit with a handsome body. When working Sennits of this nature, take care to have the lengthwise strands about twice as long as the side strands at the start.

B: This shows the completed product.

Fig. 202A: The Eight-Strand Single Cube Sennit. It comes from *Alston's Seamanship,* and was originally intended as a means of finishing off a fender. When worked in Spritsail Sheet fashion by alternately crowning over and under with each strand from its respective side, the result will be a perfect cube as shown here.

B: The completed Cube Sennit. It forms a body of very handsome appearance. When the work is finished, all ends of strands may be trimmed and then tucked back into the body of a Sennit such as this and the preceding designs of a similar nature.

Fig. 203: The Six-Strand Round Crown Sennit. It is made by arranging the cords into 2 equal sets of 3 strands each. First one set and then the other is alternately crowned to the right. To prevent confusion, it is best to extend the lower set each time another crown is formed and then bring the top set down alongside the braid. As each lower set is brought up to form the next crown, it is necessary to pass the strands between 2 strands of the upper crown.

Fig. 204A: The Eight-Strand Double Cube Sennit (16 strands). This pictures the face of the braid after the correct starting formation of the strands has been arranged. They are laid out in the same manner as for the single method.

B: This illustrates the braid after being worked down a short way. It builds into an extremely handsome and symmetrical pattern and may be carried to an enormous size by working with large line.

Fig. 205: The Twin Loop Higginbotham, or Double Idiot's Delight, as it is sometimes called, may be formed in similar manner to the Single Higginbotham, except that it is started by tying 2 Slip Overhand Knots instead of 1, and the braid is then worked by alternately employing the eye from the bight of each loop on its respective side, which is stuck through the eye of the previous bight from the opposite side, with the eye of the right bight going through the eye of the left bight in the manner shown at the top of the braid. It does not require much patience to work this Sennit, as it rapidly builds into a neat, compact, symmetrical braid.

Fig. 206: The Twin Bugler's Sennit. This extraordinary braid was developed by placing 2 Bugler's Sennits face-to-face at the start and then braiding them through each other by using the same principle as in the preceding example, except that in this case the eye from the bight of each loop is run through the eye of the 2 previous bights from the opposite side instead of 1 as in the former method. As may readily be observed, they are then interlaced in the same manner as in the previous pattern before continuing with the braid. This is one of the most handsome and pleasing Sennits developed.

Fig. 207: The Six-Strand Diagonal Reverse Weave Sennit. It is braided across the front. The outside strand goes over 1 and under 2 from first one side and then the other. Each side has the opposite or reverse weave from the other side.

Fig. 208: The Nine-Strand Twin Row Channel Sennit. Key: Under 1, over 2 and under 1, alternating from each side across the front with the outside strands. This illustration shows a back view of the Sennit. It forms a row on each side of the braid which resembles a Three-Strand Sennit, and has a Channel in the middle.

Fig. 209: The Eleven-Strand Twin Row Channel Sennit. Key: Under 1, over 2 and under 2 across the front from each side with the outside strands from their respective sides. This example presents a uniform braid with an upraised row on each side, which forms a channel in the middle in similar fashion to the preceding braid.

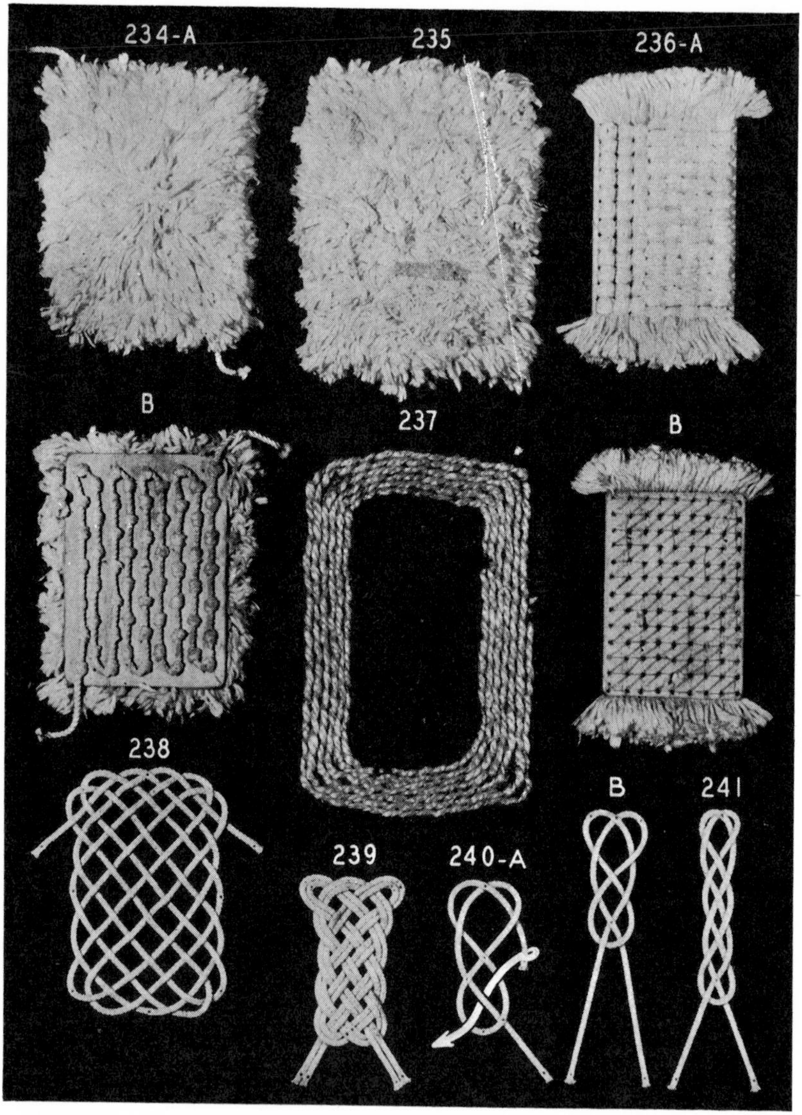

PLATE 57 Mats

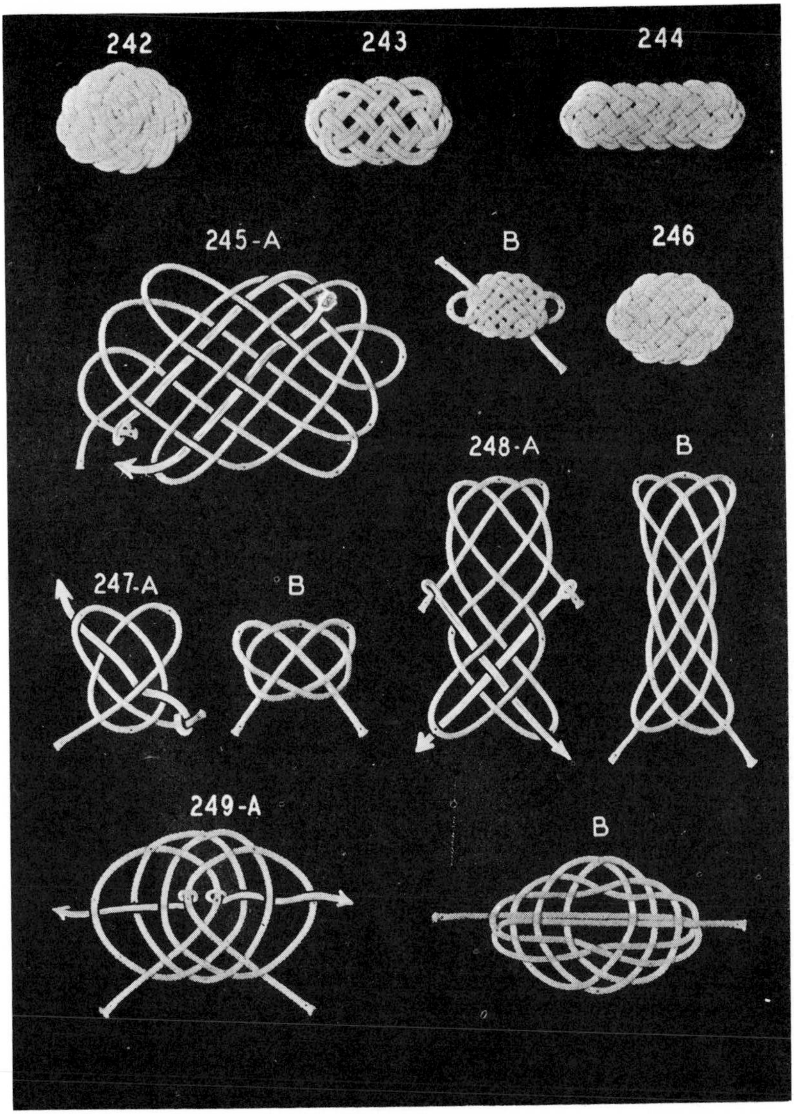

PLATE 58 Mats

Plate 54—MATS

Fig. 210A: The Single Diamond or Triangle Mat is begun by forming two interlacing bights in the manner shown. The end of the line on the left is then crossed under the line on the right in order to form additional bights to expand the weave.

B: With this line, proceed in the formation of each succeeding bight by running the working end through the weave in the manner shown, after doubling it back to form another bight each time. The drawn-in line indicates how the weave is closed after the operation has been repeated often enough to expand the weave to the proper size.

C: This shows the completed design.

Fig. 211: The Double Diamond or Triangle Mat is worked in the same manner as the single, except that it has double strands to give the weave a larger, more compact body.

Fig. 212: The Single Queen Anne Mat is begun with the line laid out in the position shown here.

B: Next form bights with both working ends, with one bight going over and the other bight going under its own part in the manner indicated. The bights are now passed through each eye that was previously formed in order to enlarge the weave. After this has been done, the operation will appear as illustrated with the drawn lines indicating how the ends are passed through to complete the weave.

C: This shows the same weave, as it looks when finished. By using the same key as previously described, this mat can be extended to any size desired, merely by a repetition of additional bights, before closing the mat with the last pass, after the desired size has been reached.

Fig. 213: The Single Queen Anne Mat is shown here after the weave has been filled in by extending the work with additional passes as previously explained.

Fig. 214: The Double Queen Anne Mat is worked with double strands; otherwise it is the same as the single method.

Fig. 215A: The Single Napoleon Bend Mat Weave is shown here with the line laid out in the form of an Overhand Knot with the bights pulled out and crossed over as indicated to start the weave.

B: The bight on the right is now crossed over on top of the bight on the left, and the working parts of the line are next passed through the weave as indicated. This will close up the pattern and complete the operation.

C: This shows the finished mat. It may be double or triple passed if a larger mat is desired.

Fig. 216: The Double Napoleon Bend Mat Weave is shown here with the strands doubled and pulled up in place to form a compact mat weave.

Fig. 217A: The Single Extended Napoleon Bend Mat Weave shows how the bights can be pulled out and crossed over to give additional length to the weave. They are then closed up as the drawn lines indicate.

B: This shows the completed mat design. Mats such as these were very popular among the old time sailormen, who used them for floor mats and for the bottom of stairs on shipboard.

Plate 55—MATS

Fig. 218: The Woven Bight Mat on Wire Mesh represents an unusual way of making a mat design and is easy to construct. The bights are led up and down the frame and crossed with the horizontal strands in the manner illustrated.

Fig. 219: The Crossed Diagonal Mat Weave on Wire Mesh is easy to duplicate and has the appearance of a mat that employs Square Knot work.

Fig. 220: A Mat Such as This may be duplicated without undue difficulty by following the pattern. Double strands are worked across the frame between each square in a horizontal direction. These strands are led over another vertical strand in the middle of each square, then under the mesh, back over the next vertical strand, and under the mesh again and so on. All vertical or filler strands are seized with an Overhand Knot at the beginning of the weave and also again at the finish. The double strands that are worked across the weave may likewise be seized with Overhand Knots on each side. Draw the seized knots up hard and fast so they won't pull out.

Fig. 221A: The Wide Rectangular Mat as it is shown here represents the symmetrical weave referred to in Plate 57, Fig. 238 which is an improvement over the former type. It may easily be duplicated by observing the general trend of the pattern and following the

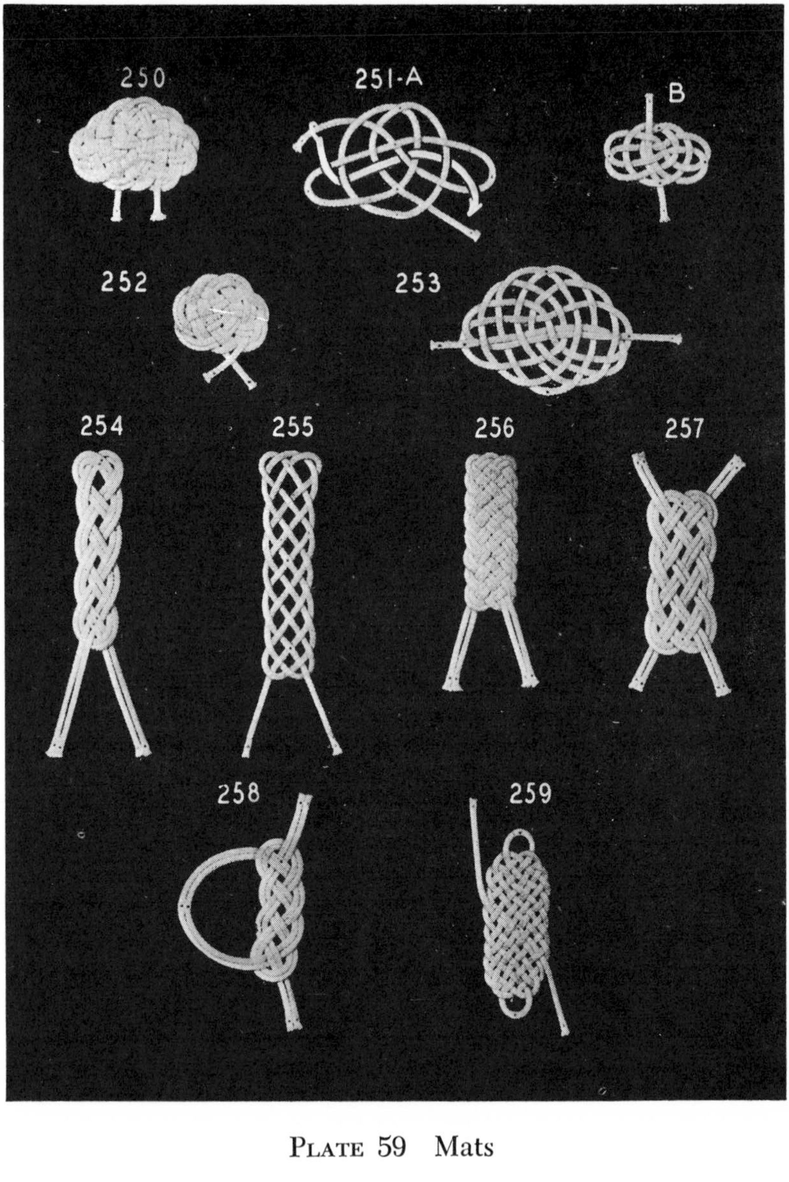

PLATE 59 Mats

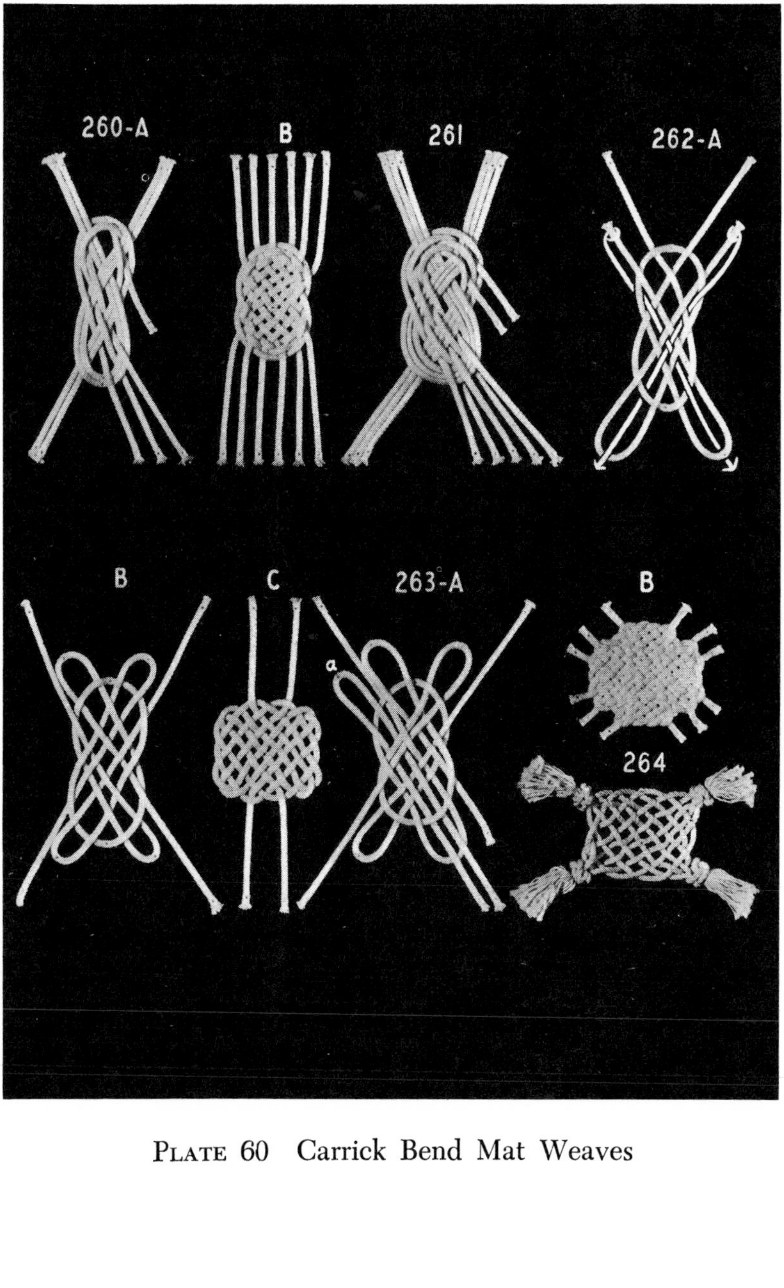

Plate 60 Carrick Bend Mat Weaves

drawn lines. It is best to employ a diagram with the use of pins to secure the cord at different intervals while working on a pattern of this type. It has 3 points at each end and 5 points on each side, with 4 bights crossing the weave from each end.

B: The finished mat, which can be doubled or tripled to fill the weave and add more body to the mat.

Fig. 222: Shows the same mat with the strands doubled and pulled up into a compact shapely design.

Fig. 223A: An almost Square Mat of 2 cross bights on each end may be worked by following the illustration.

B: Appearance of the same mat when the weave is finished.

Fig. 224: The almost Square Mat Doubled.

Fig. 225: The Single Oriental Weave may be converted into a mat by closing the ends as observed in the formation at the bottom part of the design. It has 4 diagonal crosses running each way.

Fig. 226: As the Oriental Mat Weave appears when worked taut with 2 passes. Both ends of the mat are closed and all four parts are employed in doubling this mat. After the job is finished the ends of the line are cut off and seized or sewn to the other parts.

Fig. 227A: The Sailor's True Lover Mat Weave is similar to the one shown in the *Encyclopedia of Knots and Fancy Rope Work.* It is started from a Carrick Bend in a loop, or what is more commonly known as a Sailor's Breastplate. (See Plate 45, Fig. 123.) The bights are then pulled out and crossed over in the manner shown with the drawn lines indicating how the weave is closed. The name *Prolong* or *Prolonged* was applied to this mat by several authors in the middle of the last century. They evidently called it by this name for the reason that it can be lengthened or prolonged; for similar reasons the same name might also apply to any number of other mats with the same characteristics. However, Sailor's True Lover Mat Weave seems to be the most popular name for it at the present time. Capt. William Alford tells us he has known it by this name since 1895.

B: The same mat finished.

Fig. 228: A Sailor's Breastplate or Single, Carrick Bend Design. It may be worked into a mat from this formation.

Fig. 229: The Sailor's Breastplate or Carrick Bend Design Doubled. By using 2 or 3 passes and pulling this pattern up snugly and compactly it may be employed as a serviceable table pad on which to set small hot dishes.

Plate 56—MATS

Fig. 230: The Diagonally Woven Mat on Expanded Metal is an example of mat weaving which is popular in the U. S. Navy. Mats such as this and the three following designs represent only a fraction of the many ideas that can be utilized in weaving rope and white line on diamond shape metal frames and on straight horizontal and vertical wire mesh. They are distinctive in appearance and make excellent deck mats for use at the bottom of ladders, doors, etc. 20 x 30 makes a convenient size for most mats of this type. The ends of the strands can be finished off by splicing or sewing them into the nearest part of the rope, or by seizing them to the rim of the frame.

Fig. 231: Represents a Vertically Woven Mat on Wire Mesh. Mats of this type, when made with care, have undoubted commercial value, as they are useful in the home as well as on shipboard. Wire mesh of about 1 inch square will serve most purposes. The size of the line that is used will of course be determined by the breadth of the wire mesh. In cases where a rope border is used the ends of the line forming the border are long-spliced together.

Fig. 232: The Oblique Woven Mat on Wire Mesh is made by using white line that is large enough to fill the squares. This line is wound around the metal squares in the manner shown, which produces a spiral effect.

Fig. 233: The Tuft Mat on Wire Mesh is another way of obtaining an unusual mat design. It is made by seizing a quantity of swab twine around the horizontal wires of each mesh and on the outer rim. When this mat is completely filled in, it presents a beautiful design that is fluffy and similar in characteristics to the puff-ball style of mat making. The tufts of swab twine or mop cord may be cut to any desired length that is suitable for the purpose involved.

Plate 57—MATS

Fig. 234A: The Single-Sided Angora Mat may be constructed by using a 20 x 30 piece of plywood or any other soft wood, with ¼ inch holes drilled in staggered lines from top to bottom until the board

265

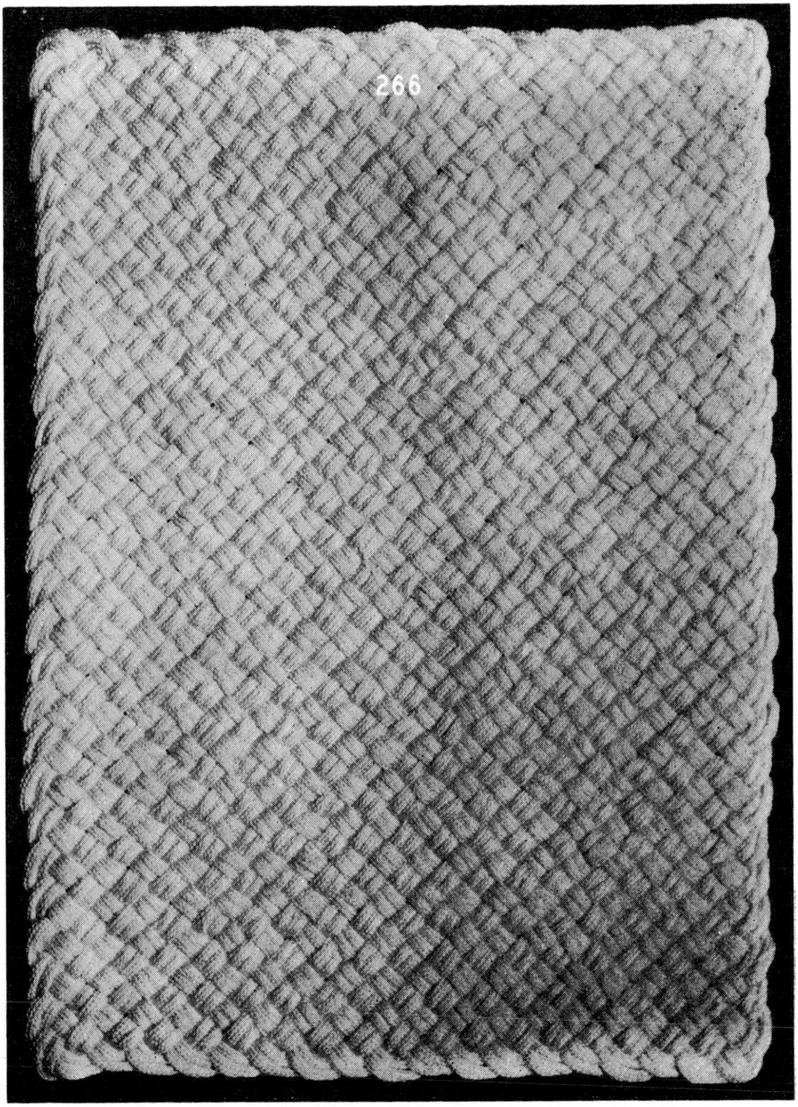

PLATE 62 Finished Rectangular Mat Design

is completely filled with holes, which should be about 1½ inches apart in vertical formation. Begin the mat by pulling a bight of swab twine or woolen yarn through each hole with the aid of an attached line. As the bights of twine are pulled through the holes, another larger line is used to run underneath the eye of each bight of twine. This will serve as a jackstay to which to anchor the tufts of twine, which are then pulled taut from the opposite side and cut to the desired length. The formation of the jackstay as it is run up and down each line of holes is shown in Fig. B, which gives a back view of the work. This makes a very soft mat that is useful in a bathroom, etc.

B: Back view of the Single Sided Angora Mat that was described in Fig. 234A.

Fig. 235: The Double-Sided Angora Mat. This mat is made in the same general way as the single one except that as each bight of material is pulled through each hole, it is cut. This produces the same effect on each side and eliminates the use of a jackstay. Otherwise, it is of the same nature as the former design.

Fig. 236A: A Puff-Ball Mat similar in technique to pillow-top making. (See Plate 32.) may be constructed along the same lines as the two previous methods. After the necessary holes have been drilled for each row, which in this case must match both vertically and horizontally, a long length of cylindrically shaped swab twine must be laid between each vertical row of holes, with the ends extending out far enough to form a fringe. The material is then seized to the board by using sail twine across the material in a horizontal manner and from one hole to another. The manner in which the sail twine is woven across the back in a continuous operation to connect all holes is shown in Fig. B. After this is completed the material is cut in the usual manner, which produces a puff-ball effect. The right side of the mat shows the material already cut, while on the left side it is still intact. This mat has a soft but firm surface and will last indefinitely.

B: Back view of the Puff-Ball Mat as explained in Fig. 236A.

Fig. 237: Door Mats such as this were frequently made by sailors of bygone years and, to a certain extent, are still made at the present time. The flakes can be made either round, square or elliptical with the heart completely filled in or left coiled as in this illustration. Unlaid strands of manila may be braided together with a three-strand Sennit to form the flakes. (See Plate 51, Fig. 164.) These braided lines are then coiled together in the form of flakes and sewn or spliced from one row to another to hold the mat together.

Fig. 238: A Wide Rectangular Mat of unique formation. This peculiar weave was accidentally discovered while attempting to develop a more symmetrical form of this type of pattern that would work out uniformly and with the ends meeting at the finish. This idea was later improved upon by Chief Boatswain's Mate R. J. Rouis, U. S. N., who perfected the design shown in Plate 55.

Fig. 239: The Prolong Mat Doubled. Otherwise, the same as Plate 58, Fig. 248.

Fig. 240A: A Single Sennit Mat such as this represents only one of a number of ways to convert Sennit braids into narrow mat weaves. It is practically the same as a Four-Strand Flat Sennit and can be followed without difficulty once the proper start has been made. See Plate 51 for Flat Sennit Braiding.

B: After the mat has been closed it will appear as shown here.

Fig. 241: An Extended Sennit Mat of the same order can be formed by pulling the bottom bight out and crossing it over again, then closing it in the usual manner. This procedure may be repeated as many times as desired to add additional length to the mat.

Plate 58—MATS

Fig. 242: A Mat with a Carrick Bend Heart Doubled; otherwise, the same weave as shown in Plate 59, Fig. 253.

Fig. 243: The Napoleon Bend Mat Weave Doubled with both ends closed is the same weave, otherwise, as shown in Plate 54, Fig. 216. In the eighteenth and nineteenth centuries this mat was commonly known as an Ocean Plat among seafaring men; however, the modern sailors of nowadays almost universally refer to it as a Napoleon Bend.

Fig. 244: The Extended Napoleon Bend Mat Weave Doubled embraces the same key as Plate 54, Fig. 217. This mat has 6 points on each side. It may be enlarged further without increasing the width by a repetition of the same key.

Fig. 245A: This Mat was developed by using a Napoleon Bend pattern with the style of weaving adapted to the Turkish Round Weave, which may be found in the *Encyclopedia of Knots and*

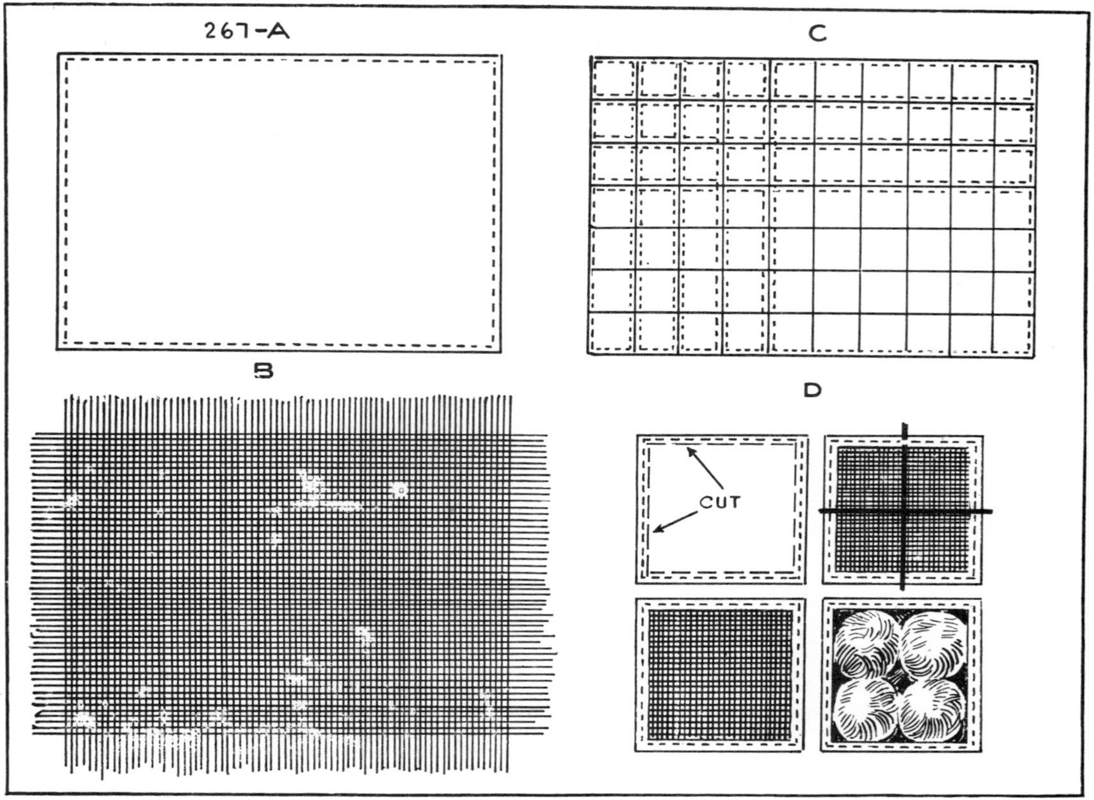
267-A
B
C
D
CUT

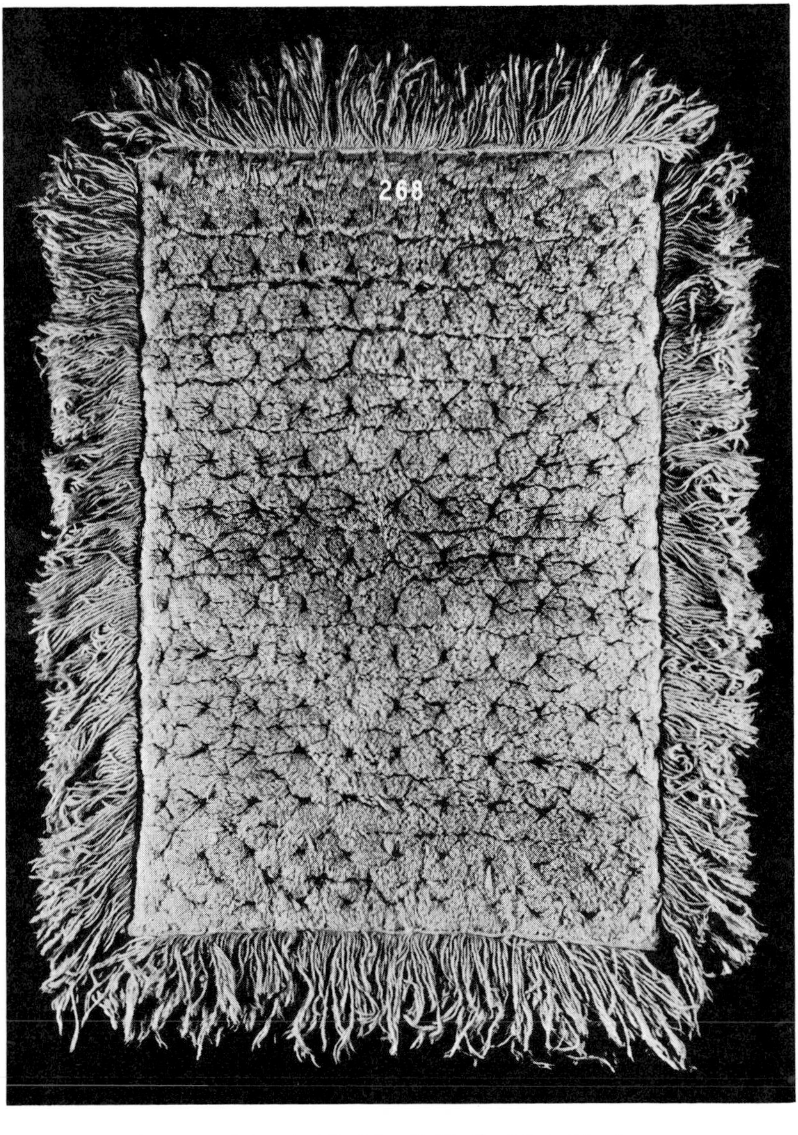

PLATE 64 A Finished Bath Mat Design

Fancy Rope Work. This gives it a broad body and an otherwise pleasing appearance. It has 6 diagonal crosses running each way.

B: As the same weave appears when finished.

Fig. 246: Represents the same mat as previously described after it has been doubled.

Fig. 247A: A Simple Mat Weave may be devised by closing the weave after the first step has been taken to form a Triangle Mat (Plate 54, Fig. 210).

B: This illustrates the same weave completed. It may be doubled or triple passed as in all other cases if desired.

Fig. 248A: The Single Prolong Mat was developed by Chief Boatswain's Mate Sam E. Franks, U.S.N. The Turkish Round Weave also serves as a base for this pattern, which is then prolonged in narrow rectangular form by using the same principles as for most other forms of mat weaving.

B: As the same design appears when finished.

Fig. 249A: A Single Mat of Four Hitches may be formed in the manner shown, with drawn lines indicating how the design is closed.

B: This shows the same mat after the ends of the line have locked the Hitches together.

Plate 59—MATS

Fig. 250: The Mat of Four Hitches Doubled. Otherwise, it is the same as the previous method shown in Plate 58, Fig. 249.

Fig. 251A: A Single Hitched Mat with a Carrick Bend Heart. This mat is formed by going a step further in the development of the last design. It is closed in the manner indicated.

B: As the same mat appears when finished.

Fig. 252: The Hitched Mat with a Carrick Bend Heart Doubled.

Fig. 253: Another Mat with a Carrick Bend Heart. This pattern is based on the layout for Plate 58, Fig. 249; with the same form of construction in the interior of the body as Fig. 251.

Fig. 254: An Extended Sennit Mat Doubled. Otherwise, it is the same as Plate 57, Fig. 241.

Fig. 255: The Extended Single Prolong Mat. It is extended by working the mat the same way as for Plate 58, Fig. 248.

Fig. 256: The Extended Prolong Mat Doubled.

Fig. 257: The Expanded Oriental Mat Weave Doubled represents a slight extension over the original pattern. It has 5 diagonal crosses running each way.

Fig. 258: A Braided Mat Weave in a loop with ornamental effect.

Fig. 259: Represents an expanded version of Plate 58, Fig. 245. This pattern has 10 diagonal crosses running each way.

Plate 60—CARRICK BEND MAT WEAVES

Fig. 260A: Shows a Double Carrick Bend Mat that may be expanded by following the key illustrated here. It is begun by tying a Carrick Bend with 2 pieces of doubled line. Another piece of line is then run between each pair of doubled lines as shown, with the end of the working part on the right side of the design, which is left incomplete in this picture. The working ends of the extra parts are followed through between each pair of doubled lines to complete the job. It will be necessary to pick up the extra parts of line by tucking under them at times with the working end of a line that is being passed from the opposite direction, in order to make the proper over and under tucks, which brings the passes out in their correct sequence to complete the pattern.

B: After each doubled part has been filled in as previously explained the mat will assume the shape portrayed here. Ends may be cut off when the slack has been drawn out of the finished mat work. Such designs as these are novelties which can be used for decorative purposes or for such things as hot-plate holders, etc.

Fig. 261: Shows a Triple Carrick Bend Mat which follows the same procedure as the double method, except that triple strands are used in this case. Only one part of the design has been filled in here.

Fig. 262A: An Enlarged Carrick Bend Mat may be constructed by using additional bights to expand the weave in the manner shown, after first forming a Carrick Bend with single lines to begin the operation. The key to the work is easily understood by following the drawn-in lines which divulge the proper way to proceed.

B: After additional bights have been laid through the top part of the design, similar to the previous passes on the bottom, the nature of the work will then assume the appearance shown at this stage.

C: The finished design is slightly oblong in shape, as can be observed from the accompanying illustration.

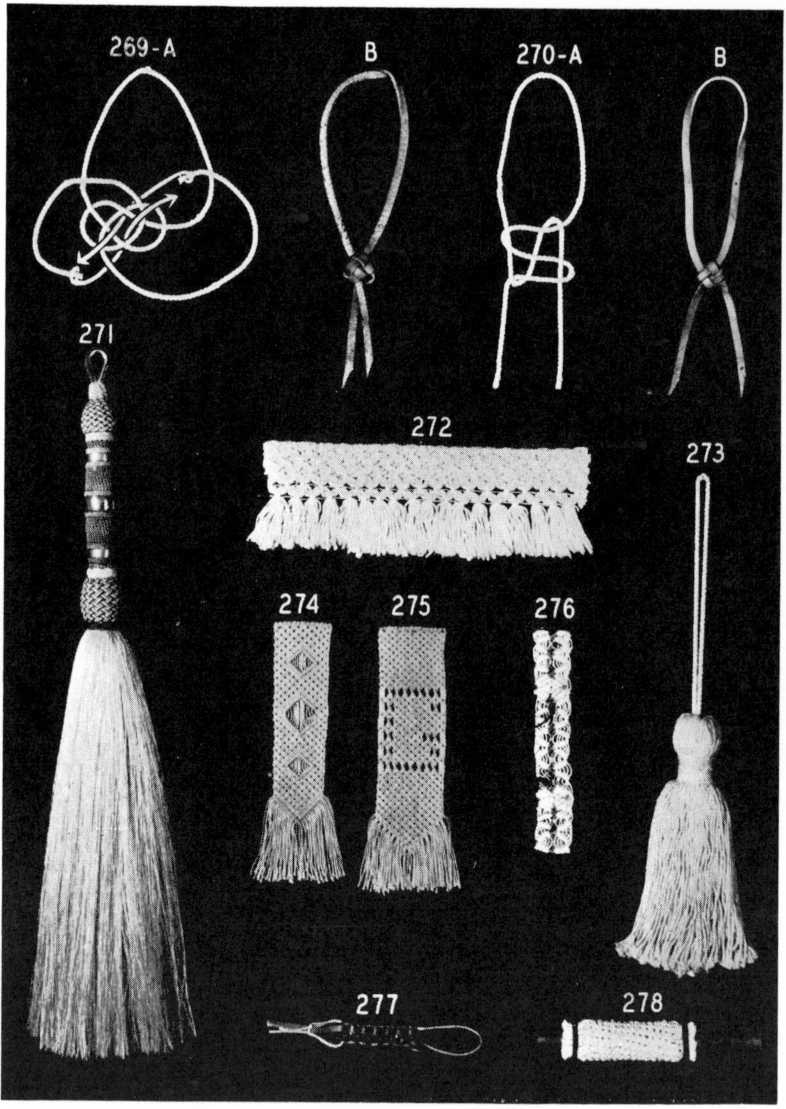

PLATE 65 Miscellaneous Designs

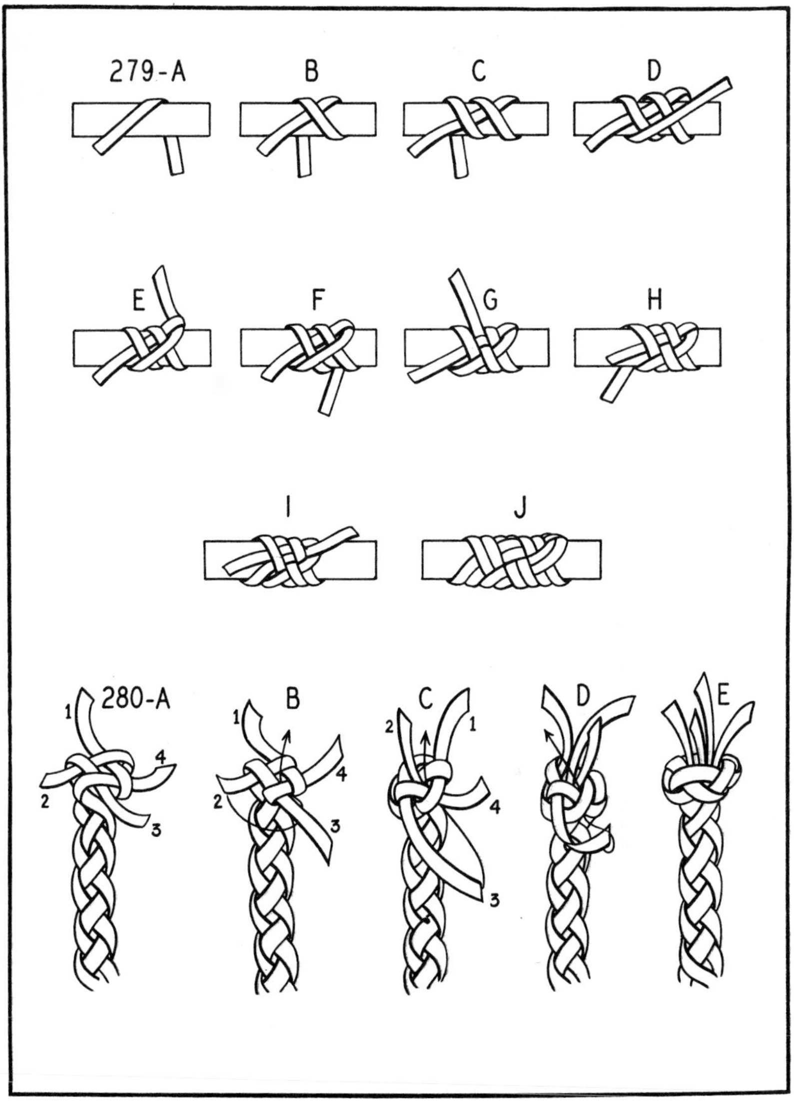

Plate 66 Sliding and Terminal Turk's Heads

Fig. 263A: An Extended Carrick Bend Mat such as this may be developed from the previous example by the use of additional bights to expand the work. The extra bights are worked into the pattern by employing the lines in the manner shown. Follow the drawn-in lines. They are used to help clarify the operation at this point. This type of mat may be enlarged to suit any requirements simply by following the same key when adding more working parts. See bight marked "a".

B: This shows the shape the mat will assume after being filled in and worked up snug with the ends cut short.

Fig. 264: Portrays a Carrick Bend Mat which is worked in similar fashion to the preceding designs. In this case it is developed into an oblong shape with the 4 ends on each corner formed into Diamond Knots with frayed-out tassels.

Plate 61—DRAWING OF RECTANGULAR MAT DESIGN

Fig. 265: The Rectangular Mat Design that is shown with an open illustration on this plate was submitted by Capt. G. T. Mundorff, Jr., U. S. N. It is one of the handsomest patterns for a mat design we have ever come in contact with, has an excellent lead, and can be worked into a uniform, symmetrical shape after careful deliberation in the formation of the key layout. The key to the system of construction lies in the "V" formation at each corner of the mat, as is clearly illustrated in the drawing. Depending upon the size and the proportion, 1, 2 or 3 separate pieces of line may be required, but the method of weaving and finishing this mat remains the same in all cases. There are very few methods in the weaving of mats by which the ends may be brought out together in such a manner that additional passes can be made, and that are, at the same time, susceptible of enlargement to any desired size, so long as the proportion is not 1 : 1. This mat design fulfills these conditions, meeting all requirements along this essential line, and should be thoroughly mastered by all diligent students of this artistic work. It will be noted there are 17 points on each end and 25 points on each side, not counting the "V" formations in each corner.

Plate 62—FINISHED RECTANGULAR MAT DESIGN

Fig. 266: This shows how the picturesque Mat previously explained appears after being worked up neatly into shape. An enlarged copy of the diagram will help considerably for working mats of this kind. As the weaving proceeds, the cord can be pinned at certain intervals to hold the pattern in place. Such mats are very decorative and can also be used as stair treads and as door mats.

Plate 63—INITIAL STEPS IN MAKING A BATH MAT

Fig. 267: This shows the first step in the preparation of a Canvas and Swab Twine Bath Mat. For a 23 x 33 inch mat, No. 4 or No. 6 canvas can be used, which is sewn down around the edge as shown in this illustration, to start the operation.

B: Using the contents of 2 deck swabs, lay half of the yarns lengthwise on the canvas, and the other half crosswise. Now lay a second piece of canvas over these yarns in the form of a sandwich, and sew the whole thing together in 2 inch squares, using a heavy duty canvas sewing machine, although it can be sewn by hand if no machine is available.

C: This illustrates the proper way to sew the squares described in the last paragraph.

D: The canvas is now cut with a sharp knife about 3/16 inch on the inside of the sewing as indicated in the top panel on the left. After this has been completed the yarns are exposed as shown in the bottom panel on the left. Using a flat pointed wooden stick, under-run the lengthwise section of strands and cut them crosswise at each intersection. Now under-run the crosswise section of strands and cut them lengthwise at each intersection. This operation is illustrated with the use of a heavy line, both lengthwise and crosswise, in the top panel on the right. After the swab twine is cut, a ball will form at each corner of a 2 inch square, as shown in the bottom panel on the right. The mat is now completed. To prevent the yarns from pulling out, soak the mat in very hot water for about two hours.

PLATE 67 Coxcombing

PLATE 68 Comb Hanger Designs

PLATE 64—A FINISHED BATH MAT DESIGN

Fig. 268: The Bath Mat previously described will appear as it is pictured here, after being completed. A mat of this kind will last indefinitely.

PLATE 65—MISCELLANEOUS DESIGNS

Fig. 269A: The Carrick Diamond Neckerchief Design shows how the line is laid out and joined with a Carrick Bend. The ends are then pulled through the middle of the knot in the manner indicated.

B: This illustrates the same design in leather after being worked up snug.

Fig. 270A: The Japanese Crown Neckerchief Design is begun by laying the line out and lacing each part around and through the other part as pictured here.

B: This shows the completed design in leather after being worked up snug.

Fig. 271: A Comb Hanger Design that is modeled in the most attractive style and represents a beautiful work of art in this type of pattern. The core is formed with a rubber heart. A sufficient amount of rope yarn is laid around the heart to make a complete cover. Cork foundations are used for the 2 large Turk's Head designs which have 2 passes and consist of 13 and 15 strands respectively. A Running Sennit was used on the thimble which forms the eye. The number of strands used will depend upon the size of the seizing around the base. The work is continued with Spiral Hitching and Turk's Head seizings, which are followed at different intervals with brass bands. The work is finished off by seizing the yarns around the core before the last series of Turk's Heads are formed at the lower end as illustrated.

Fig. 272: McNamara Lace, such as this, represents the usual way of forming designs in stripped canvas. After the horizontal threads have been withdrawn from the canvas for the proper distance, the remaining vertical threads are joined together with Clove Hitches to form diamond shaped designs as shown. The work is finished off with tassels that are formed by taking half of each set of previous threads and joining them together with Clove Hitches in the usual manner. In bygone years sailors used this type of work in the construction of wall bags, etc., for decorative effect.

Fig. 273: The Hand Swab is made by first tying a Figure-of-Eight Knot in both ends of a short piece of line. A quantity of swab twine is middled and then laid around the line after it is doubled. A seizing is next applied near the middle of the body of the swab twine and about 3 inches from the Figure-of-Eight Knots on each end of the line which have previously been brought together. The swab twine is now folded back over the seizing and another seizing is applied above the Figure-of-Eight Knots. This last seizing will be very hard and rigid if the seizing twine is tied to something a distance of 6 or 8 feet away. The opposite end is then wound around the Hand Swab by means of turning it in the hands while applying leverage with the arms and body. It is used for washing paint work on naval and merchant vessels.

Fig. 274: A Book Mark can be square-knotted by using cord of any color. Cut an even number of strands seven times the desired length of the book mark. Hammer two headless nails three or four inches apart into a piece of wood. Double one strand over these nails and fasten it to each nail by means of a Clove Hitch. This strand will later become the 2 outside strands of the book mark. To this strand, between the nails, loop each of the other strands by means of a Lark's Head knot. Omitting the first 3 and the last 3 of the new strands just looped over, divide the rest of the strands into groups of 4 and make a row of Square Knots in the usual way. Below this row, continue making Square Knots, bringing the work down to a point.

Now untie the strands on the nails and fasten the work to a piece of wood by means of a couple of nails or upholsterer's tacks. There should be 4 unused strands at each side. Using the 4 strands on the left, tie 1 Square Knot; using the 4 strands on the right, tie another Square Knot. The outside strands run through the Lark's Heads, and this gives the book mark a neat and firm edge at the top.

From this point the work continues in the same manner as with a belt, and any designs may be used in the making. Initials can be

PLATE 69 Comb Hanger Designs

PLATE 70 Comb Hanger Designs

worked in by means of Spirals or Half Hitching, as shown in the illustration. When the desired length of 6 or 7 inches is reached, the work may be finished off in the same way as a belt, or the ends may be cut off even and left as a fringe. The fringe is improved by unlaying the strands and dipping them into water to straighten them out.

Fig. 275: A Book Mark is shown here with the initial "G" worked in the pattern to illustrate the previous explanation.

Fig. 276: A Woman's Head Band for keeping the hair in place is shown in this illustration. 12 cords are used in its construction, with an elastic attachment included. It is of simple construction and can be duplicated easily.

Fig. 277: Square Crowning in Leather is begun by first splitting the leather up a distance from both ends. The work is then started by crowning the four strands alternately, or first one way and then the opposite way, until the work is as long as desired.

Fig. 278: Square Knot Pointing represents a way of covering a cylindrical object with this type of work, which is nothing more than a series of Square Knots joined together.

Plate 66—SLIDING AND TERMINAL TURK'S HEADS

Fig. 279A: The Sliding Turk's Head is begun by passing a line around the object to which it is to be attached, in the manner shown.

B: After a complete turn is taken, the work will correspond with the diagram.

C: The line is then passed around the object for the second time over the standing part of the line, as illustrated here.

D: Now continue by bringing the working end over the round turns in the manner shown.

E: At this stage of the operation pass the working end under the standing part as indicated.

F: Next, bring the working end up between the 2 round turns that were previously made, in order to cross over and then under the two diagonal parts.

G: After the 2 previous tucks have been made, the work will appear as shown here, with the working end passed over the first part then under the next part.

H: Now lead the working end of the strand around and up under the same turn that covers the standing part. Then parallel the standing part by passing the working end of the line through the knot alongside of it, making the necessary over and under passes to reach the opposite side.

I: This picture of the knot shows the example after it has been completed.

J: Continue by following the standing end around with the working end until each part of the knot has been doubled. Then crop the ends off short after all slack has been taken out of the work. This design may be used as a sliding attachment for such things as whistle lanyards, watch fobs, hat bands, etc.

Fig. 280A: A Terminal Turk's Head may be formed on the end of a braided thong of four parts of leather or on any other type of line in the following manner: After the braid has been worked to the required length, a crown may be tied by overlapping the strands in the manner shown, with strand 1 going over strand 4 and under strand 2. Strand 2 is likewise carried over strand 1 and under strand 3. Strand 3 goes over strand 2 and under strand 4. Then strand 4 goes over strand 3 and under strand 1 to complete the operation of forming the crown.

B: After the previously explained steps have been taken, the next stage of the operation is shown by the drawn-in line which illustrates how strand 2 is taken around and over strand 4 on the lower part of the crown, then tucked up through the middle of the work by going under the same strand, as indicated.

C: After this stage of the operation has been completed, strand 3 is next passed around and over strand 1, then through the middle of the knot which brings it out under the same strand in a similar manner to the previous tuck.

D: With strands 2, 3 and 4 already tucked up through the middle of the knot as previously explained, strand 1 is now ready to be tucked in similar fashion, as indicated by the drawn-in line.

E: The Terminal Turk's Head in its final form is shown here after all the strands have been tucked in their proper places and pulled taut. Any number of strands may be tied in this manner with a repetition of the same key. This knot serves a variety of purposes. It may be used to finish off the ends of Sennit Braids or as a stopper when change to another key of braiding is desired while making dog leashes, whistle lanyards, etc.

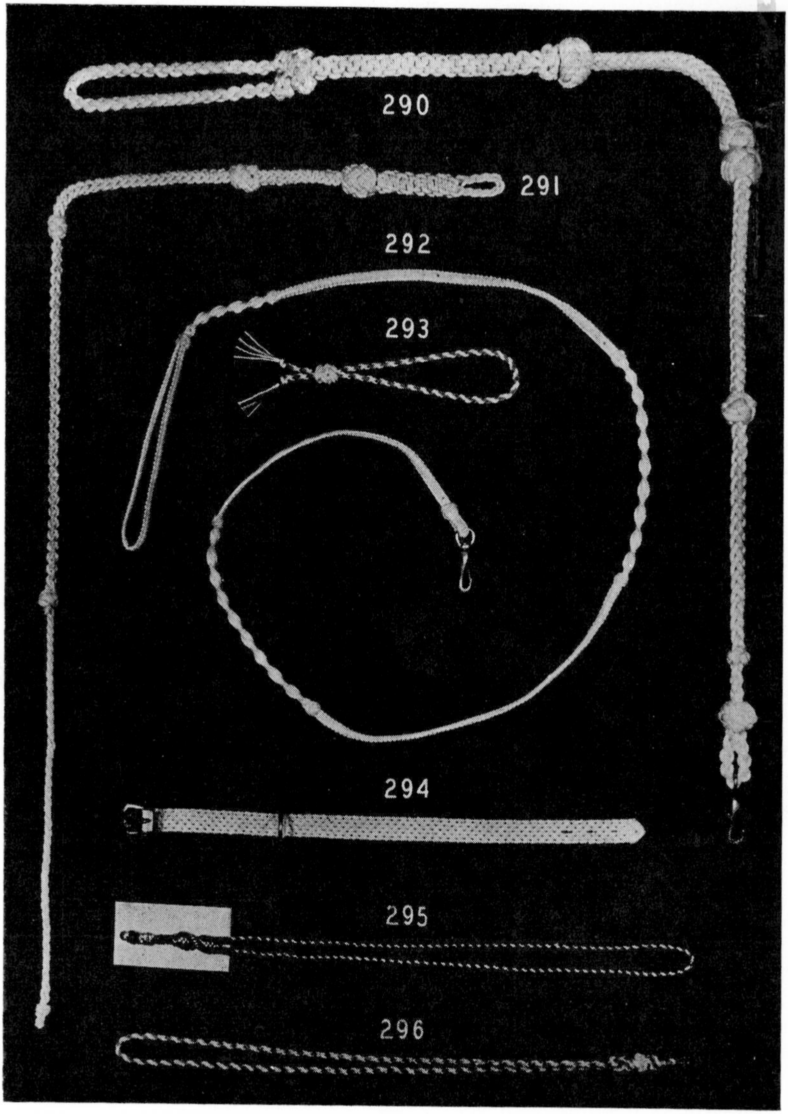

PLATE 71 Dog Leashes, Collar and Whistle Lanyards

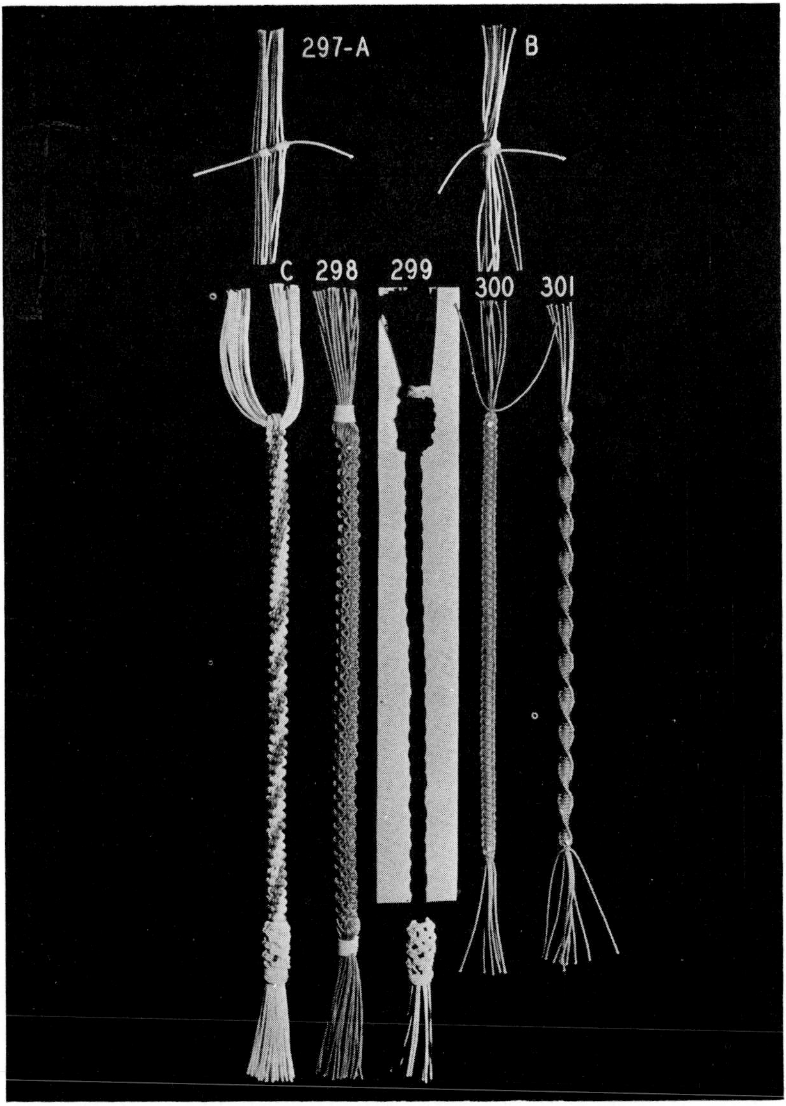

PLATE 72 Bath Robe Cords

PLATE 67—COXCOMBING

Fig. 281: A Three-Strand Coxcomb such as that shown here may be formed as follows: Three strands are seized on top of the object the Coxcomb is to be attached to. Now proceed by tying a left-hand Half Hitch with one strand and a right-hand Half Hitch with another strand, then a left-hand Half Hitch with the third strand. Continue alternating the strands in this manner by always using the last strand for each succeeding Half Hitch. In this case strand 1 has been half hitched to the left, and strand 2 to the right, while strand 3 is likewise half hitched to the left. This procedure is repeated until the desired length of Coxcomb is completed. Coxcombing, which in reality is nothing but another name for Half Hitches, when applied around any kind of object, has many different uses, and is effective as a decorative type of work for handbag handles and ornamental covering on handrails, bucket handles, rings, etc. When using Coxcombing for any type of Square Knot work, such as handbags, etc., a filler is required. It can also be used on shade pull rings and belt buckles. Any reasonable number of strands may be used for this kind of work, but it is seldom practical to go beyond six. In each case the type of Coxcomb will vary, depending upon the number of strands used and the way the hitches are applied.

PLATE 68—COMB HANGER DESIGNS

Fig. 282: The Hackamore Comb Hanger Design has a Hackamore Knot formed in the bight of a rope. Continue by unlaying the strands of the rope, which are then formed into a Six-Strand Diamond Knot. After this knot is worked up and pulled taut, the yarns are then unlaid and frayed out with a comb in order to produce the same effect as that shown in the photograph. Comb hangers such as this and the following designs provide a novel and useful place to keep a comb.

Fig. 283: The Combination Comb Hanger Design is formed in the following manner: First unlay the rope for the required distance and then seize the parts together with a temporary whipping. This will hold the strands in place while the job is being completed. Then tie a Lanyard Knot which is followed by a Double Lanyard and Star Knot respectively. After the Star Knot has been pulled up in a snug, uniform manner, the ends are then formed into a Turk's Head Weave. A Five-Strand Turk's Head with 5 passes is next tied below the Turk's Head weave in the manner shown. This operation can best be performed with the use of a sail needle and small white line. Finish off by fraying out the yarns, the same as for the previous example.

Plate 69—COMB HANGER DESIGNS

Fig. 284: The Double Lanyard Knot Comb Hanger Design is tied as follows: First seize an eye in the rope, then unlay the strands down to the seizing. A Lanyard Knot is then formed, which is followed by a Double Lanyard Knot, with a Walled Crown and another Lanyard Knot following in that order. This completes the design. The strands are then frayed out and trimmed to any suitable length.

Fig. 285: The Star Knot Comb Hanger Design has a Three-Strand Coxcomb formed with small white line around the loop above the Star Knot. Next, bend the two parts together to form the eye, which is then seized. Then form a Lanyard Knot for a base, followed by a Star Knot and a Matthew Walker Knot respectively. To finish the design, a Five-Strand Turk's Head with 2 passes may be placed around the base of the eye in the manner shown.

Fig. 286: The Single Diamond Knot Comb Hanger Design is tied as follows: Bring the two parts of rope together and tie a Two-Strand Diamond Knot to form the eye. Follow this operation with a Lanyard Knot and Walled Crown to complete the design.

Plate 70—COMB HANGER DESIGNS

Fig. 287: The Double Diamond Knot Comb Hanger Design has the eye formed and Coxcombed in the same way as for Plate 69, Fig. 285. The strands are then unlaid and a Double Diamond Knot

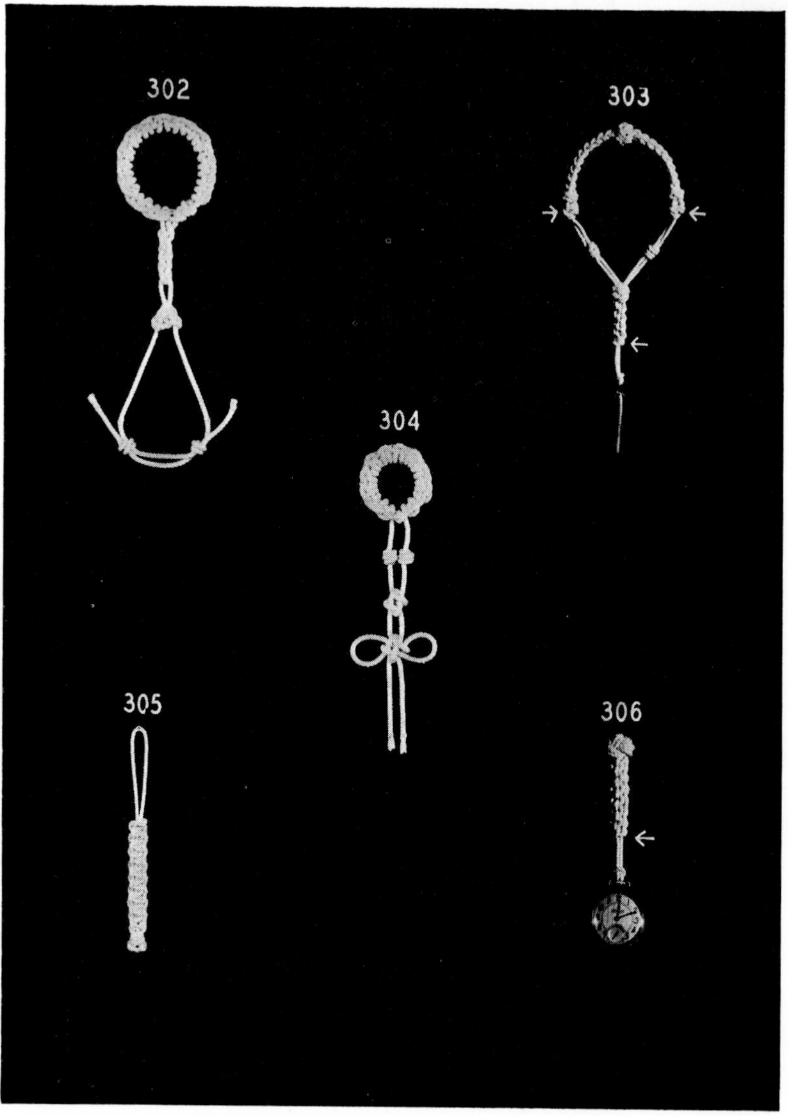

PLATE 73 Tatting, Knife Lanyard and Watch Fobs

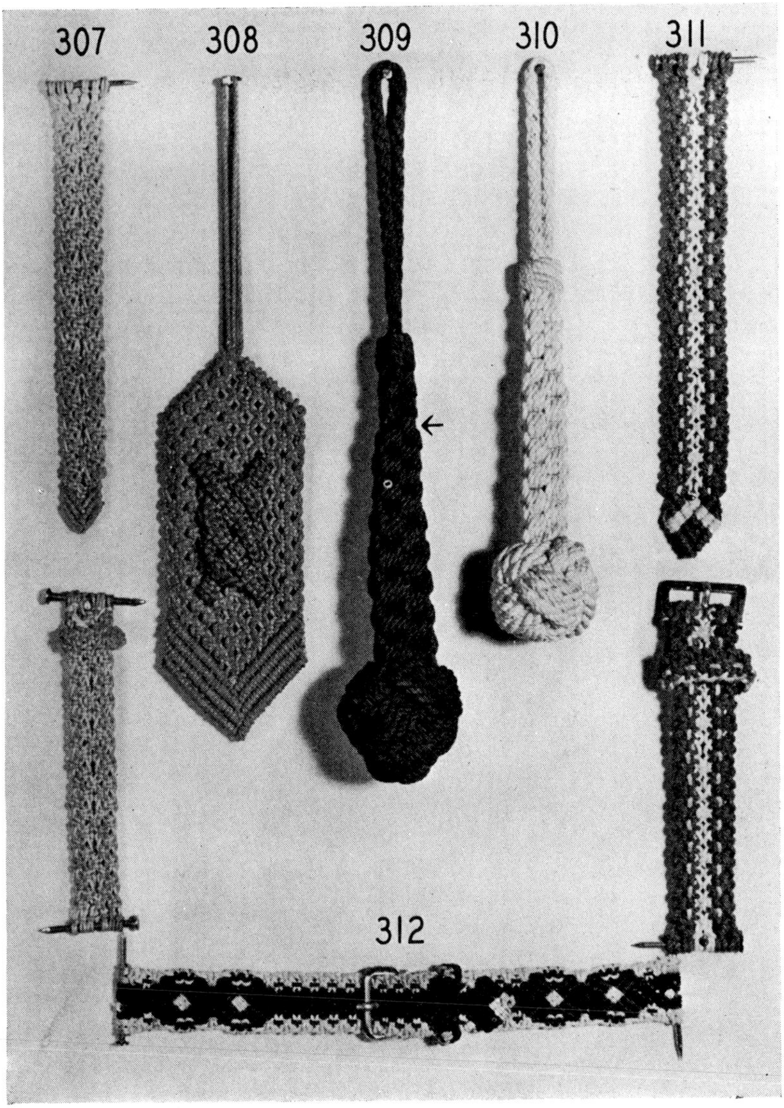

PLATE 74 Watch Fobs and Wrist Watch Straps

is tied and pulled up snug. This operation is followed by a Single Diamond Knot to complete the design. To finish off, place a Five-Strand Turk's Head with 2 passes around the base of the eye in the manner illustrated.

Fig. 288: The Sailor's Breastplate Comb Hanger Design has a Carrick Bend formed in the eye of a line as illustrated. Next, bring the 2 parts of rope together and apply a seizing, then proceed with a Lanyard Knot which is followed with a Turk's Head weave. The yarns are then frayed out in the usual manner. Any combination of knots to suit individual taste may be used in the construction of these designs.

Fig. 289: The Sennit Knot Comb Hanger Design includes a Sennit Knot, followed by a Matthew Walker Knot, which are formed in their respective sequence, after the eye has Coxcombing applied the same as for Fig. 287. A Five-Strand Turk's Head with 2 passes is likewise employed at the base of the eye in this case, the same as for the previously mentioned example.

Plate 71—DOG LEASHES, COLLARS AND WHISTLE LANYARDS

Fig. 290: Represents an Ornamental Dog Leash. Many original ideas may be used in the formation of fancy dog leashes of this type. The one shown here is begun with a Four-Strand Round Sennit that is used to form the hand loop in the end. This braid is stopped off on each part with Terminal Turk's Heads, after the required amount of loop has been formed. The ends are next brought together and seized by an Extended Terminal Turk's Head with top and bottom parts doubled. From this point the work is transformed into an Eight-Strand Crown Sennit which is carried down for a short distance and then seized or stopped off with an ordinary Terminal Turk's Head. The strands are next led out and formed into an Eight-Strand Square Sennit. A triple passed Three-Strand Turk's Head is applied at the base as illustrated. Another Three-Strand Turk's Head is seized on the opposite end of this braid with 3 passes, which is followed by another Three-Strand Turk's Head that is triple passed around a built-up mousing. Two strands are now dropped and the work is continued with a Six-Strand Half Round Sennit which is carried down to the point where the next Extended Terminal Turk's Head with double passes at top and bottom is applied. Another strand is dropped at this stage and a Five-Strand Crabber's Eye Sennit follows. It is stopped off with a small Three-Strand Turk's Head with a single pass. The work is again tapered down at this point by dropping another strand and the braid is changed into a Four-Strand Round Sennit, which is seized off, after being doubled back to form an eye for the snap, with an Extended Terminal Turk's Head triple passed on top and bottom to finish the design. (See Plates 51 to 53 for the different Sennit keys.)

Fig. 291: A Dog Leash Design of a simple pattern which differs somewhat from the preceding example. It is begun with a Cable Laid Three-Strand Sennit, then brought together in the form of an eye, and continued with the formation of a Spiral Sennit. 2 additional strands are now added. These strands represent both the standing and working end of the double passed Six-Strand Turk's Head. Work is continued with an Eight-Strand Square Sennit which is then tapered down into a Six-Strand Half Round, Four-Strand Round and finally a Three-Strand Cable Laid Sennit with Turk's Heads at proper intervals as illustrated. The example is finished off with a Matthew Walker Knot. These two ideas were submitted by Capt. Wm. Alford.

Fig. 292: This Dog Leash consists of Flats and Spirals. Cut 12 strands 6 feet long for the filler. Cut another strand 60 feet long and double it about 6 inches down over the filler strands. Then tie a Flat 12 inches long with this doubled strand. Now form the handle by tying the Flat together. Continue tying Flats and Spirals until the required length is reached. Add the dog leash snap and tie the Flat together. To complete the design, a Turk's Head is added where the handle loop and the snap are joined.

Fig. 293: A Hat Band is started about 6 inches from the end of 8 strands where a Four-Strand Double Crown is formed. Then form a Four-Strand Double Terminal Turk's Head. Continue by tying a Four-Strand Double Round Braid, and add a Four-Strand Double Crown and Terminal Turk's Head. (See Plate 66, Fig. 280.) Next add a Sliding Turk's Head around the 2 parts in the manner shown. (See Plate 66, Fig. 279.)

Fig. 294: This Dog Collar is started from the buckle. First, Square Knots are tied for a length of about 5 inches. At this point a nickel

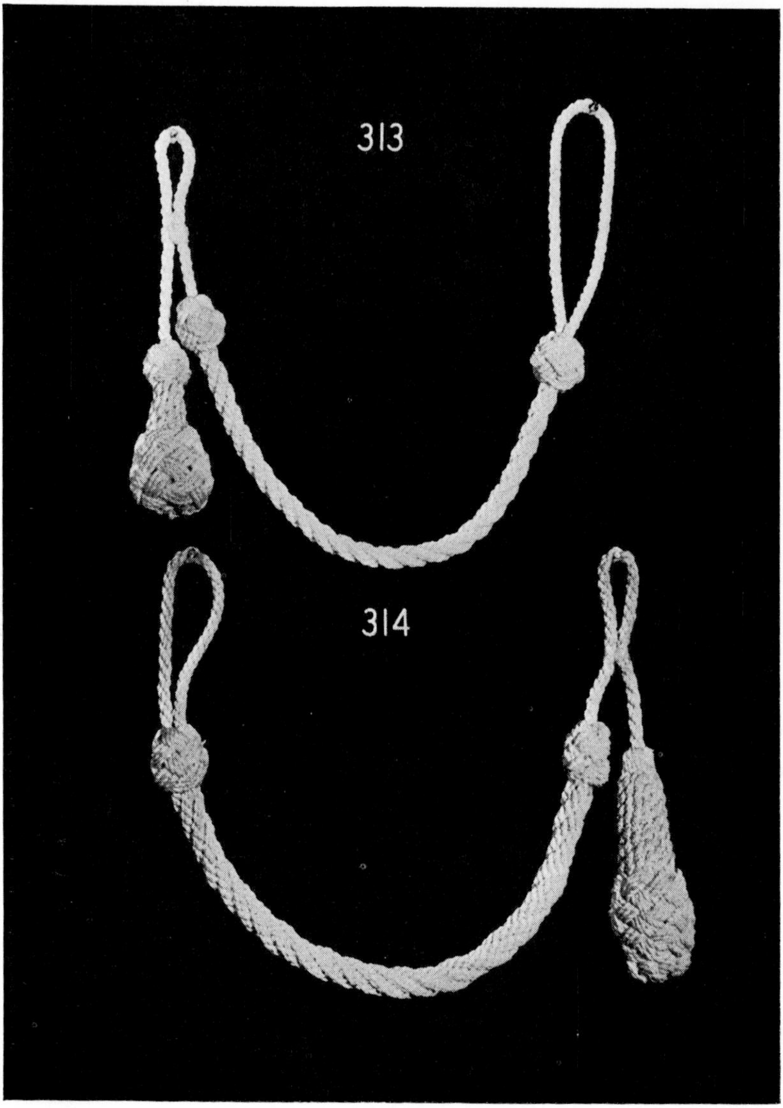

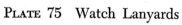

Plate 75 Watch Lanyards

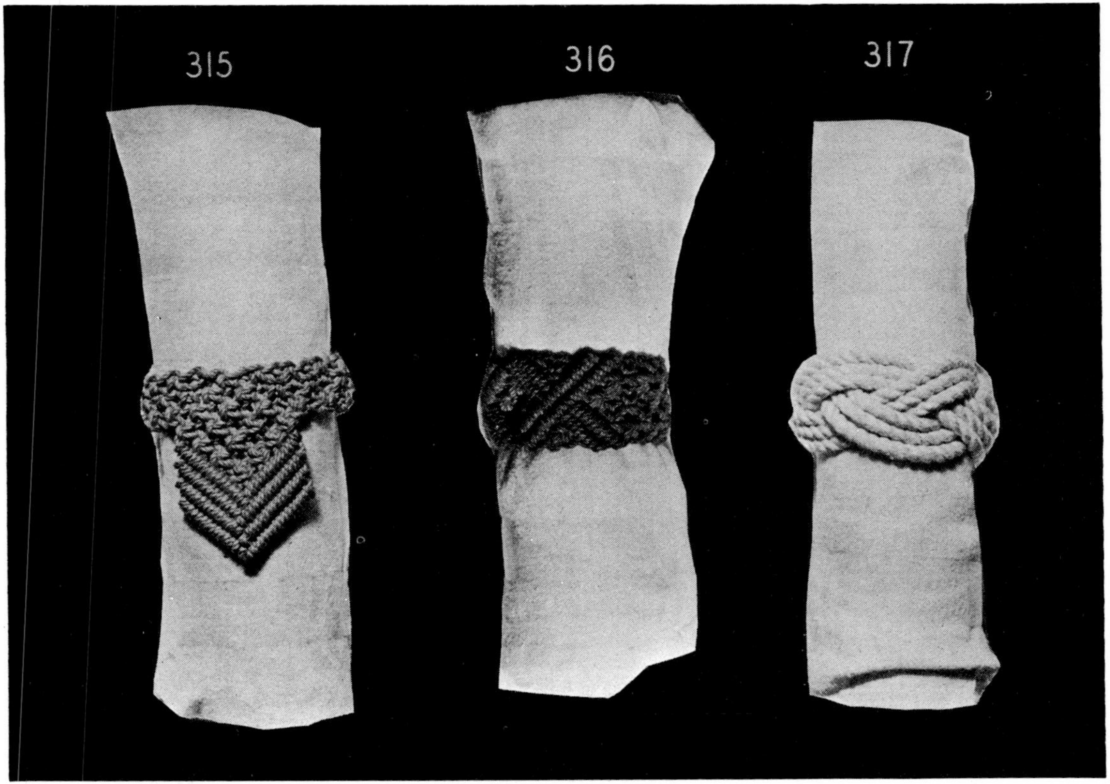

Plate 76 Napkin Rings

plated Dee is added by tying one Half Hitch on it with each of the 12 strands. Continue to the required length and finish off with 2 rows of Half Hitches.

Fig. 295: This Whistle Lanyard was made with material known as Gimp, and it consists of a Four-Strand Round Braid finished off with a Square and Spiral Crown Braid.

Fig. 296: The Whistle Lanyard shown here is begun by doubling 2 strands over a nail, or they may be passed through a whistle ring. Next, tie a Four-Strand Round Braid and work it down to the required length. Continue by tying a Crown on the braid. This will form a Sliding Crown Braid. Then bury the ends in the Crown and cover them with a Turk's Head as illustrated.

Plate 72—BATHROBE CORDS

Fig. 297A: This Two-Tone Bathrobe Cord Design is formed as follows: Cut 4 white and 4 colored strands 35 feet long. Cut another strand 40 feet to be used as a Filler. See Plate 17 for instructions as to the proper method of shortening strands when they are too long to handle. Middle the 8 strands and tie 2 Half Hitches in the middle of the Filler strand with each strand.

B: Illustrates the work after 2 rings of Half Hitches have been tied.

C: The same Bathrobe Cord shows how 16 strands 8 inches long have been middled and a Square Knot tied with the working strands to form the tassel on the right side. The other end shows how a Square Knot Crown and Turk's Head has been added. (See Plate 3.) The Spiral Half Hitches are worked to a length of 24 inches and the same distance is worked on the opposite side. This will make a cord about 60 inches long.

Fig. 298: Shows a Sixteen-Strand Round Square Knot Bathrobe Cord. Middle the strands; first tie one half, and then the other. The tassel and crown are added in the manner previously explained.

Fig. 299: Illustrates a Cable Laid Bathrobe Cord with a tassel added at each end. Cut 5 strands 36 feet long, seize and fasten one end over a hook and hold taut at the other end. Then twist the 5 strands to the right almost to the point of kinking. At this stage of the operation, have someone grasp the line in the middle, thus forming a bight, while at the same time placing a hand on the forward part of the line near the hook in order to bend the end of the bight back over the hook. There are now 3 lengths, consisting of 15 strands, which are held taut while being uniformly adjusted to proper length. Now twist to the left almost to the point of kinking and then seize both ends. Add the tassel and crown in the manner previously explained.

Fig. 300: Illustrates a Square Knot Flat Bathrobe Cord.

Fig. 301: Illustrates a Spiral Bathrobe Cord. The Cords illustrated in this plate can be used in the making of whistle lanyards, dog leashes, and pocketbook handles.

Plate 73—TATTING, KNIFE LANYARDS AND WATCH FOBS

Fig. 302: A Tatting Design of unusual distinction is shown in the accompanying illustration. It includes a ring of Tatting which is formed by tying Lark's Heads with the working end of the line around the standing part, after the ring has been adjusted to the required size. A Four-Strand Round Braid is next formed with the 2 strands by dropping the bight of one strand down in a crossed over position, then crisscrossing the braid back and forth with the other strand to achieve the effect illustrated. A Two-Strand Diamond Knot is then added and the design is finished off with Sliding Blood Knots.

Fig. 303: A Knife Lanyard such as the one shown here may be formed as follows: Using a Lark's Head, attach the middle of a suitable line to the ring in the end of a knife. Lead the 2 strands down a short distance, then add 2 more strands, as indicated by the arrow. Next, form a series of Four-Strand Crowns, reversing them each time, to any suitable length. After this operation is completed, add a Four-Strand Double Diamond Knot on top of the Crown Braid. At this junction split the strands into two separate pairs, lead them down a short way and form Blood Knots with 4 passes as illustrated. Spread the strands apart in the shape of a fork in order to judge the proper distance required so that each set of designs will be spaced evenly. At the arrows, 2 additional strands are added on each side, and the work is continued with Double Stopper Knots tied with each set of 4 strands. Now form Turk's Heads weaves

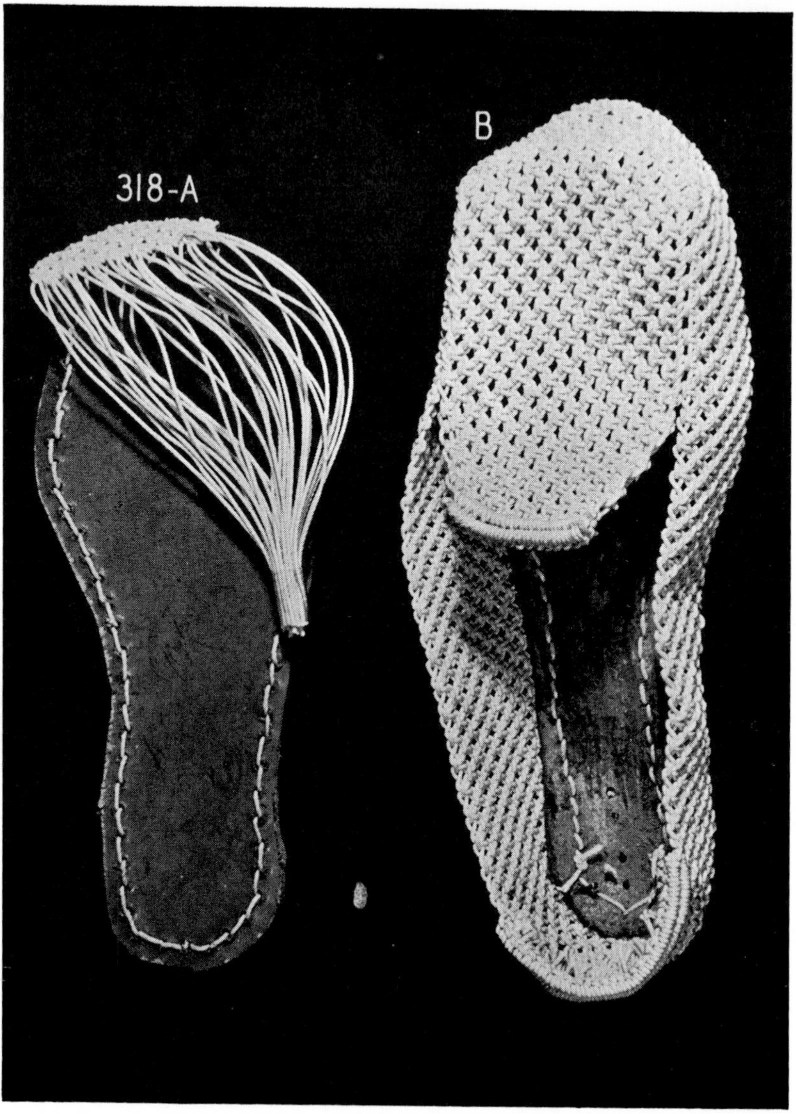

PLATE 77 Moccasin Sandal

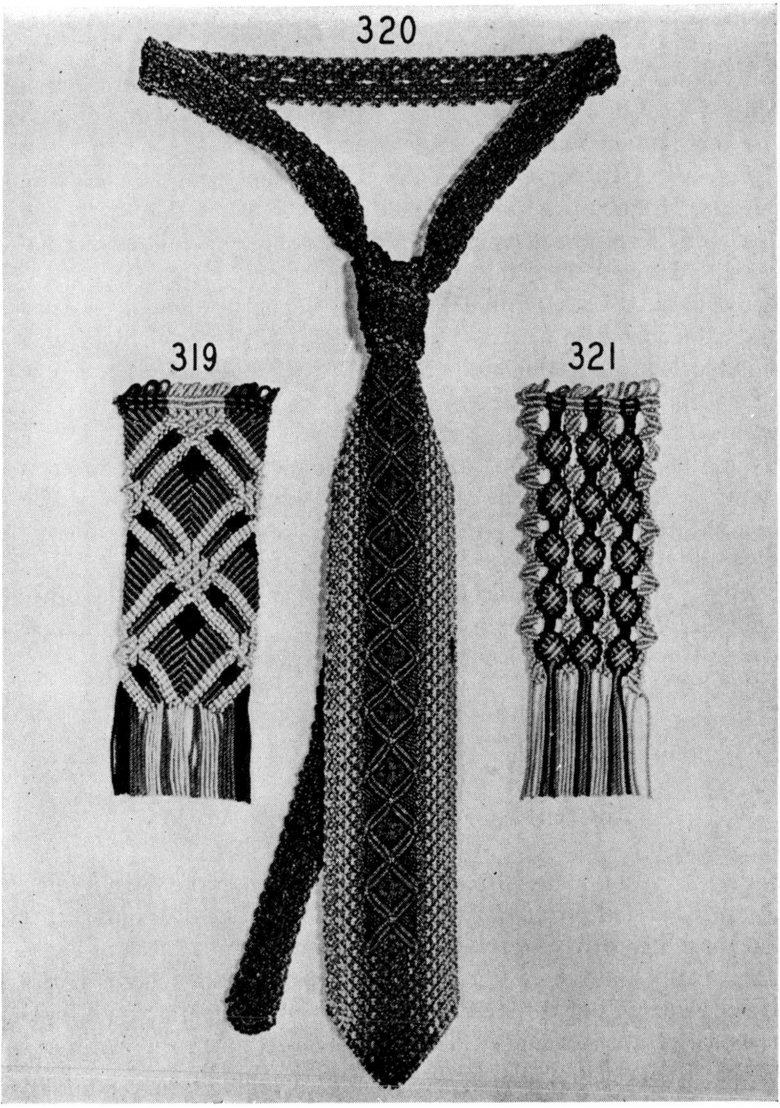

PLATE 78 Cravat and Book Marks

behind the Stopper Knots, then proceed with a Four-Strand Round Braid with each set until the necessary length is reached to bring the end of each braid together in the middle of the design. Now whip and marry the strands the same as for a splice, then apply a Shroud Knot or any other suitable knot to bring them together. Pull the knot up taut and cut the ends off.

Fig. 304: A Tatting Design somewhat different from the preceding pattern. It embraces Blood Knots, then a Japanese Crown and a Dragonfly Knot as illustrated. There are many possibilities of combining various designs along this line.

Fig. 305: A Watch Fob Design. It is begun by doubling a cord and attaching it to a nail or hook. Then allow enough line for a suitable loop and add another cord. These four strands are now formed into a series of several Square Knots which are finished off with a Double Diamond Knot with the ends cut short.

Fig. 306: A Watch Fob Design of a somewhat different pattern is shown here. It is begun by attaching a doubled strand to the handle of a watch, with a Lark's Head Knot. Lead them down a short way, then add 2 more strands at the point indicated by the arrow. Now continue by alternately Crowning first one way and then the other until the braid is the proper length for the fob. It is then finished off with a Double Stopper Knot and the ends are cut short.

Plate 74—WATCH FOBS AND WRIST WATCH STRAPS

Fig. 307: The material most suitable for making a Wrist Watch Strap is braided Nylon #24 strength fishline. Cut 8 strands 3 feet long and then drive a six-penny nail part way into a piece of wood horizontally and double the 8 strands over the nail, tying 8 Lark's Head Knots. Using 16 strands, tie 18 rows of Square Knots for a distance of about 2 inches. Then continue to tie 18 more rows of Square Knots, skipping a Square Knot in the middle after completing each row for a distance of about 2 inches more, and finish off with three rows of Half Hitches. Cut 8 more strands 3 feet long and place horizontally on a six-penny nail inserted part way into a piece of wood and double the 8 strands over the nail, then tie 8 Lark's Head Knots. Using 16 strands, tie Square Knots for a distance

ho
d 9°

$1\frac{5}{8}$"

Strands need to be 9x and ...
(they are doubled over ∴ only $4\frac{1}{2}$x, really)

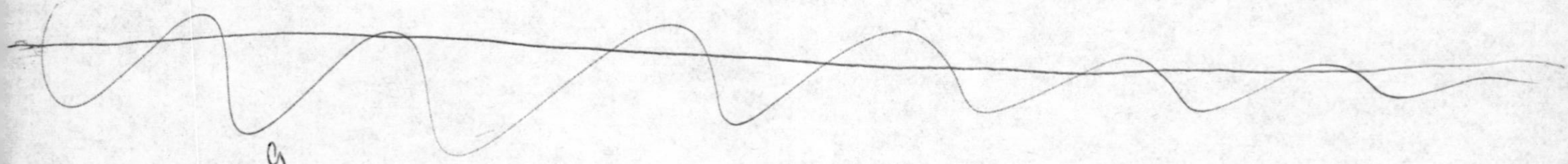

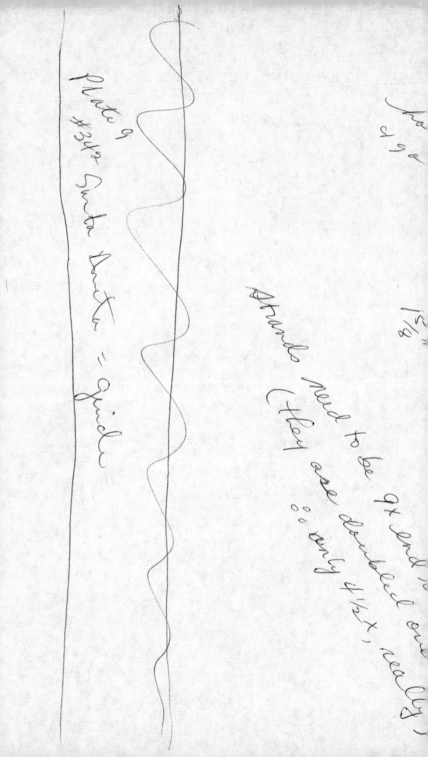

Plate 9
#342 Santa Donita = Guide

8"

9"

measure Doug's belt to see how wide 12 strands will be

there

2" strap & btm/sides

th

of about 3 inches. Then form the belt loop in the manner mentioned in Plate 5.

Remove the pins from the wrist watch, and then remove the nails from the straps, and insert pins in the same openings where the nails were. Replace the pins in the watch and the work is complete.

Fig. 308: This Twenty-Four Strand Watch Fob is begun by first doubling 2 strands over a nail. Then, about 2 inches down, with a doubled strand, tie a Square Knot. The strands on the left and right sides are used as a filler. Then add the necessary amount of strands on the right and left sides and fill in with Square Knots. Finish off with 4 rows of Half Hitches.

The Carrick Bend Design is formed from two Flats 3½″ long. To start this Bend, loop 2 doubled strands down and up through the Square Knot work, and then about 2 inches apart do the same thing. (See Plate 79, Fig. 322.)

Fig. 309: The Watch Fob Lanyard shown here is started with a Cable Laid Sennit of 3 strands which are joined together and seized after the eye is formed. At this point another double strand is added by separating the 6 strands from the Sennit, then tying an Overhand Knot with an extra piece of line around the seizing between the separated strands. This gives the work 2 more strands with which to form an Eight-Strand Matthew Walker Knot. After the Matthew Walker Knot is tied, 2 more double strands are added and the work is continued with a Four-Strand Triple Passed Reverse Crown to the point indicated by the arrow, where 2 more double strands are added, which converts the braid into a quadruple passed affair of the same nature. Continue this procedure to the required length. Then bring the strands down and form a Wall around the base of the last crown as for a Stopper Knot. A Turk's Head is then tied around the design with a separate piece of line as indicated. Any suitable number of passes can be used in the preparation of the Turk's Head, which is sewed to the body of the work for additional security and neatness.

Fig. 310: Another Watch Fob Lanyard similar in nature to the one just described.

Fig. 311: The Wrist Watch Strap shown here is constructed the same way as the example in Fig. 307.

Fig. 312: Another Wrist Watch Strap which is likewise made the same way as the one in Fig. 307.

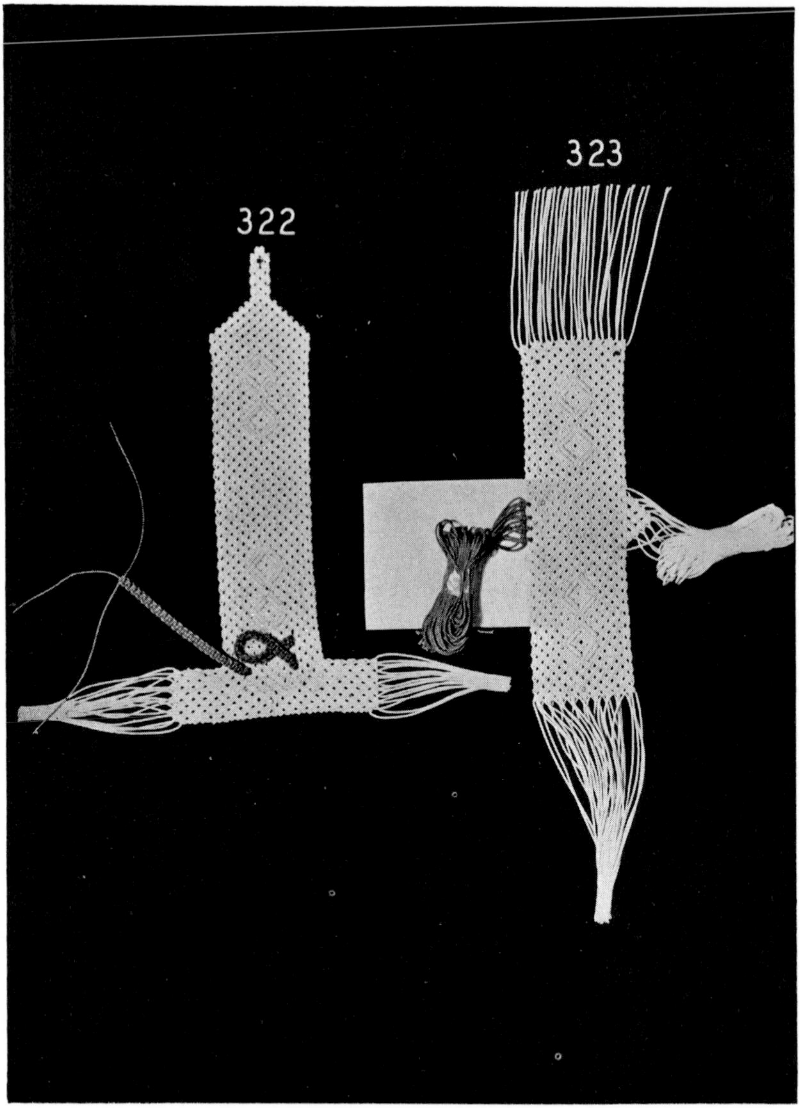

PLATE 79 Cigarette Cases

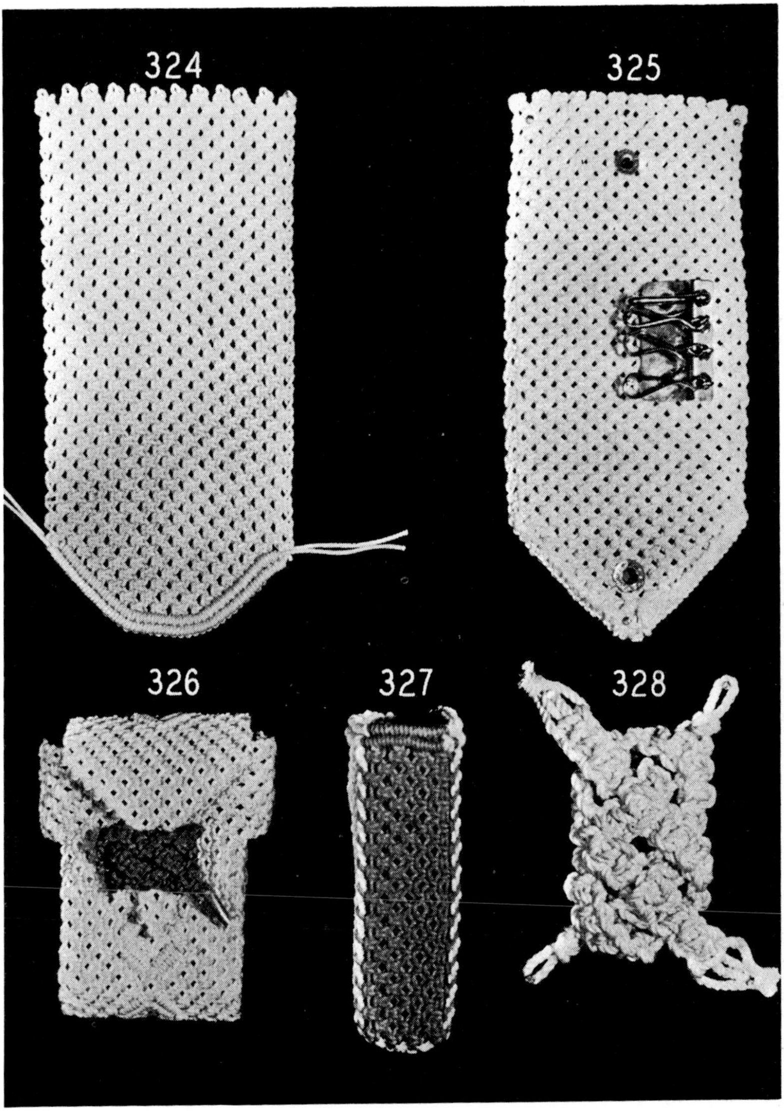

PLATE 80 Key and Cigarette Cases

Plate 75—WATCH LANYARDS

Fig. 313: An Interesting Design for a Watch Lanyard of the shirt pocket variety. These novel ideas may be made to suit individual taste, with any appropriate combination of knot work, such as the different types that are explained in the previous plate.

Fig. 314: Another handsome method for constructing a Shirt Pocket Watch Lanyard. This and the preceding example have the same general Cable laid principles as previously explained for watch fobs. Turk's Heads are applied as indicated with the work being finished off with Spiral Crown fillers which are also covered with Turk's Heads on the ends.

Plate 76—NAPKIN RINGS

Fig. 315: This Napkin Ring is formed in the following manner: Cut 6 strands 24 inches long and tie 3 rows of 16 Square Knots. Then join together both ends and finish off in the same way as for a belt loop which is explained in Plate 5.

Fig. 316: This Square Knot Diamond Design Napkin Ring is formed in the same manner as the one mentioned in Fig. 315.

Fig. 317: This Three-Strand Triple Pass Turk's Head is formed as explained in Plate 50.

Plate 77—MOCCASIN SANDAL

Fig. 318A: This style Moccasin Sandal is started from the toe. First make Shoemaker's stitches all around the sole about ¼ inch apart. To make this stitch, double a strand and thread both ends, and then pass one needle from the top through to the bottom and the other needle from the bottom through to the top. Continue by looping 9 double strands between 9 stitches around the toe and tie 9 SK. This part of the work will cover the top of the foot and act as the tongue. Cut 1 strand from each knot and finish off on the tongue with 2 rows of HH.

Now loop 10 double strands on the left and right sides of the toes and tie 10 SK on each side. As you move back, pass the outside strand through the stitch on one side and do the same on the other side of the tongue. In this way, continue to tie SK all round. Then join both sides at the heel and finish with a double row of HH.

B: Illustrates a finished Moccasin.

Plate 78—CRAVAT AND BOOK MARKS

Fig. 319: This Beautiful Book Mark was made with 32 strands Half Hitched in 3 different colors.

Fig. 320: This artistic Cravat was made with soft material, and is a very serviceable article. Cut 22 strands 8 times the desired length. These strands are doubled, making 44 in all. The cravat is started from the large end in the same manner as for a belt, which is explained in Plate 4. Work the tie to a point in the usual manner and after all strands have been added, tie 7 SK toward the middle from both sides. The design is formed in the following manner:

(*) #16 to right, HH with 17 to 22. 28 to left, HH with 27 to 22.
15 " " " " 16 to 21. 29 " " " " 28 to 23.

Tie 7 SK with 21–24, 1–4, 3–6, 5–8, 7–10, 9–12 and 11–14 and repeat three times.

20 to left, HH with 19 to 14.
21 " " " " 20 to 15.

Tie 7 SK with 13–14, 41–44, 39–42, 37–40, 35–38, 33–36, 31–34 and repeat three times.

24 to right, HH with 25 to 30.
23 " " " " 24 to 29.

Tie SK with 29–32. Using strands 20–25 as F, tie a Granny Knot with strands 17–19 and 26–28. Repeat from (*) to a distance of about 11 inches. Continue to cut 2 strands on each side until there are 20 working strands. See Plate 81, giving instructions on how to elimi

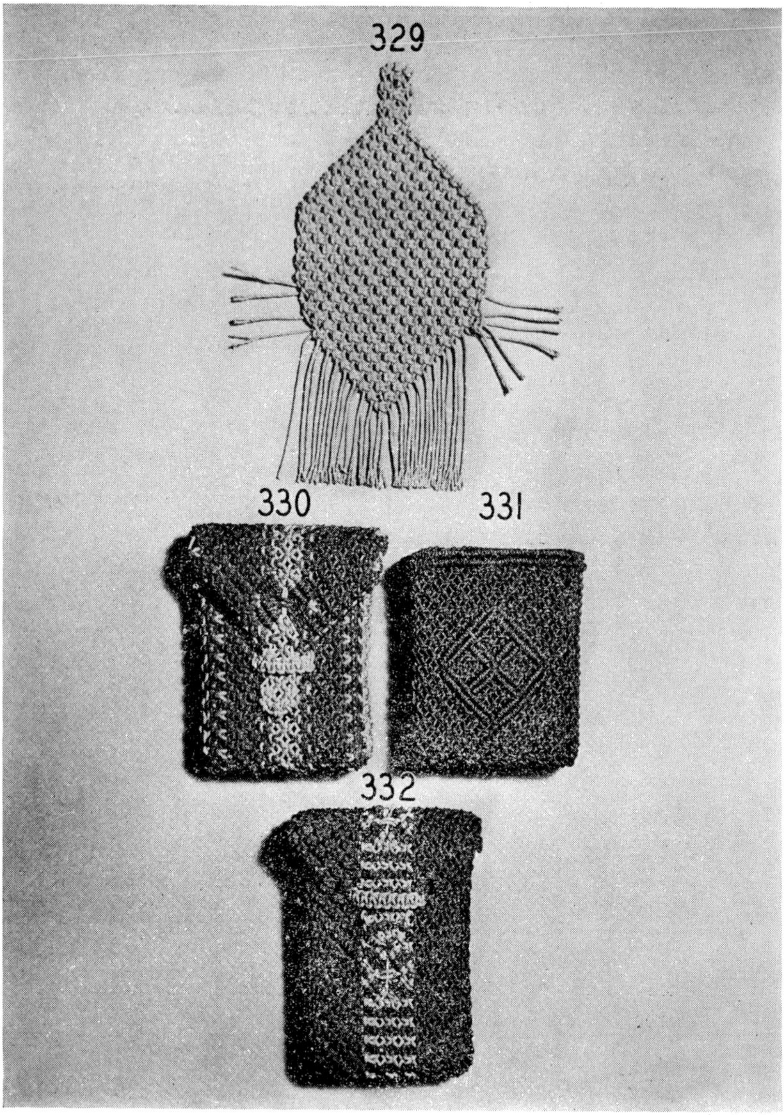

PLATE 81 Cigarette Cases

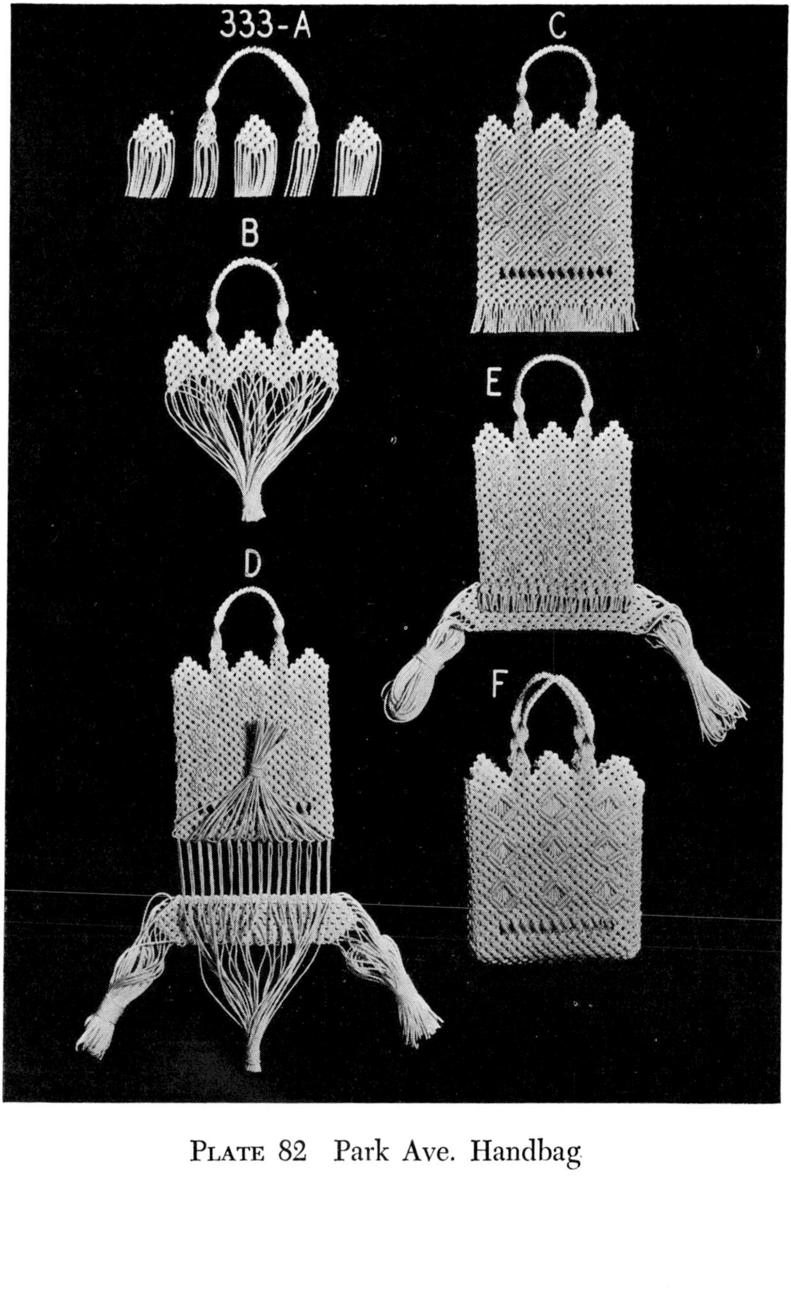

PLATE 82 Park Ave. Handbag

nate strands. Then tie SK for another 35 inches. Finish with 2 rows of HH and the work is completed.

Fig. 321. Another Book Mark made with 28 strands Half Hitched in three different colors.

Plate 79—CIGARETTE CASES

Fig. 322: This is the first type of Cigarette Case known to have been made by Square Knotters. It is started in the same manner as a belt or an envelope handbag. Cut 18 strands 7 feet long. These strands are doubled, making 36 in all. (For abbreviations see Plate 4.) Using 4 strands doubled, form the tongue about 1 inch long, consisting of 15 SK. Place 7 brads to the left and 7 brads to the right diagonally ¼ inch apart. Then, double a strand over the first brad on the left and join it to the tongue with a SK by using the inside strand of the double strand just added with the adjoining strand as a F. Repeat on the right side. Continue adding strands on the left and right sides, then fill in straight across with SK. After the flap part is finished, add 4 more rows of SK. To form the HH design in this case or in any handbag, always start with the middle knot, in this case #5, which includes strands 17–20 as the F strands.

#17 to left, HH with 16 to 13.	20 to right, HH with 21 to 24.
18 " " " " 17 to 14.	19 " " " " 20 to 23.

Tie 6 SK with strands 11–14, 21–24, 17–20, 15–18, 19–22 and 17–20.

14 to right, HH with 15 to 18.	23 to left, HH with 22 to 19.
13 " " " " 14 to 17.	24 " " " " 23 to 20.

Tie SK with 17–20. This completes the first design. Continue to fill in the necessary SK on the sides and then add another design. The work is brought to a point 10 inches from the tip of the tongue. Then the 36 strands are parted, 18 strands on the left are formed into a strap of SK about 1 inch long in that direction, and the same thing is done with the other 18 strands to the right. This is the same procedure that is used in forming a belt loop. (See Plate 5.)

The Double Carrick Bend is formed by inserting a double strand between 2 of SK as illustrated. Then 1 strand is added as a F on which a 24 SK Flat is tied. Then a crossed loop is formed and the ends are tucked through and made secure on the inside. Now, on the opposite side, insert another double strand, add 1 strand as a F, and tie a 24 SK Flat. (Generally 2 strands are used as a F.) Take this Flat and place it over the loop, and then under and over the cross, under the loop, over its own part, and under the loop. Then insert the ends through and make secure on the inside of case. The illustration in colored cord shows the preliminary stages in the forming of this knot.

To tie the horizontal pieces to the back of the case, cut 1 strand from each of the 4 SK. Then, on the reverse side, pass the F strand of knot 1 through the 6th opening on the side, and then tie SK with the strands on the right and left of the F. Pass the F strand of knot 2 through the 7th opening on the side and tie SK with the strands on the right and left of the F. Do the same thing with the F strands of knots 3, 4 and 5. Repeat on the opposite side. To make the sides more secure, bury the strands after tying the SK.

Fig. 323: This type of Cigarette Case is formed in the same way as the one in Plate 80, Fig. 327, and is the same style as the handbag in Plate 101. Cigarette cases or handbags such as these, can be started in the middle or about 6 inches from one end of the working strands. There are 18 strands, cut 7 feet long. These strands are doubled, making 36 in all. Continue to form this case so there are 12 openings or 24 rows of SK on the side; then 4 openings or 8 rows of SK for the bottom. Make 12 more openings or 24 rows of SK for the other side.

On the left side we illustrate how 8 double strands 2 feet long have been inserted between the 13, 14, 15 and 16th openings, and 4 SK have been tied. Illustration on the right side shows how 10 SK have been tied, strand 1 woven through the 12th opening, and strand 16 woven through the 17th opening on the opposite side. Continue to use this system until 24 rows of SK have been formed for the end. Do the same thing on the opposite end. There are now 104 working strands, or 26 knots, at the top or mouth of case. Bear in mind when tying a horizontal row of HH, that 1 F strand is cut from each knot. This is portrayed in the upper part of this illustration, leaving 25 working strands. In the lower illustration, the strands are not cut and there are 36 strands. Cut 1 F strand from each of the 26 knots.

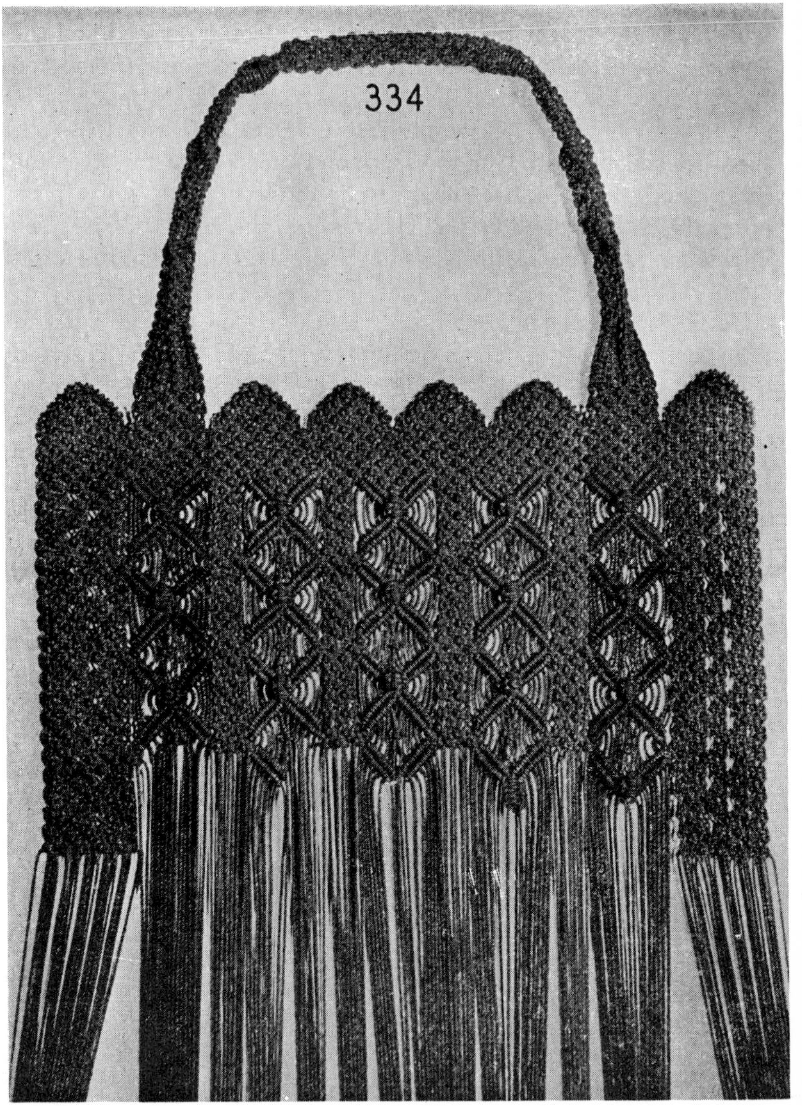

PLATE 83 Polynesian Handbag

Plate 84 Epsom Downs Handbag

To form the HH around the top or mouth of the case add 1 strand, and using it as a F, tie 2 HH on it with strands 1–78. Then add another strand and tie another row of HH. When tying the second part of HH with strand 2, insert strand 1. Continue using this system to the end. Finally, bury both ends of the 2 F strands.

Cut a piece of wood 1″ x 2¼″ x 2¾″, and place it inside of the case. Wash case and when it has dried, remove block and cut strands short. This completes the work.

Plate 80—KEY AND CIGARETTE CASES

Fig. 324: This Key Case is started from 24 brads placed in a board ⅛ inch apart. Then, double 2 strands 2 feet long over each brad and tie 12 SK. Continue by tying 40 rows of SK and finish off with 2 rows of HH. Strands 3 and 47 are cut. Strand 3 is used as a F to the right and strand 45 is used as a F to the left. The 2 outside strands and the 2 F strands are buried on the reverse side of the case.

Fig. 325: This Key Case is started in the same way as the one mentioned in Fig. 324. It is finished with 2 rows of HH coming to a point. The Eyelet is added at the point and a spring snap fastener is added in the middle near the top. The swivel type key case frame is then added in its proper place.

Fig. 326: This finished Cigarette Case is the one explained in Plate 79, Fig. 322.

Fig. 327: This finished Cigarette Case is the one explained in Plate 79, Fig. 323.

Fig. 328: Illustrates a Double Carrick Bend formed with large cord.

Plate 81—CIGARETTE CASES

Fig. 329: Shows how a Cigarette Case is started and how the 4 strands on each side are dropped.

Fig. 330: Shows a completed Cigarette Case which will hold a regular size pack of cigarettes.

Fig. 331: Shows a completed Cigarette Case finished off at the top with Half Hitches.

Fig. 332: This Cigarette Case and all envelope type pocketbooks are started from the tongue. The tongue can be started either from brads or on F strand. (For abbreviations see Plate 4.)

Cut 22 strands 6 feet long. Double them, making 44 strands in all.

To make the tongue use 6 strands and tie 3 rows of 7 SK. Then free the F strands and, using 8 strands, tie 3 SK. Now place the tongue forward on the table and secure it with glass-top push pins or brads. Fasten the 2 outside strands (1 strand to each of the 2 brads placed 4 inches apart), using a Clove Hitch. After adding all the strands, free the outside strands and bring the work to a point in the usual manner. Then tie 8 rows of SK for the top of the case.

At this point 4 strands are cut on the left side and 4 on the right side. It is very important to become adept in this system of eliminating strands. These strands must be cut so that the flap will be wider than the back; otherwise, there would be an opening at the sides. Cut strands 2 and 4; then with strand 1 tie 1 HH around strand 2. Using strands 2 and 3 as F, tie 1 SK with strands 1 and 4. Repeat the foregoing on the right side. Then work to a point in the usual manner. Again cut strands 2 and 4; then with strand 1 tie 1 HH around strand 2. Using strands 2 and 3 as F, tie one SK with strands 1 and 4. Repeat the foregoing on the right side. Now 8 strands have been cut, leaving 36 working strands in all.

From the place where the last strand was cut, form 26 rows of SK or 13 openings, for the back; 8 rows of SK or 4 openings, for the bottom; and 24 rows of SK or 12 openings, for the front of case.

To form the strap for the tongue to go through, insert one 12 inch strand and one 18 inch strand, both doubled, between the 10th and 12th row down, 3 SK from the left. Using the 2 shorter strands as F, tie a 9 SK Flat with the 2 longer strands. Between the 10th and 12th row down, 3 SK from the right, insert the 4 strands. Using two strands, tie a SK inside the case and bury the ends by partially opening a SK with a pricker. Do the same with the other 2 strands.

To add the sides to this case (or to any handbag), loop two 48 inch strands doubled through opening 14 and tie SK, loop two 36 inch strands doubled, through opening 15, then loop two more 36 inch strands doubled through opening 16 and tie SK. There are now 12 working strands for the side. Now, tie 2 SK with strands 3–6 and 7–10. Insert strand 1 on the left through opening 18 and tie SK. In-

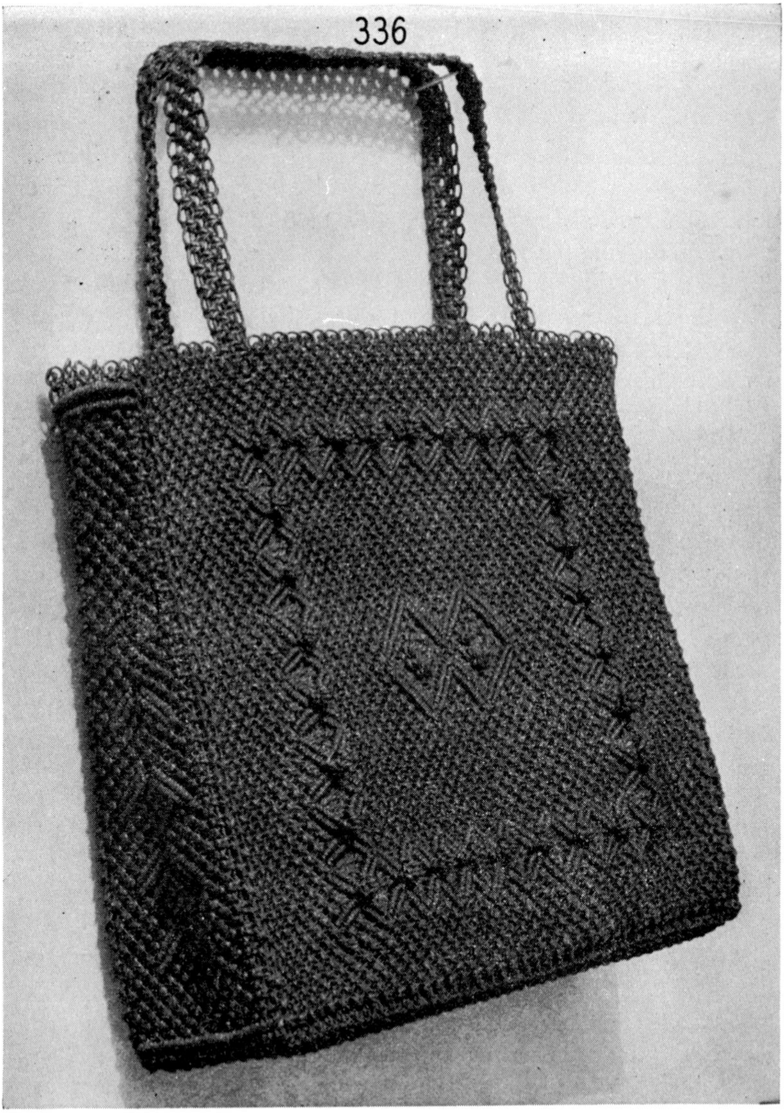

PLATE 85 Champs-Elysées Handbag

PLATE 86 Champs-Elysées Handbag

sert strand 12 through opening 13 and tie SK. Then tie SK with 5–8. Continue this procedure until 24 rows of SK have been formed. Repeat the foregoing instructions on the right side.

There are now 60 strands, consisting of 15 SK. Cut 1 F strand from each of the 15 SK, leaving 45 working strands in all.

Insert strand 1 from the left (long one) through the nearest loop in the back of the case. A strand may be added and used as the F, if desired. Using this strand as F, tie HH on it with strands 2 to 45, inclusive. Continue to use the same strand as F. Insert it through the nearest loop in the back of the case on the right, and continue to tie another row of HH toward the left. During the process of tying the second part of HH with strand 44, insert strand 45 through the loop; when tying the second part of HH with strand 43, insert strand 44; etc. When all the strands have been tied in this manner, the F strand and strand 2 are woven through the back of the case and buried through a SK which has been partially opened with a pricker. Pull all strands taut.

Cut a piece of wood 1″ x 2½″ x 3″. Wash the case and place the piece of wood inside it. After the case has dried, remove the wooden form and cut all strands close.

PLATE 82—PARK AVENUE HANDBAG

Fig. 333A: The Park Avenue Handbag.

This fashionable Handbag is started from brads in the same manner as a belt. Cut 24 strands 6 feet long. These strands are doubled, making 48 in all. With 8 double strands make your first pattern, then make 2 more similar patterns. Cut 8 strands 5 feet long, middle these strands and form the handle with a Flat of 8 SK, then a Spiral with 16 Half Knots; next tie 9 SK. Now finish the other half of handle.

B: The first pattern or scallop is tied to the handle with SK, using strands 15–18, the second with SK, using strands 23–28 and 39–42, the third with SK, using strands 47–50. Continue adding 3 more rows SK across. Then fill in with the necessary SK before starting the HH designs as illustrated.

C: First design:

(*) #31 to left, HH with 30 to 27.
32 " " " " 31 to 28.

Tie SK with 25–28.

34 to right, HH with 35 to 38.
33 " " " " 34 to 37.

Tie SK with 37–40. Fill in the middle with 4 SK using strands 31–34, 29–32, 33–36 and 31–34.

28 to right, HH with 29 to 32.
27 " " " " 28 to 31.

37 to left, HH with 36 to 33.
38 " " " " 37 to 34.

Tie SK with 31–34.
Second design:

11 to left, HH with 10 to 7.
12 " " " " 11 to 8.

Tie SK with 5–8.

14 to right, HH with 15 to 18.
13 " " " " 14 to 17.

Tie SK with 17–20. Fill in the middle with 4 SK using strands 11–14, 9–12, 13–16 and 11–14.

8 to right, HH with 9 to 12.
7 " " " " 8 to 11.

17 to left, HH with 16 to 13.
18 " " " " 17 to 14.

Tie SK with 11–14.
Third design:

51 to left, HH with 50 to 47.
52 " " " " 51 to 48.

Tie SK with 45–48.

54 to right, HH with 55 to 58.
53 " " " " 54 to 57.

Tie SK with 57–60. Fill in the middle with 4 SK using strands 51–54, 49–52, 53–56 and 51–54.

48 to right, HH with 49 to 52.
47 " " " " 48 to 51.

57 to left, HH with 56 to 53.
58 " " " " 57 to 54.

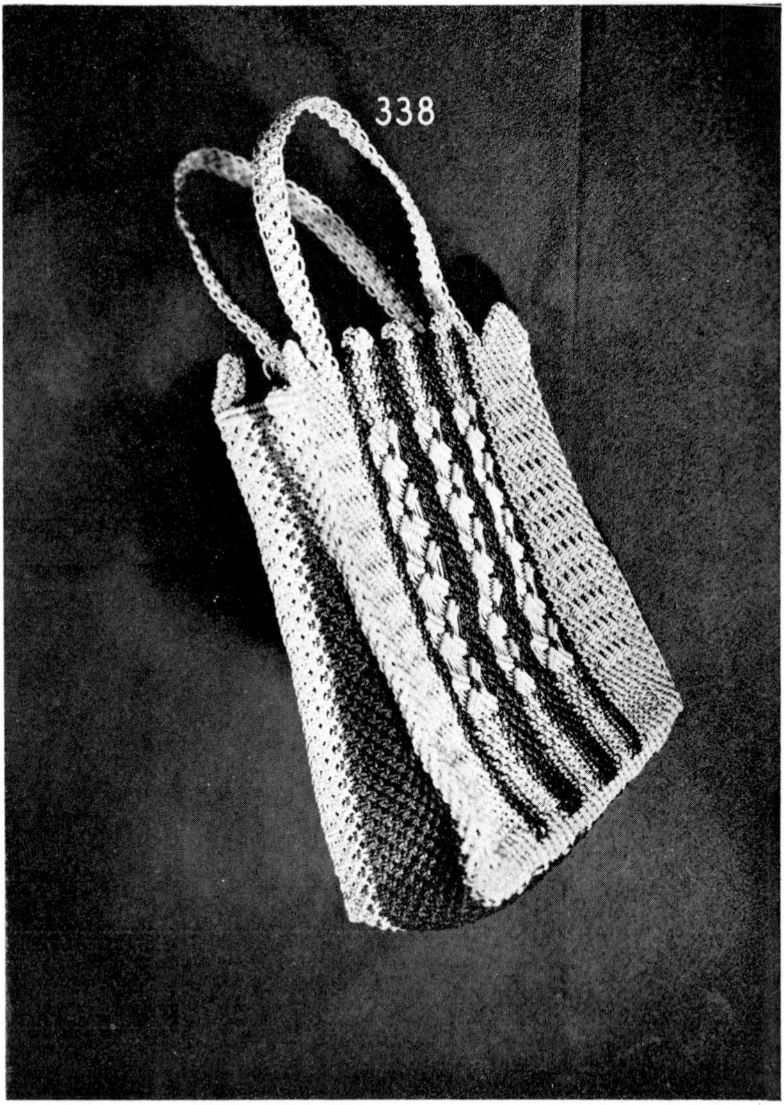

PLATE 87 Parisian Handbag

PLATE 88 Shantung Handbag

Tie SK with 51–54. Continue to fill in with SK and repeat design from (*). After completing 9 HH designs, tie 2 rows of SK. Then tie 11 Spirals of 6 Half Knots with strands 11–14, 15–18, 19–22, 23–26, 27–30, 31–34, 35–38, 39–42, 43–46, 47–50 and 51–54. Then tie 5 more rows of SK. This completes one side. Now form another similar pattern for the other side of handbag.

D: Cut 20 strands 4 feet long for the bottom. Start 18 inches from one end and with these strands tie 32 rows of SK. This bottom will then have 16 openings on each side where the F strands from knots 1 to 16 are passed through openings from the front and back of handbag.

E: Then with the strands on the right and left side of each knot, tie a SK on the 2 F strands on the inside of the handbag. When both front and back of handbag have been attached to the bottom in this manner, weave the sides in as explained in Plate 81. After 30 rows of SK have been added to each side, cut 1 strand from each SK on both ends. Then loop 1 strand through opening 1 on the front or back of bag. Now tie 1 row of HH with strands 2–14, and then, using the same strand as F, tie another row of HH with strands 14–2. When tying the second part of HH with strand 13, insert strand 14, and when tying the second part of HH with strand 12, insert strand 13; etc., clear across. Finally, bury the F strand and strand 2 inside of bag. Repeat the same procedure on the other end of bag.

Cut a block of wood to the approximate size of the inside of the bag. Wash the bag with soap and water. Rinse thoroughly in cool water with a little vingar added; then fit the bag over the block and allow it to dry in the shade. When dry, remove the block and cut all strands closely.

Satin or silk is the best material for a lining, and about ¼ yard is ample. To cut the lining, measure the outside of the bag and allow ¼ inch for seams. Cut 2 pieces for the front and back, 2 pieces for the sides and one piece for the bottom. Sew the bottom to the front and back, next sew in the two sides, and then lap the top over on the outside of the lining and sew the edge all the way around. If desirable, the lining may first be sewed to the bag and the zipper added. It is advisable to pin the lining in first, and then sew it, removing one pin at a time as the work progresses. The zipper is first pinned at both ends and then sewed in. Most zippers are 1 inch wide. With 20 strands used on the sides, a zipper of this type just fits. If 24, 28, 32 strands, etc. are used on the sides a much larger opening is formed. Therefore, it will be necessary to extend the zipper to the desired width with two strips cut from the lining and then sew it on top of the zipper tape. This will make a much neater job as the zipper tape will not be exposed and any desired width can be attained. Pass the threaded needle alternately up and then down through the zipper tape, in between every second HH. This completes the work.

F: Illustrates a completed Park Avenue Handbag.

Plate 83—POLYNESIAN HANDBAG

Fig. 334: The Polynesian Handbag.

These illustrations and text represent a most modern type of handbag. (For abbreviations see Plate 4.)

Cut 60 strands 6 feet long and also cut 16 strands 15 feet long for a 15 inch handle. This is the amount of cord needed for the front of the handbag. Start in the same manner as in making a twenty-strand belt, and fill in with 15 SK. Then form 5 more similar patterns with 20 strands. There are 152 working strands.

The handle is formed first by middling the 16 strands and tying 4 SK around. Then tie 11 more round rows of SK; next, tie one Spiral with 12 Half Knots; then, with 8 strands, tie 2 Flats with 6 SK in each; next, 4 Spirals with 4 strands in each; then form 6 rows of SK, tying every other row of SK in the opposite direction, by doing this, the handle at this point will appear square. Continue by tying 4 Spirals with 4 strands in each. Now form 6 more rows of SK, tying each row in the opposite direction from the preceding row, and tie 4 Flats with 7 SK, using 4 strands in each. Continue by tying 5 more rows of SK. Repeat the same directions for the other half of handle.

Join	the	1st	scallop,	or	point,	to	the	handle,	tie	SK	with	19–22.
"	"	2nd	"	"	"	"	"	"	"	"	"	35–38.
"	"	"	"	"	"	"	"	3rd	"	"	"	55–58.
"	"	3rd	"	"	"	"	"	4th	"	"	"	75–78.
"	"	4th	"	"	"	"	"	5th	"	"	"	95–98.
"	"	5th	"	"	"	"	"	handle	"	"	"	115–118.
"	"	6th	"	"	"	"	"	"	"	"	"	131–134.

Continue by tying 5 more rows of SK and bring the work to a point at the following places by tying 5 SK with 27–30, 51–54, 75–78, 99–102 and 123–126.

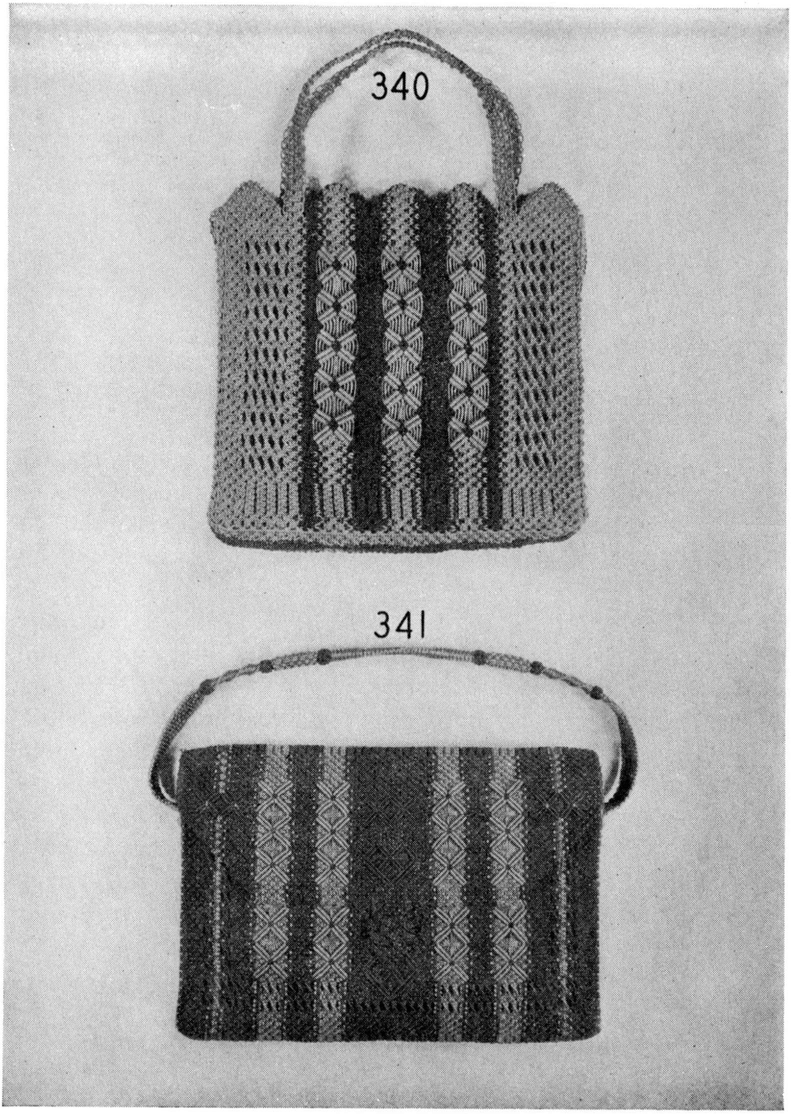

PLATE 89 Parisian and Longchamps Handbags

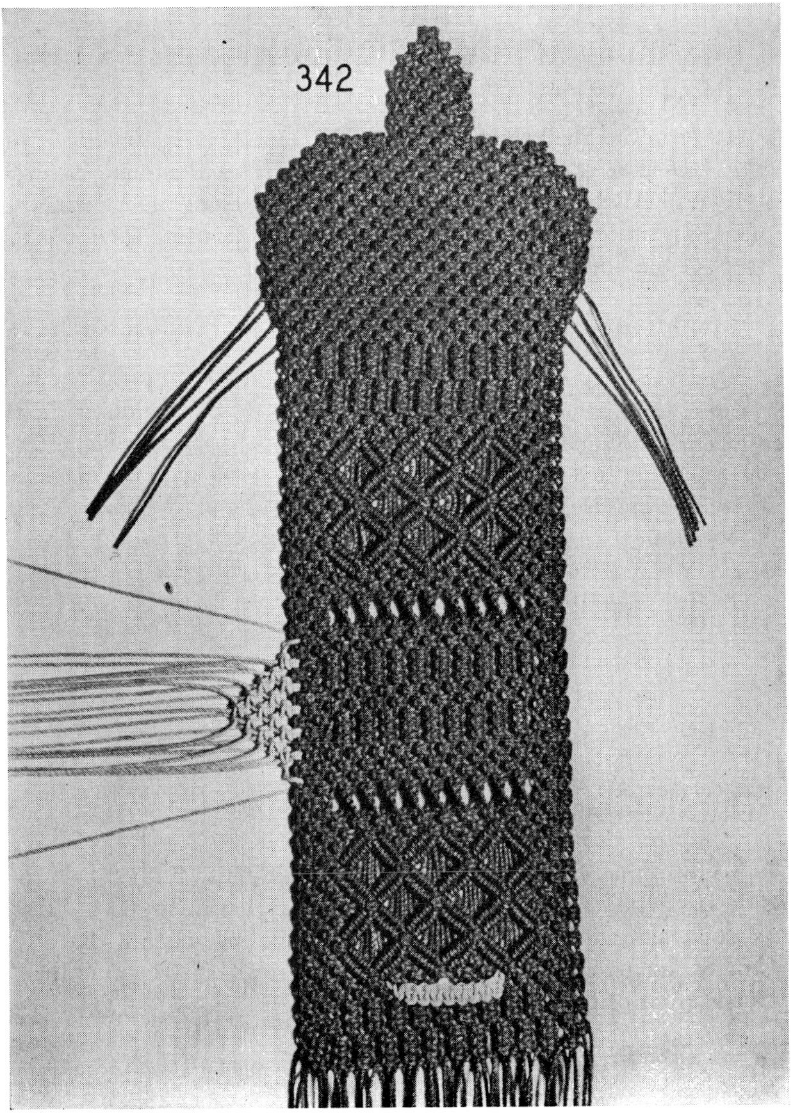

PLATE 90 Santa Anita Handbag

The first design:

#70 to right, HH with 71 to 76.	83 to left, HH with 82 to 77.
69 " " " " 70 to 75.	84 " " " " 83 to 78.

To form the Shell Knot, use strands 76 and 77 as F, then tie 1 inside HH with strand 75 and then 1 inside HH with strand 78. This is done alternately 5 more times. Continue by passing the 2 F strands, up, over and down between the 2 rows of HH, bring them out in front of the Shell Knot and tie SK with 75–78.

75 to left, HH with 74 to 69.	78 to right, HH with 79 to 84.
76 " " " " 77 to 69.	77 " " " " 78 to 84.

Now, using strands 75 and 78 as F, tie SK in the middle with 76 and 77. Continue by tying 15 SK with strands 61–64, 65–68 and 63–66, repeating this procedure 4 more times. Tie SK with 67–70. Continue by tying 15 SK with strands 85–88, 89–92 and 87–90, repeating 4 more times. Tie SK with 83–86.

70 to right, HH with 71, 72, 73, 74, 76, 75.
69 " " " " 70 to 75.
83 " left, " " 82, 81, 80, 79, 77, 78.
84 " " " " 83 to 78.

Second design:

46 to right, HH with 47 to 52.	59 to left, HH with 58 to 53.
45 " " " " 46 to 51.	60 " " " " 59 to 54.

To form the Shell Knot, use strands 52 and 53 as F, then tie 1 inside HH with strand 51 and then 1 inside HH with strand 54. This is done alternately 5 more times. Continue by passing the 2 F strands, up, over and down between the 2 rows of HH, bring them out in front of the Shell Knot and tie SK with 51–54.

51 to left, HH with 50 to 45.	54 to right, HH with 55 to 60.
52 " " " " 51 to 45.	53 " " " " 54 to 60.

Now, using strands 51 and 54 as F, tie SK in the middle with 52 and 53. Tie SK with 59–62. Continue by tying 15 SK with 37–40, 41–44 and 39–42, repeating this procedure 4 more times. Tie SK with 43–46.

46 to right, HH with 47, 48, 49, 50, 52 and 51.
45 " " " " 46 to 51.
59 " left, " " 58, 57, 56, 55, 53 and 54.
60 " " " " 59 to 54.

Third design:

22 to right, HH with 23 to 28.	35 to left, HH with 34 to 29.
21 " " " " 22 to 27.	36 " " " " 35 to 30.

To form the Shell Knot, use strands 28 and 29 as F, then tie 1 inside HH with strand 27 and then 1 inside HH with strand 30. This is done alternately 5 more times. Continue by passing the 2 F strands, up, over and down between the 2 rows of HH, bring them out in front of the Shell Knot and tie SK with 27–30.

27 to left, HH with 26 to 21.	30 to right, HH with 31 to 36.
28 " " " " 27 to 21.	29 " " " " 30 to 36.

Tie SK with 35–38. Fill in the outside with 10 rows of SK using strands 1–20. Then tie SK with 19–22. Using strands 27 and 30 as F, tie SK in the middle with strands 28 and 29.

22 to right, HH with 23, 24, 25, 26, 28 and 27.
21 " " " " 22 to 27.
35 " left, " " 34, 33, 32, 31, 29 and 30.
36 " " " " 35 to 30.

Fourth design:

94 to right, HH with 95 to 100.	107 to left, HH with 106 to 101.
93 " " " " 94 to 99.	108 " " " " 107 to 102.

To form the Shell Knot, use strands 100 and 101 as F, tie 1 inside HH with strand 99 and then 1 inside HH with strand 102. This is done alternately 5 more times. Continue by passing the 2 F strands, up, over and down between the 2 rows of HH, bring them out in front of the Shell Knot and tie SK with 99 and 102.

99 to left, HH with 98 to 93.	102 to right, HH with 103 to 108.
100 " " " " 99 to 93.	101 " " " " 102 to 108.

Now, using strands 99 and 102 as F, tie SK in the middle with 100 and 101, then with 107–110. Continue by tying 15 SK with strands 109–112, 113–116 and 111–114, repeating this procedure 4 more times. Then tie SK with 115–118.

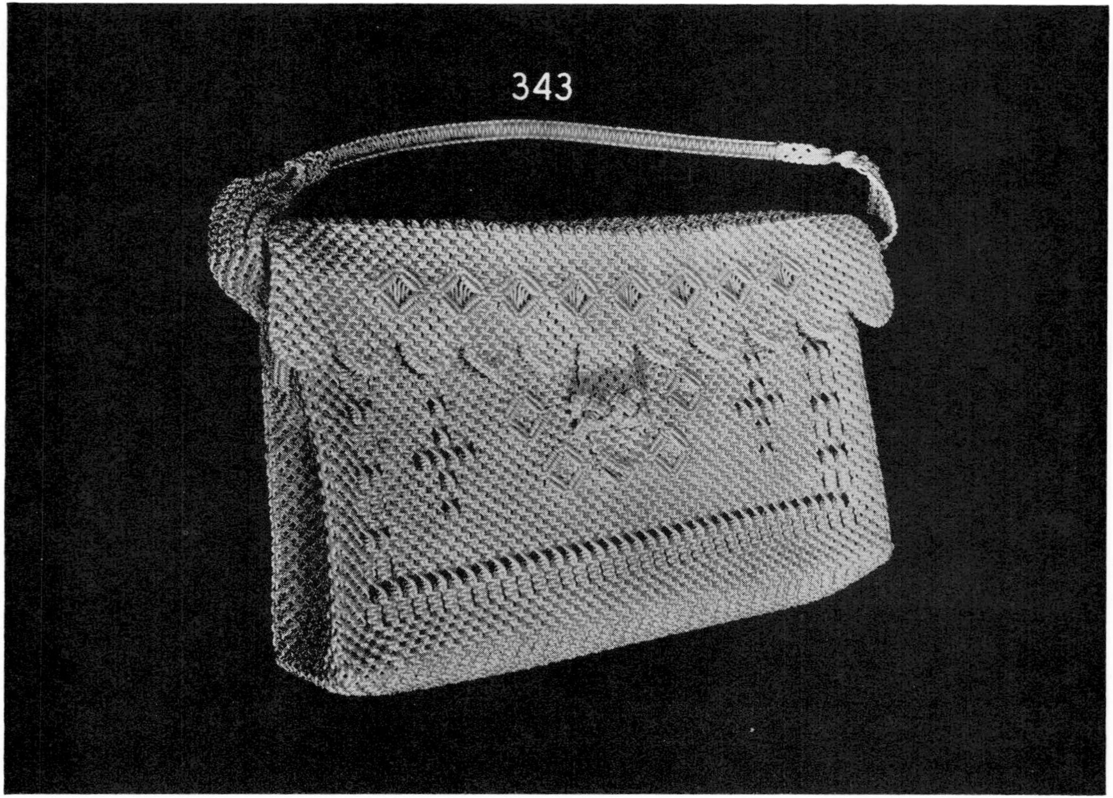

343

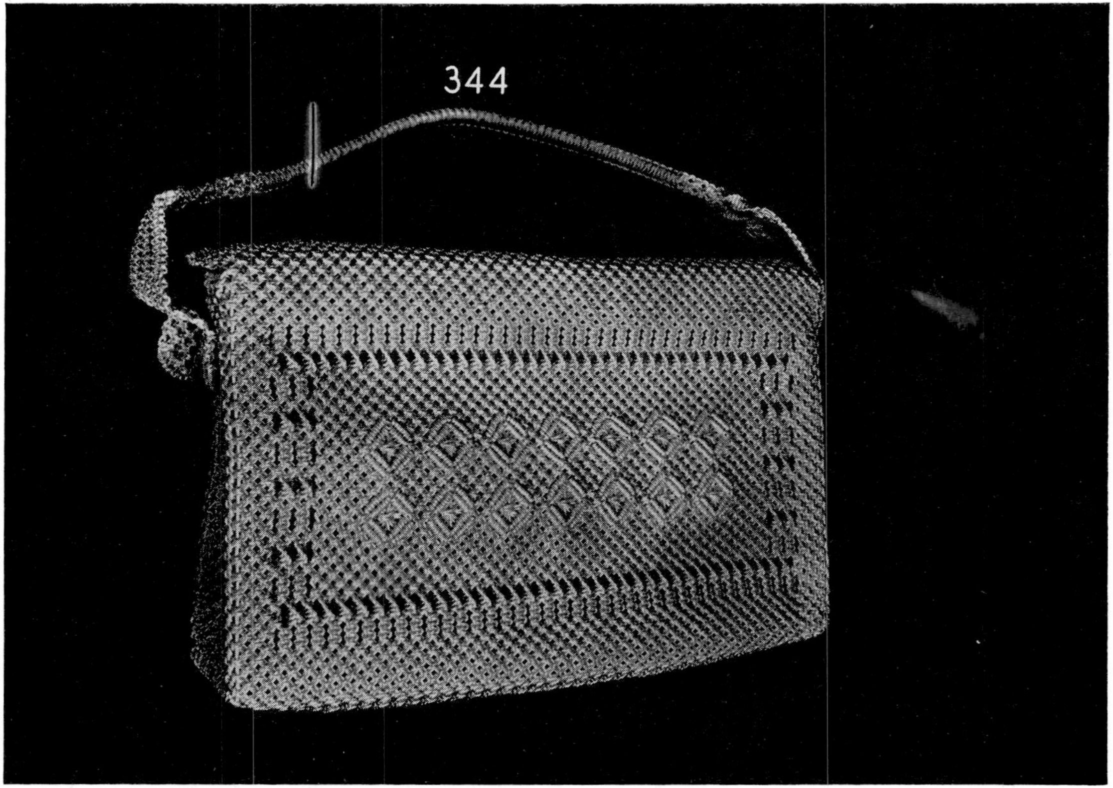

Plate 92 Taj Mahal Handbag

94 to right, HH with 95, 96, 97, 98, 100 and 99.
93 “ “ “ “ 94 to 99.
107 “ left, “ “ 106, 105, 104, 103, 101 and 102.
108 “ “ “ “ 107 to 102.

Fifth design:

118 to right, HH with 119 to 124.
117 “ “ “ “ 118 to 123.

131 to left, HH with 130 to 125.
132 “ “ “ “ 131 to 126.

To form the Shell Knot, use strands 124 and 125 as F, then tie 1 inside HH with strand 123 and 1 inside HH with strand 126. This is done alternately 5 more times. Pass the 2 F strands up, over and down between the 2 rows of HH, bring them out in front of the Shell Knot and tie SK with 123 and 126.

123 to left, HH with 122 to 117.
124 “ “ “ “ 123 to 117.

126 to right, HH with 127 to 132.
125 “ “ “ “ 126 to 132.

Now using strands 123 and 126 as F, tie SK in the middle with 124 and 125. Tie SK with 115–118. Fill in the outside with 10 rows of SK using strands 133–152. Tie SK with 131–134.

118 to right, HH with 119, 120, 121, 122, 124, 123.
117 “ “ “ “ 118 to 123.
131 “ left, “ “ 130, 129, 128, 127, 125, 126.
132 “ “ “ “ 131 to 126.

Each step in the formation of these designs is illustrated at the bottom of each vertical row of designs.

First vertical row shows how the design is placed in the middle by using strands 27 and 30 as F, and then tying SK with strands 28 and 29.

Second vertical row of designs shows how strand 46 is used as F, held to the right, and HH are tied on it with strands 47, 48, 49, 50, 52 and 51; strand 45 as F, held to the right, and HH are tied on it with strands 46 to 51.

Third vertical row of designs shows how strand 83 has been used as F, held to the left, and HH are tied on it with strands 82, 81, 80, 79, 77 and 78; strand 84 as F, held to the left, and HH are tied on it with strands 83 to 78.

Fourth vertical row of designs shows how the Shell Knot is formed by using strands 100 and 101 as F, tying 1 inside HH with strand 99, and then tying 1 inside HH with strand 102. This is done alternately 5 more times.

Fifth vertical row of designs shows how the 2 F strand on which the Shell Knot was tied has been passed up, over and down between the 2 rows of HH, and then brought out in front of the Shell Knot, and SK tied with strands 123–126.

Plate 84—EPSOM DOWNS HANDBAG

Fig. 335: The Epsom Downs Handbag.

This handbag is started the same way as a belt explained in Plate 4. Cut 16 strands 12 feet for a handle 19″ long, and then start 3 feet from one end for the handle. Cut 70 strands 6 feet long, which are doubled. Then form 7 points or scallops with 20 strands in each one.

Join the	1st	scallop, or point	to the	handle,	tie SK with	19– 22.
" "	2nd	" " "	" "	"	" " "	35– 38.
" "	3rd	" " "	" "	2nd	" " "	55– 58.
" "	4th	" " "	" "	3rd	" " "	75– 78.
" "	5th	" " "	" "	4th	" " "	95– 98.
" "	6th	" " "	" "	5th	" " "	115–118.
" "	"	" " "	" "	handle	" " "	135–138.
" "	7th	" " "	" "	"	" " "	151–154.

Continue to form the design as illustrated.

Repeat the above instructions and form another pattern with 172 strands.

Generally, it is more practical to use 28 strands for the bottom and sides, because this eliminates the necessity of dropping strands on the sides in order to fit in a zipper of sufficient width. Made in this way, the bag will take a zipper 1¾ inches wide, a size which is readily obtainable. See Plate 82 for instructions on how to insert the bottom, sides, and to make the lining. This completes the handbag.

Plates 85 and 86—CHAMPS ELYSÉES HANDBAG

Fig. 336: The Champs Elysées Handbag. Side view.

This modern 2½″ x 8″ x 10″ handbag with the Shell Knot design is started from brads. First cut 8 strands 14 feet long for the handle,

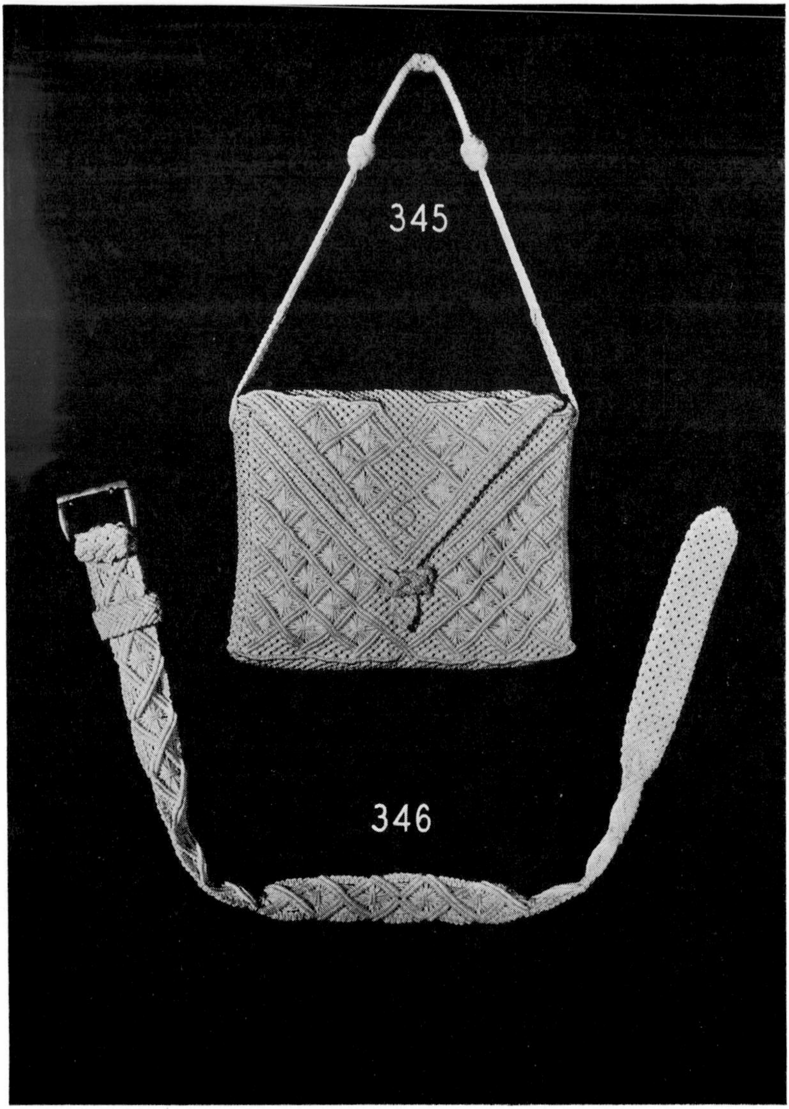

PLATE 93 Zanzibar Handbag and Belt

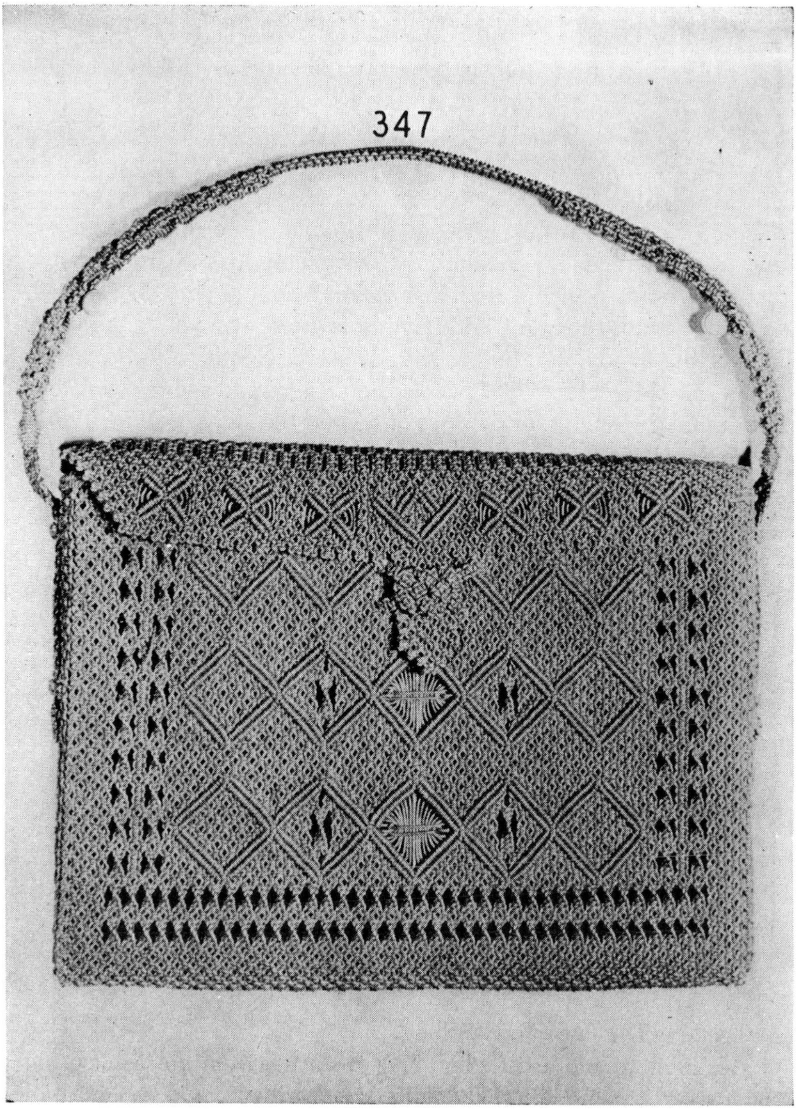

PLATE 94 Venetian Handbag

and then start 3 feet from one end and tie a SK strap 13 inches long. Next, cut 68 strands 8 feet long.

Place in a board a double row of 7 brads ¼ inch apart. Then loop 1 double strand over each of the 14 brads and tie 7 SK. Then tie 3 rows of SK. Next, tie these 28 strands to one part of the handle and tie SK with 27–30. Place in a board a double row of 20 brads ¼ inch apart. Then loop 1 double strand over each of the 40 brads and tie 20 SK. Next, tie these 80 strands to the other part of handle and tie SK with 35–38. Join the other end of the handle to these 80 strands and tie SK with 115–118. Continue by placing in a board a double row of 7 brads ¼ inch apart. Then loop 1 double strand over each of the 14 brads and tie 7 SK. Then join these strands to the other part of the handle and tie SK with 123–126. Continue to tie, in all, 7 rows of SK across. Then put in the design, and work down to a depth of 32 openings, or 64 rows of SK, on the sides.

Repeat the above instructions and form a similar pattern with 152 strands.

Cut 40 strands 8½ feet long for the bottom. Start 3 feet from one end and tie 76 rows of SK or 38 openings to correspond with the 38 SK across the front and back of handbag. After half the side has been inserted, drop 20 strands, 4 at each of the following rows in the middle: 32nd, 28th, 24th, 20th and 16th. Then fill in the remainder of the side with 20 strands. Repeat the foregoing on the opposite end.

See Plate 82 for instructions on how to insert the bottom and sides, to add lining and zipper, and to finish a handbag of this type.

Fig. 337: The Champs Elysées Handbag shown here illustrates a front view of the same bag explained in the foregoing text.

Plate 87—PARISIAN HANDBAG

Fig. 338: The Parisian Handbag.

This modern and artistic handbag is started from the point using the method explained in Plate 4.

First cut 8 strands 14 feet long for the handle and then start 3 feet from one end and tie a SK strap 13 inches long. Next cut 60 strands 8 feet long. The first scallop or point is made with 24 strands. The front of the bag is formed with 136 strands.

See Plate 82 for instructions on how the scallops or points are joined to the handle; also how to insert the bottom, sides, add lining, zipper, and finish a handbag of this type.

Plate 88—SHANTUNG HANDBAG

Fig. 339: The Shantung Handbag.

This attractive handbag is started from the point in the manner explained in Plate 4, with 14 double strands. There are 156 strands on each side of this bag. The handle is formed with 8 strands. The bottom is formed with 36 strands.

See Plate 82 for instructions on how the scallops or points are joined to the handle, how to insert the bottom, sides, add lining, zipper, and finish a handbag of this type.

Plate 89—PARISIAN AND LONGCHAMPS HANDBAGS

Fig. 340: The Parisian Handbag. Front view.

This is the same bag as the one in Plate 87.

Fig. 341: The Longchamps Handbag.

Represents another beautiful example of an envelope handbag. This illustrates the opposite side of the bag which is explained in Plate 95, Fig. 348. For instructions on how to make a similar bag, see Plate 90.

Plate 90—SANTA ANITA HANDBAG

Fig. 342: The Santa Anita Handbag.

This envelope handbag is started from the tongue in the same manner as one would start a belt from brads.

Cut 30 strands 9 times the over all length. The tongue consists of 16 strands with 31 SK. Place 6 brads ⅛ inch apart on the left side and 6 brads on the right side of the tongue, horizontally. Next, join the 12 strands on the left and the 12 strands on the right to the tongue with 2 SK. Now, place 5 brads on the left and 5 brads on the right diagonally, ¼ inch apart, and double 2 strands over each brad. There are now 60 working strands. Fill in with the necessary SK, making

Plate 95 Longchamps Handbag and Belt

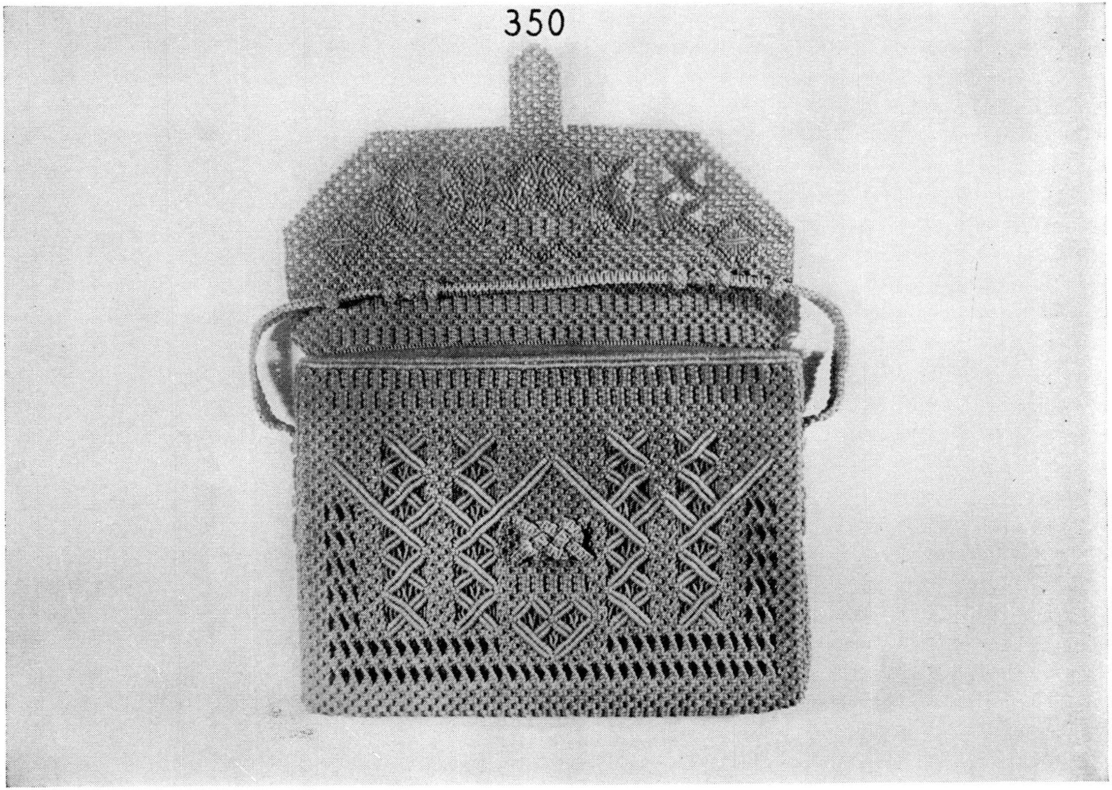

Plate 96 Sepoy Handbag

6 rows in all. At this point, 4 strands are cut on the left side and 4 on the right side. See Plate 81 on how to eliminate these strands. After the 8 strands have been eliminated, add 4 more rows of SK, thus completing the tongue and the flap.

Now start to form the back of the handbag, which consists of 13 openings on each side, or 26 rows of SK. Tie 10 Flats of 3 SK with strands 7–10, 11–14, 15–18, 19–22, 23–26, 27–30, 31–34, 35–38, 39–42 and 43–46. Tie another row of 9 Flats of 3 SK with strands 9–12, 13–16, 17–20, 21–24, 25–28, 29–32, 33–36, 37–40 and 41–44. Fill in both sides with SK, and the work is brought even with the last row of Flats. Continue by tying 2 more rows of SK. Tie 4 SK with 7–10, 19–22, 31–34 and 43–46. Now start to form the HH design, using the 4 middle strands as fillers; off knot #7, strands 25–28; knot #4, strands 13–16; and knot #10, strands 37–40.

(*) #25 to	left,	HH	with	24 to 21.	16 to	right,	HH	with	17 to 20.
26 "	"	"	"	25 to 22.	15 "	"	"	"	16 to 19.
28 "	right,	"	"	29 to 32.	37 "	left,	"	"	36 to 33.
27 "	"	"	"	28 to 31.	38 "	"	"	"	37 to 34.
13 "	left,	"	"	12 to 9.	40 "	right,	"	"	41 to 44.
14 "	"	"	"	13 to 10.	39 "	"	"	"	40 to 43.

Tie 4 SK with 7–10, 19–22, 31–34 and 43–46.

10 to	right,	HH	with	11 to 14.	31 "	left,	"	"	30 to 27.
9 "	"	"	"	10 to 13.	32 "	"	"	"	31 to 28.
19 "	left,	"	"	18 to 15.	34 "	right,	"	"	35 to 38.
20 "	"	"	"	19 to 16.	33 "	"	"	"	34 to 37.
22 "	right,	"	"	23 to 26.	43 "	left,	"	"	42 to 39.
21 "	"	"	"	22 to 25.	44 "	"	"	"	43 to 40.

Tie 3 SK with 13–16, 25–28 and 37–40. Fill in the sides with the necessary SK and repeat from (*).

Tie 1 row of SK under the designs. Then, tie 9 Spirals with 6 Half Knots in each, using strands 9–12, 13–16, 17–20, 21–24, 25–28, 29–32, 33–36, 37–40 and 41–44. Fill in the sides with the necessary SK and tie 2 more rows of SK. This completes the back of handbag with 13 openings on each side, or 26 rows of SK.

Now form the bottom of the bag by tying 10 Flats of 3 SK with strands 7–10, 11–14, 15–18, 19–22, 23–26, 27–30, 31–34, 35–38, 39–42 and 43–46. Fill in the sides with SK and tie 2 more rows of SK. Tie 9 Flats of 3 SK with strands 9–12, 13–16, 17–20, 21–24, 25–28, 29–32, 33–36, 37–40 and 41–44. Fill in the sides with the necessary SK and tie 3 rows of SK. This completes the bottom of the bag with 5 openings, or 10 rows of SK.

Now form the front of the bag by tying 9 Spirals with 6 Half Knots in each, using strands 9–12, 13–16, 17–20, 21–24, 25–28, 29–32, 33–36, 37–40 and 41–44. Form 2 more rows of SK and continue from (*) to make the HH designs. After the designs have been completed, fill in the sides with the necessary SK and make 2 more rows of SK. Form 9 Flats of 3 SK with strands 9–12, 13–16, 17–20, 21–24, 25–28, 29–32, 33–36, 37–40 and 41–44. Fill in the sides with SK and tie 10 more Flats of 2 SK with strands 7–10, 11–14, 15–18, 19–22, 23–26, 27–30, 31–34, 35–38, 39–42 and 43–46. Fill in the sides with SK, and the front of the bag is completed.

Cut 10 strands 18 inches long, and insert 2 double strands in openings 14, 15, 16, 17 and 18, tie 5 SK with each set of 4 strands. The first weave is made with strand 1 through opening 19, and the second weave with strand 20, is made through opening 13; etc., until 24 rows of SK are completed. Repeat the foregoing on the opposite end. When putting in one end of the bag, make sure that the 1 strand nearest the back of the bag is at least 1 foot longer than the rest of the strands. This strand will be used as a F, on which the HH are tied. Another method that can be used is to loop a double strand through opening 1 and form the HH on these 2 strands. For still another method, use only 1 strand as the F for the 2 rows of HH. After both sides have been set in, cut 1 strand from each knot. There are 5 knots for the left side, 5 knots for the right side, and 13 knots for the front. This means that 23 strands are eliminated, and there are now 69 working strands. Continue by taking the strand nearest the back, loop it through opening 1 on the left and use it as a F, tying HH with strands 2–69. Then take the same strand, and using it as a F, tie HH with 69–2. When tying the second part of HH with strand 68, tuck strand 69 through. Continue in this manner until all the strands have been HH and tucked through. Then bury the F strand and strand 2 through SK with a pricker.

The Double Carrick Bend or a Flat is now formed in the front of the handbag for the hold-down through which the tongue will pass.

The handle is formed with either SK or Sennit Braiding. See Plates 51 to 53 and Plate 72 for any number of different kinds of handles that can be made. Attach the handle to the sides of the handbag, and make it secure on the inside. See Plate 82 for additional instructions on how to wash, dry and insert lining and zippers on all bags.

351

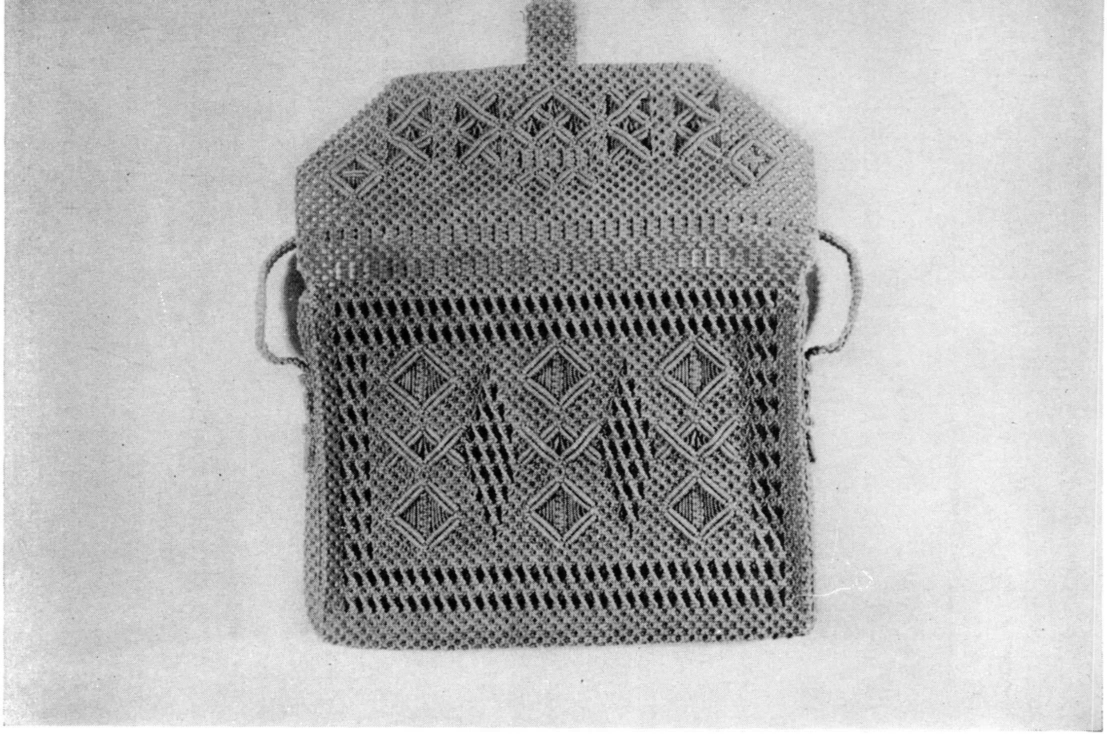

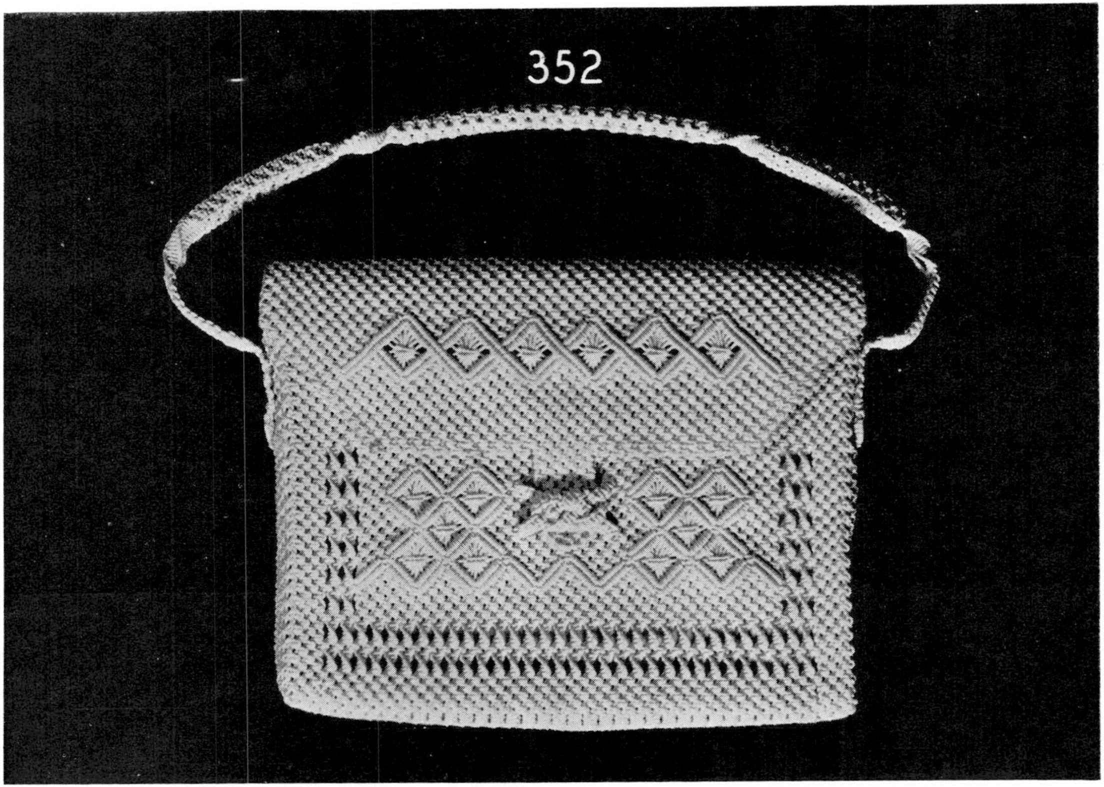

PLATE 98 Saigon Handbag

PLATES 91 AND 92—TAJ MAHAL HANDBAG

Fig. 343: The Taj Mahal Handbag. Front and side views.

This white envelope handbag is started from the point in the same manner as a belt. The tongue and 10 scallops have 16 strands in each. Cut 88 strands 15 feet long. These strands are doubled, making 176 in all. After the flap is finished, 4 strands are dropped on each side.

Join	the	1st	point	or	scallop	to	the	2nd	scallop;	tie	SK	with	15–18.
"	"	2nd	"	"	"	"	"	3rd	"	"	"	"	31–34.
"	"	3rd	"	"	"	"	"	4th	"	"	"	"	47–50.
"	"	4th	"	"	"	"	"	5th	"	"	"	"	63–66.
"	"	5th	"	"	"	"	"	tongue		"	"	"	79–82.
"	"	tongue		"	"	"	"	6th	"	"	"	"	95–98.
"	"	6th	"	"	"	"	"	7th	"	"	"	"	111–114.
"	"	7th	"	"	"	"	"	8th	"	"	"	"	127–130.
"	"	8th	"	"	"	"	"	9th	"	"	"	"	143–146.
"	"	9th	"	"	"	"	"	10th	"	"	"	"	159–162.

The handle is made separately with 16 strands and is tied to the sides on the inside of the handbag.

See Plate 90 for instructions on how to insert the sides and finish a handbag of this type. See Plate 82 for instructions on how to put in the lining and zipper.

Fig. 344: This shows a back view of the Taj Mahal Handbag.

PLATE 93—THE ZANZIBAR HANDBAG AND BELT

Fig. 345: The Zanzibar Handbag.

The handbag shown here represents another attractive design in silk, with an unusual pattern of knot work which should not be too difficult for the experienced square knotter to follow. The Collection Knot shown in this design is similar to those described and illustrated in Plate 10. Note the attractive Turk's Heads and Coxcombing on the handle.

Fig. 346: The Zanzibar Belt.

The belt pictured here is of the same general pattern as the handbag. These designs were submitted by First Class Boatswain's Mate R. B. Ausve, U. S. N.

PLATE 94—VENETIAN HANDBAG

Fig. 347: The Venetian Handbag.

Any combination of colors desired by the individual may be used. See Plate 90 for instructions on how this envelope bag may be formed.

PLATE 95—LONGCHAMPS HANDBAG AND BELT

Fig. 348: The Longchamps Handbag—back view.

This is the same handbag as the one described in Plate 89, Fig. 341.

Fig. 349: The Longchamps Belt follows the same pattern as the handbag of this name.

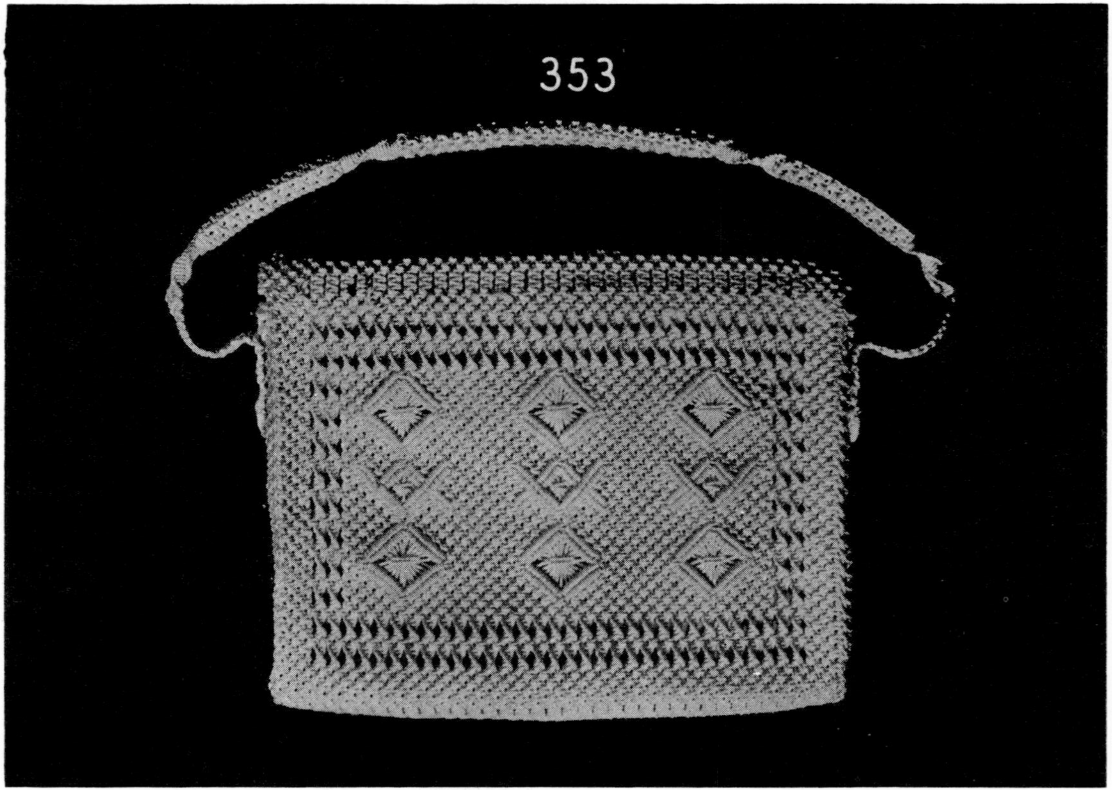
353

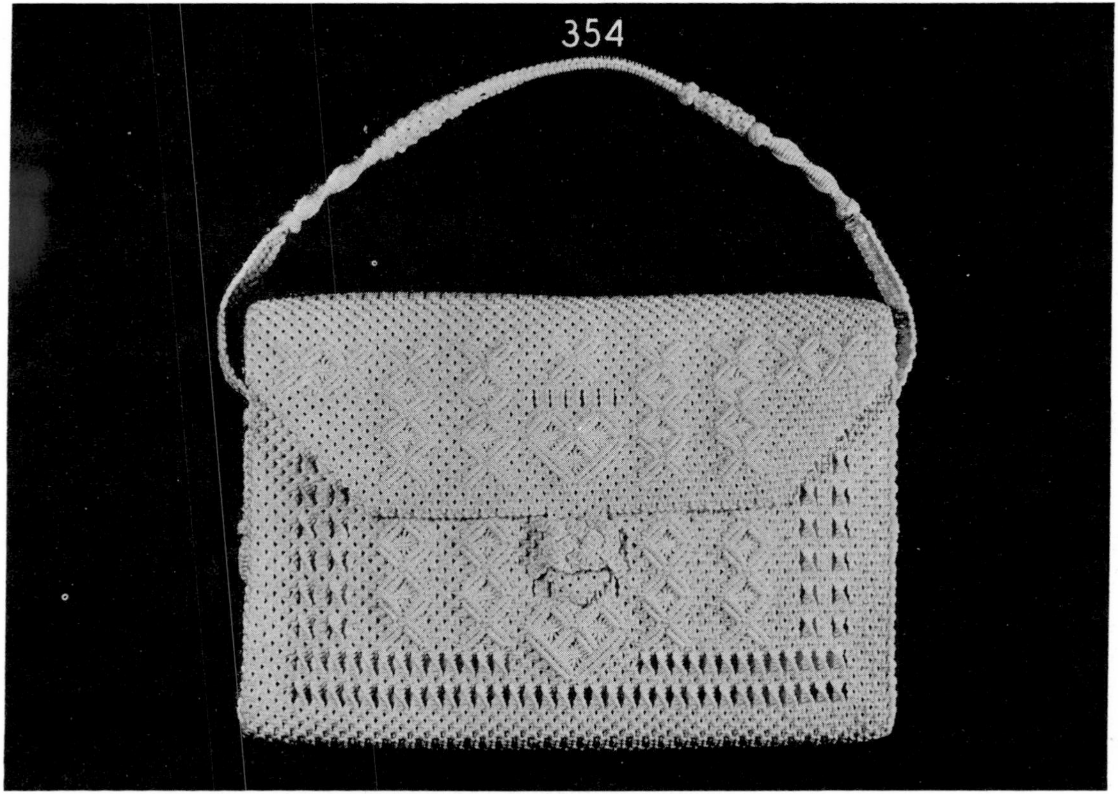

PLATE 100 Singapore Handbag

PLATES 96 AND 97—THE SEPOY HANDBAG

Fig. 350: The Sepoy Handbag—front view.
See Plate 90 for instructions on how this envelope bag is made.
Fig. 351: The Sepoy Handbag—rear view.

PLATES 98 AND 99—THE SAIGON HANDBAG

Fig. 352: The Saigon Handbag—front view.
See Plate 90 for instructions on how this envelope bag is made.
Fig. 353: The Saigon Handbag—rear view.

PLATE 100—THE SINGAPORE HANDBAG

Fig. 354: The Singapore Handbag.
See Plate 90 for instructions on how this envelope bag is made.

Plate 101—DURBAN HANDBAG WITH PURSE AND KEY CASE

Fig. 355: The Durban Handbag.

This bag is made with 176 strands, and measures 1½″ x 8″ x 11″. Cut each strand 14 feet long and start about 6 inches from one end. It is possible to start in the middle of the bottom and work up to the top, repeating the same procedure for the other side. The sides have 28 strands in each. This bag has a double row of HH on top. See Plate 79, Fig. 323, for instructions on how this type of bag is made.

The handle is shaped in the form of a fork and then worked together on the sides.

Fig. 356: Illustrates a Change Purse.

Fig. 357: Illustrates a Key Case closed. For full instructions see Plate 80, Fig. 325.

Plates 102 and 103—ANGLO-SAXON HANDBAG

Fig. 358: The Anglo-Saxon Handbag. Front view.

This Handbag represents a style in use up to 1925. It is beautiful to look at, but it has served its purpose. It is from these antiquated ideas in construction and design, that the present day style originates.

This envelope bag can be started either from the tongue or the front, as it has two parts. Cut 50 strands 10 feet long for the tongue, flap and back. These strands are doubled, making 100 in all. The tongue is started from brads with 6 double strands. There are 49 SK in the tongue.

Place in a board, to the left and right of the tongue, ¼ inch apart diagonally, 24 brads on each side. Then loop a double strand over the brad on the left and tie a SK with these 2 strands and 2 strands from the tongue. Do the same thing on the right side. After adding 3 sets of double strands on both sides, form the first Spiral with 6 Half Knots, using the 4 middle strands. Continue in this manner

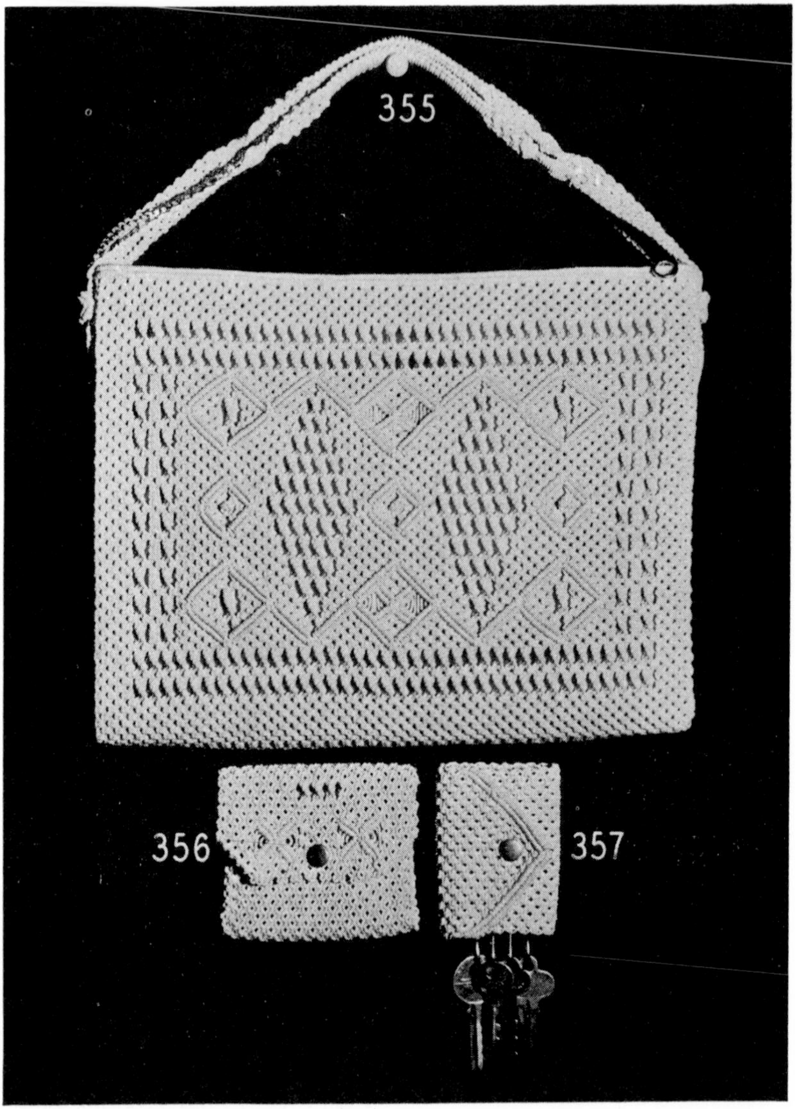

PLATE 101 Durban Handbag

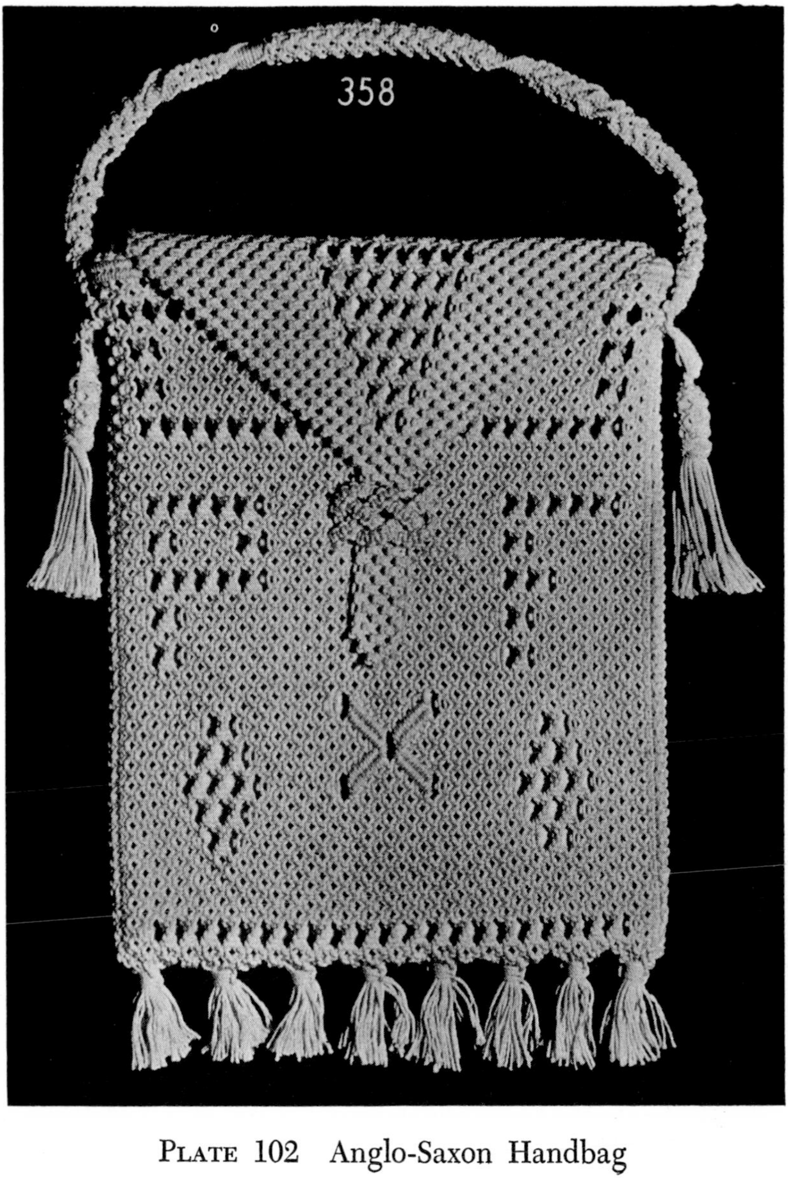

PLATE 102 Anglo-Saxon Handbag

until there are 100 working strands with 27 Spirals in 7 rows. From 6 more rows of SK; now form 2 rows of HH. Using strand 1 as F, tie HH with strands 2–100, then using strand 100 as F, tie HH with 99–1. Form 2 more rows of SK. Tie 21 Spirals of 6 Half Knots with strands 9–12, 13–16, 17–20; etc. Continue to form the design as illustrated to a depth of 72 rows of SK or 36 openings.

Cut 50 strands 8 feet long for the front. Then secure 1 strand about 3 feet long to some object, loop the 50 strands doubled over this F strand, and tie 50 Lark's Head Knots. Then with the same strand as F, tie HH with strands 1–100 and 100–1. Now bury the two F strands. Then tie two rows of SK, and form 21 Spirals of 6 Half Knots, starting with strands 9–12. Next, tie 8 rows of SK, then tie 21 Spirals. Continue forming the design as illustrated until there are 72 rows of SK, or 36 openings. The Double Carrick Bend can now be added. (See Plate 79, Fig. 322.)

Cut 2 strands 10 feet long and then loop 1 strand through opening 1 on the front and loop the other strand through opening 1 on the rear. Using 2 strands of the 4 as F, about 2 feet long, tie SK with the 2 longer strands. Continue to weave the longer strands through the openings on both sides of the bag, and tie 2 SK in between each weave. Continue doing this until both sides of the bag are joined together. Repeat the foregoing instructions on the opposite end.

To join both sides at the bottom 16 strands from the front on the left and 16 strands from the rear on the left are seized with the outside strand, tying 6 HH around the 31 strands. Repeat on the opposite side. Now, pair the remaining strands off in groups of 12 from each side and tie 6 Half Hitches with the outside strand in each group. Cut the tassel to any length desired.

Cut 16 strands 8 feet and form the handle 22 inches long, which includes the tassels. Attach the handle to the sides of bag and the work is completed.

Fig. 359: The Anglo-Saxon Handbag—rear view.

Plate 104—CAMERA CASE

Fig. 360: This Camera Case is formed in the same way as all envelope handbags.

Cut 30 strands 8 feet long. These strands are doubled, making 60 in all. 4 strands are cut on each side after completion on the flap. The design on the flap is formed as follows:

25 to left, HH with 24 to 19.
26 " " " " 25 to 20.

Tie SK with 17–20.

28 to right, HH with 29 to 34.
27 " " " " 28 to 33.

Tie SK with 33–36.

Using strands 22–31 as F, tie a Granny Collection Knot with strands 21 and 32.

20 to right, HH with 21 to 26.
19 " " " " 20 to 25.

33 to left, HH with 32 to 27.
34 " " " " 33 to 28.

Tie SK with 25–28.

The hold-down for the tongue bears the initials "E. W." formed with 6 strands. The black cord is the F when tying vertical rows of HH, and when forming the letters, the black cord ties 2 HH horizontally.

See Plate 90 for instructions on how to insert the sides and finish this case. The correct size of Camera Cases must, of course, be proportioned in relation to the actual size and shape of camera involved.

Cut 16 strands 6 feet for a handle 12 inches long. Start by middling the 16 strands, then tie 4 SK with 1–4, 5–8, 9–12 and 13–16; next round row tie 3 SK with 3–6, 7–10 and 11–14. Repeat the foregoing instructions 5 more times. Next, using strands 2–15 as F, tie a Spiral of 16 Half Knots with strands 1 and 16. Continue by tying 4 Flats of 6 SK with strands 1–4, 5–8, 9–12 and 13–16. Then with strands 2–7 as F, tie a Spiral of 16 Half Knots with strands 1 and 8, and with strands 10–15 as F, tie a Spiral of 16 Half Knots with strands 9 and 16. Now tie 4 SK pointing to the right; then in the next row tie 3 SK pointing to the left. Continue to tie 5 more rows of SK and reverse every other row of knots. Now tie 20 SK and finish with 2 rows of HH. Now tie the other half of handle. Weave the 16 strands through both ends and make secure on the inside of case.

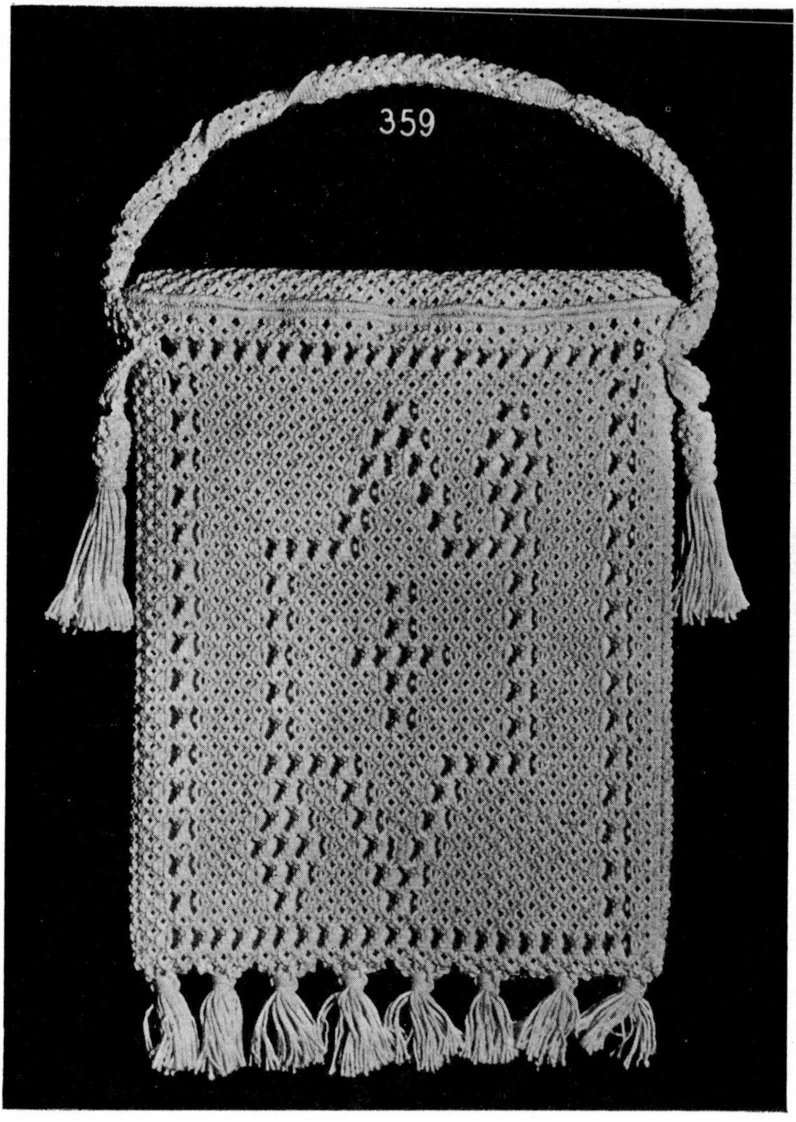

PLATE 103 Anglo-Saxon Handbag

PLATE 104 Camera Case

Index